Welcome to the EVERYTHING® series!

These handy, accessible books give you all you need to tackle a difficult project, gain a new hobby, comprehend a fascinating topic, prepare for an exam, or even brush up on something you learned back in school but have since forgotten.

You can read an *EVERYTHING®* book from cover to cover or just pick out the information you want from our four useful boxes: e-facts, e-ssentials, e-alerts, and e-questions. We literally give you everything you need to know on the subject, but throw in a lot of fun stuff along the way, too.

We now have well over 100 *EVERYTHING®* books in print, spanning such wide-ranging topics as weddings, pregnancy, wine, learning guitar, one-pot cooking, managing people, and so much more. When you're done reading them all, you can finally say you know *EVERYTHING®*!

FACTS

Important sound bytes
of information

SSENTIALS

Quick handy tips

ALERT

Urgent warnings

QUESTIONS?

Solutions to
common problems

THE
EVERYTHING®
Series

Cari amici!

Whenever I opened a language textbook in high school or college, I felt like Dante approaching the entrance to Hell: "Abandon all hope, you who enter." I'd dread being called on in class, afraid of making a mistake in pronunciation or grammar.

A few years later, though, I studied at a total-immersion language school in Florence, Italy, and everything changed. It was the sink-or-swim method: speak, read, write, and listen in Italian every day, no other language allowed. Soon enough, I was conversing with shopkeepers, listening to news broadcasts, and writing essays in Italian. A whole new world opened up, and I was able to learn about the art, history, and culture of Italy in its native language.

One reason I wrote *The Everything® Learning Italian Book* was to build on my experience as a private tutor and as the About.com Italian language guide. Many people have asked for a book that isn't a conventional textbook, but one with information that's accessible and easily understood. There's no avoiding grammar and vocabulary, but it helps if it's offered in a nonintimidating, engaging way.

Enjoy the journey, and remember that Dante's trip ended in Paradise!

A presto!

Michael San Filippo

THE
EVERYTHING®
LEARNING
ITALIAN BOOK

Speak, write, and understand basic Italian in no time

Michael P. San Filippo

Adams Media Corporation
Avon, Massachusetts

DEDICATION

For Elias, Nicholas, Chaston, Daniel, Trevor,
and their great-grandfather Michael.

• • • • • •

EDITORIAL
Publishing Director: Gary M. Krebs
Managing Editor: Kate McBride
Copy Chief: Laura MacLaughlin
Acquisitions Editor: Bethany Brown
Development Editor: Julie Gutin
Production Editor: Khrysti Nazzaro

PRODUCTION
Production Director: Susan Beale
Production Manager: Michelle Roy Kelly
Series Designer: Daria Perreault
Cover Design: Paul Beatrice and Frank Riveria
Layout and Graphics: Colleen Cunningham, Rachael Eiben,
Michelle Roy Kelly, Daria Perreault

An Everything® Series Book.
Everything® is a registered trademark of Adams Media Corporation.

Published by Adams Media Corporation
57 Littlefield Street, Avon, MA 02322 U.S.A.
www.adamsmedia.com

ISBN: 1-58062-724-2
Printed in the United States of America.

J I H G F E D C B A

Library of Congress Cataloging-in-Publication Data
San Filippo, Michael.
The everything learning Italian book: speak, write, and understand
basic Italian in no time / by Michael P. San Filippo.
p.   cm. -- (The everything series)
Includes index.
ISBN 1-58062-724-2
1. Italian language–Textbooks for foreign speakers–English. I. Title. II. Series.
PC1129.E5 S26 2002   458.2'421–dc21
                                              2002008503

Many of the designations used by manufacturers and sellers to distinguish their products are claimed as trademarks. Where those designations appear in this book and Adams Media was aware of a trademark claim, the designations have been printed with initial capital letters.

This publication is designed to provide accurate and authoritative information with regard to the subject matter covered. It is sold with the understanding that the publisher is not engaged in rendering legal, accounting, or other professional advice. If legal advice or other expert assistance is required, the services of a competent professional person should be sought.

—From a *Declaration of Principles* jointly adopted by a Committee of the American Bar Association and a Committee of Publishers and Associations

Illustrations by Barry Littmann.

This book is available at quantity discounts for bulk purchases.
For information, call 1-800-872-5627.

Visit the entire Everything® series at everything.com

Contents

Acknowledgments

My thanks to everyone who assisted with the research and writing of this book. I am grateful to my editor Bethany Brown for her expertise and my agent Jessica Faust for her guidance. I am also indebted to my friend Gabrielle Euvino for her encouragement and support.

Introduction

VIN SANTO AND CANTUCCI. Romulus and Remus. Campari and soda. There are many familiar Italian pairs that seem inseparable. The Italian language and culture is another dynamic duo that makes for a compelling and fascinating combination. Discovering more about the culture will inevitably lead to greater knowledge of the language, and vice versa.

Why is Italian important? Readers of this book may have many motivations for learning the language. For students studying a subject with ties to Italy or fulfilling a language requirement, learning Italian can be essential. Tourists wanting to get more out of their visit to *il bel paese*, professionals traveling to Italy to conduct business, and people of Italian descent investigating their genealogical roots can also benefit from learning Italian.

Italy has made many important contributions to Western culture, and the language is an integral part of its achievements. The history of Italy includes the Etruscan civilization, the Roman Empire, the papacy, the Renaissance, the *Risorgimento*, and two world wars of the twentieth century. The Italian artistic patrimony is estimated to comprise the majority of Western art. There are rich customs and traditions that vary by region, and *la cucina italiana* is one of the favorite cuisines the world over.

Learning a language is like learning a new way of life and can increase your appreciation for other cultures. Language is a way to look at the world around you and reflects the traditions and customs of the speakers. Learning to communicate in Italian can expand your horizons in profound ways.

How long has the Italian language been around for? It has its roots in the Latin language, spoken on the Italian peninsula and throughout the Roman Empire thousands of years ago. Developed as a vernacular, it has been part of the Mediterranean linguistic landscape for over a millennium, and gained literary popularity with the publication of Dante's *Divine Comedy* in the 1300s. At the time of the unification of Italy in the 1800s, Italian became its official language. Today, more than 55 million people throughout the world speak Italian.

How will *The Everything® Learning Italian Book* approach the topic? Think of this book as Dante's guide Virgilio, guiding you through the nine rings of conjugation hell and the purgatory of adverbs and adjectives. There are a variety of methods to keep you turning the pages: a mix of linguistic and cultural facts, grammatical essentials, dialogues with real-life characters, and quizzes and word searches to improve your vocabulary. And since Italian language and culture go hand in hand, you'll be learning about grammar and Gorgonzola, pronouns and Petrarca, reflexive verbs and the Renaissance.

The Everything® Learning Italian Book can serve as a one-stop resource or a stepping-off point for further study. It includes recommendations for other reference materials, CDs, tapes, and Web sites. You can also use it as a handy travel guidebook, as reference material for a language course, or the start of a lifetime of exploration of *la bella lingua italiana*.

CHAPTER 1

Presenting the Italian Language

I talian is a language full of contradictions: Its history goes back thousands of years, and yet it became the national language of Italy only recently, in the nineteenth century. How did Italian develop and how did it come to dominate the Italian peninsula? What are the Italian dialects and where are they spoken? How did Italian influence English? And why should you learn Italian?

Why Learn Italian?

Maybe you fell in love with the rolling hills of Tuscany on your first visit to *il bel paese*—or maybe you fell in love with an Italian! Maybe your grandparents emigrated from Italy, so you want to investigate your family history. Perhaps you're an aspiring musician who wants to learn what *adagio*, *allegro*, and *andante* mean, or an opera singer who wants to improve her pronunciation. For all these reasons and more, you've decided to learn Italian, improve on what lessons you've already taken, or formalize those rudimentary phrases you've been speaking when traveling to Italy.

FACTS

Every year, the president of the United States signs an executive order designating October as National Italian-American Heritage Month. Coinciding with the festivities surrounding Columbus Day, the proclamation recognizes the many achievements, contrib-utions, and successes of Italians and Italian-Americans in the United States.

No matter what your motivation—the opportunity to work overseas, cultural exchange in a land steeped in history and culture, researching your genealogy, or studying other topics such as literature or art history—you can discover new worlds when learning Italian. So raise a glass of *Montepulciano* and congratulate yourself on embarking on a new adventure. *Buon viaggio!*

Top Ten Reasons to Learn Italian

1. Understand Luciano Pavarotti when he belts out a phrase in a high C.
2. Order in Italian with confidence at an authentic Italian restaurant.
3. Improve your cultural understanding and global communication.
4. Stop relying on subtitles when watching Italian-language movies.
5. Get directions in Italian on your next visit to Rome.
6. Converse with your Italian-born grandparents.
7. Choose the right size at the Armani boutique in Florence without guessing.
8. Research your family roots and interpret old documents.
9. Study art history in the land where Michelangelo was born.
10. Read *La divina commedia* as Dante wrote it.

Love Those Romance Languages!

What comes to mind when you hear the word "romance"? Champagne and chocolates, candlelight dinners, soft music, and Valentine's Day? Not many people will think Italian, Spanish, or Portuguese. So what are Romance languages and why is Italian part of this group?

Linguistically speaking, Romance languages are descendants of the spoken form of Latin, known as Vulgar Latin. In this case, "vulgar" doesn't mean "coarse" or "off-color," but rather "common," referring to the usual, typical, everyday speech of ordinary people.

Romance languages consist of modern French, Italian, Spanish, Romanian, Catalan, the Romansch group of dialects (spoken in Switzerland), and Sardinian. Also included are such languages as Occitan and Provençal (France), Andalusian (Spain), Friulian (northeast Italy), Ladin (northern Italy), and Sicilian (southern Italy).

Many Romance languages are regional dialects rather than national languages, classified together on the basis of a shared section of vocabulary, which originated from the influence of the language of the Roman conquerors on the local native languages spoken in the Mediterranean area (where the Romance languages are clustered). Today, nearly 400 million people speak Romance languages.

ALERT

French, Spanish, Portuguese, and other Romance languages bear a striking resemblance to Italian. But even identical twins have distinguishing characteristics, so avoid assuming that one language's grammar is identical to another's, or that similar-sounding words have the same meaning or pronunciation.

Italian, like the other Romance languages, is the direct offspring of the Latin spoken by the Romans and imposed by them on the peoples under their dominion. Of all the major Romance languages, Italian retains the closest resemblance to Latin.

The Story of *La Bella Lingua*

The history of the Italian language, like a winding road along *la costa amalfitana* (the Amalfi Coast), has many twists and turns, swoops and bends. Here are just a few highlights of the origin and development of *italiano* (a term that came into use in the thirteenth century).

To Hell and Back

A towering figure of world literature, Dante Alighieri (1265–1321) is best known for his allegorical work *La divina commedia* (*The Divine Comedy*), which he began circa 1307 and worked on until his death. *La commedia* traces Dante's imaginary journey through Hell, Purgatory, and Heaven, during which he encounters historical and mythological creatures, each symbolic of a particular fault or virtue.

Dante's Latin treatise *De vulgari eloquentia* (c. 1303) promoted vernacular Italian as a literary language fit to replace Latin. *La divina commedia*, written in Italian verse, proved Dante's argument. Italian, previously treated as a spoken dialect, was recognized as a language to rival Latin, and *The Divine Comedy* has remained one of the world's greatest works of literature.

But let's not forget the other two-thirds of the linguistic trinity that revolutionized the Italian language. The love poetry of Francesco Petrarca (1304–74), especially his *Canzoniere* (*Song Book*), had enormous influence on the poets of the fifteenth and sixteenth centuries. Giovanni Boccaccio (1313–75) wrote the *Decameron*, one hundred stories that became a model for writers of fiction and other forms of prose.

La questione della lingua

Nevertheless, the language of Dante, Petrarca, and Boccaccio was a dialect spoken in Tuscany, a region of northwest Italy. It was up to writers and grammarians to continue the language's transformation into a central and classical Italian speech. The "question of the language" movement, which took place during the fifteenth and sixteenth centuries, was such an attempt to establish linguistic norms and codify the Italian language, and it engrossed writers and grammarians of all persuasions. Eventually, this radical approach to Italian did relax, and Italian continues to change in a more organic fashion, as do other living tongues.

In a land renowned for its culinary traditions, perhaps it was inevitable that the Italian national language academy would be named for a byproduct of the bread-making process. *L'Accademia della Crusca* (the Academy of the Chaff) was founded in Florence in 1582 to maintain the purity of the Italian language. Still in existence today, the academy was the first such institution in Europe and the first to produce a modern national language.

Birth of a Nation and a Language

It was not until the nineteenth century that the language spoken by educated Tuscans spread to become the language of a new nation. The unification of Italy in 1861 had a profound impact not only on the political scene but also resulted in a significant social, economic, and cultural transformation. With mandatory schooling, the literacy rate increased, and many speakers abandoned their native dialect in favor of the national language.

Italian by the Numbers

How many people claim Italian as their *madre lingua* (mother tongue)? And where is Italian spoken? In Italy, out of a total population of 58 million people, 55 million speak Italian; some of them are bilingual in Italian and another regional dialect, and some of them use Italian as a second language. Amazingly, only 2.5 percent of Italy's population could speak standard Italian when Italy became a unified nation in 1861. Italian is also spoken by a sizable number of people in Croatia, Eritrea, France, San Marino, Slovenia, Switzerland, and the Vatican State.

What passes for Italian in American movies, on TV shows, and between friends isn't always accurate. Many times the Italian-American lingo you may be familiar with is made up of petrified Italian words from over a century ago plus street slang popularized by gangster movies and an anglicized, mangled pronunciation.

Dialects, Accents, and Everything in Between

One of the first things you'll notice when eating in Italy is *la cucina locale* (the local cuisine). Every region has their own specialty and preparation techniques depending on the season, the local produce, and other ingredients. Likewise, most regions in Italy have their own accent, dialect, and sometimes their own language—as in the case of Sardinia, Sicily, Friuli, and Piemonte. Some of the major dialects include Abruzzese, Central Marchigiano, Laziale, Pugliese, Tuscan, Umbrian, and Venetian.

The various languages and dialects spoken in Italy evolved over centuries and remained distinct from "standard" Italian for a variety of reasons such as geopolitics, lack of mobility, the absence of radio or TV until the twentieth century, and the desire of many groups to maintain their cultural heritage and independence.

FACTS

Today, schoolchildren from all regions of Italy learn the standard Italian language, and perhaps also their regional dialect. Standard Italian has evolved from the times when it was a medieval Tuscan dialect, and now serves as the common language of Italy.

Italian dialects have many striking characteristics that distinguish themselves from others. For example, the Neapolitan dialect, *Napoletano*, is the most widely known because it is often employed in popular songs. The speakers of *Napoletano* clip the articles to single vowels, such as in the song title *'O sole mio (Il sole mio*—"My Sun*"*). In *Romanesco* (the Roman dialect), the letter *r* often replaces the letter *l*, so a speaker of *Romanesco* would pronounce *volta* ("once") as *vorta*. And the Tuscans are famous for their *gorgia Toscana*, similar to a raspy English "h" that makes the word *casa* ("house") sound like *chasa*.

Italian in English, English in Italian

Italian words have been migrating to English over the course of many centuries. Most musicians are familiar with terms such as *bel canto*, *cello*, *mezzosoprano*, *pianoforte*, and *solo*. Architecture has borrowed words like *cupola*, *loggia*, and *stanza*. If you like Italian food, there's no avoiding mouth-watering *ravioli*, *mozzarella*, *lasagne*, *vermicelli*, or *porcini*. And in everyday culture we speak of camera-toting *paparazzi*, *graffiti* artists, gun-slinging *mafia*, and the urban *ghetto*. So your vocabulary already consists of many familiar words that are Italian. *Figuriamoci!* (Imagine that!)

QUESTIONS?

What do Italian school kids study as their foreign language?
In the past, the most common foreign language taught in Italian schools was French; more recently, schools have switched to English.

Because of the growing influence of American culture, especially through the media, it's a two-way linguistic street. So many English words have been adopted in Italian that there's a name for them: *Itangliano* (highly anglicized Italian). These words include "club," "flirt," "shopping," "spray," and "style." It might seem as if you hear more English than Italian spoken in the tourist-heavy cities of Florence, Rome, and Venice!

PARLA INGLESE? (DO YOU SPEAK ENGLISH?)

FABIO: *Buon giorno. Parla inglese?*
(Good morning. Do you speak English?)

CHIARA: *No, mi dispiace, ma non lo parlo.*
(No, I'm sorry, I don't speak English.)

FABIO: *Purtroppo so soltanto un po' di italiano.*
(I'm afraid I speak only a little Italian.)

CHIARA: *Non fa niente. Riesco a capirla.*
(That's all right. I understand you.)

FABIO: *Mi innervosisco sempre quando parlo in italiano.*
(I always get nervous when I speak Italian.)

CHIARA: *La capisco benissimo.*
(I understand you very well.)

The Best Way to Learn Italian

The Italian national soccer team, known as *gli Azzurri* because of the blue of their jerseys, has for years ranked among the top teams in the world. They've won the World Cup three times, Italian-born players routinely sign multimillion-dollar contracts for European teams, and the Italian soccer leagues offer some of the most talented competition anywhere. The overriding reason for their success? Practice, practice, practice. And that's the secret to learning Italian or any other foreign language. Exercise your language muscles every day, and soon you too will be competing with the best of them.

The quickest and most effective way to learn Italian is the total-immersion method. This means traveling to Italy for an extended period, studying at any of the thousands of schools throughout the country, and speaking only Italian. Many programs include a home-stay component that enhances the cultural exchange. You literally eat, breathe, and dream in Italian.

ESSENTIALS

The eighteenth-century *Palazzo Gallenga Stuart* is headquarters for the *Università per Stranieri di Perugia*, the world's oldest and most prestigious center of Italian language education. State-of-the-art language labs and highly flexible course programs make this school an irresistible choice for anyone wanting to study in Italy.

Unfortunately, not everyone has the opportunity to spend weeks or months in Florence, Rome, or other Italian towns sipping *espresso*, touring ancient ruins, and taking language classes. There are other ways to learn Italian without leaving your hometown, wherever that may be.

You've already taken the most important step to learning Italian when you picked up this book, because the most important thing is to start studying! And any method is appropriate, whether it's reading an Italian textbook, taking a language course at a university or local language school, completing workbook exercises, listening to a tape or CD, or conversing with a native Italian speaker. Spend some time every day reading, writing, speaking, and listening to Italian to become accustomed to the target language. Slowly but surely, your confidence will build, your vocabulary will expand, and you'll be communicating in Italian. Maybe you'll even start talking with your hands!

CHAPTER 2

What You See Is What You Hear

How many letters are in the Italian alphabet? Where does the accent fall in the word *gondola*? What is the difference between *da* and *dà*? Or between *la* and *là*? It's time to learn the Italian ABCs, how to pronounce consonants and vowels, and what punctuation marks are used in writing. Remember, to improve your Italian, *fare la pratica con la bocca* (exercise your mouth)!

The Italian ABCs

Twenty-one letters is all it takes to produce the sweet, lyrical language affectionately called *la bella lingua* (the beautiful language). Using the Roman alphabet and with the addition of acute and grave accents (which will be explained later in this chapter), native Italian speakers are able to argue passionately about their favorite soccer team, discuss the latest elections, or order *gnocchi genovese* while sounding like characters in a Verdi opera.

What happened to the other five letters that are common in other languages using the Roman alphabet? They're found in foreign words that have infiltrated Italian, and are pronounced approximately as they are in the original language.

TABLE 2-1

THE ITALIAN ALPHABET			
LETTER	ITALIAN NAME	ITALIAN EXAMPLE	APPROXIMATE ENGLISH SOUND
a	*a*	*arancia, ape*	father, car
b	*bi*	*bagno, buono*	beer, barrel, bark
c	*ci*	*cane, cosa;*	cane, care;
		ciao, cedro	church, chest
d	*di*	*donna, denaro*	dim, dank, duck
e	*e*	*essere, edicola*	bet, met, set
f	*effe*	*fango, furbo*	farce, fill, firm
g	*gi*	*grazie, gamba;*	go, gab;
		gentilezza, gente	gem, general
h	*acca*	*che, hai*	(this letter is silent)
i	*i*	*idea, isola*	police, cheese, these
l	*elle*	*libro, lento*	loud, lark, lamb
m	*emme*	*mamma, mago*	math, music, march
n	*enne*	*nano, Natale*	number, name, nail
o	*o*	*otto, occhio*	bold, sold, rote
p	*pi*	*prego, Pasqua*	party, pay, pill
q	*qu*	*quadro, questo*	quiet, queen, quandary

LETTER	ITALIAN NAME	ITALIAN EXAMPLE	APPROXIMATE ENGLISH SOUND
r	*erre*	*riso, ragno*	rain, run, rag (but roll those Italian *rs*!)
s	*esse*	*strega, stanza*	slam, steal, smog
t	*ti*	*topo, terra*	tear, time, tongue
u	*u*	*uomo, uno*	croon, noon, root
v	*vu*	*vino, volcano*	vase, valley, vine
z	*zeta*	*zio, zaino*	reds, nets, sets

TABLE 2-2

FOREIGN LETTERS		
LETTER	**ITALIAN NAME**	**EXAMPLE**
j	*i lungo, i lunga*	jolly, jazz
k	*cappa*	kimono, poker
w	*doppia vu, vu dopio*	sandwich, welter
x	*ics*	box, unisex
y	*ipsilion, i greco*	sexy, yoga

For help in spelling and pronouncing words in Italian, here's a simple rule: What you hear is what you get. Italian is a phonetic language, which means most words are pronounced as they are written. The Italian words *cane*, *mane*, and *pane* will always rhyme (compare the English triplet "chalice," "police," and "lice," and you will see that you've got it easy). Another point to keep in mind is enunciation. Native Italian speakers open their mouths wide—not just to shout, but to get those big, round, vowel sounds. For example, if you want to pronounce the Italian letter *a*, just open wide and say "aahh!"

E ALERT

In Italy, one of the first books for school-aged children is the *abbecedario*, or primer. The name of the book comes from the Latin word *abecedarium*, which is derived from the first four letters of the alphabet, ABCD.

Constant Consonants

Italian pronunciation might pose some difficulties for the beginner. Yet it is very regular, and once the rules are understood it is easy to pronounce each word correctly. As you can see from **TABLE 2-1**, most Italian consonants are similar in pronunciation to their English counterparts. The consonants *c* and *g* are the only exceptions, because they vary according to the letters that follow them. Here are a few basic pronunciation rules for these two consonants:

- When *c* appears before *e* or *i*, it sounds like "ch" in the English word "church." In the contraction *c'è* (there is), pronounced "cheh," the letter *c* also has the same "soft c" sound. In all other cases, it has a sound similar to the English "k."
- When *g* appears before *e* or *i*, it sounds like "g" in the English word "general." When it appears before *n*, it sounds like the "ny" in "canyon." When it appears in the combination *gli*, it sounds like "ll" in the English word "million." In all other cases, it has a sound like the "g" in "good."

ESSENTIALS

Everyone knows how to pronounce *Chianti*, the famous red wine from Tuscany—phonetically it's key-AHN-tee. *Chianti* is the "key" that will help you remember how to pronounce Italian words that start with *chi*, such as *chiamare*, *chiara*, *chiave*, *chilo*, and *chissà*. Their pronunciations all begin with the sound "key." (*Chianti* is also the "key" to pronouncing Italian words with *chi* elsewhere, such as *dichiarare* and *inchiodare*. In all instances, the letter combination *chi* is pronounced "key.")

Double the Consonants, Double the Fun

In Italian, double consonants are pronounced much more forcefully than single consonants. Although it may not be obvious at first, a trained ear will notice the difference. Make it a point to listen to native speakers pronounce these words.

Any consonant except *h* can be doubled. With double *f, l, m, n, r, s,* and *v,* the sound is prolonged; with double *b, c, d, g, p,* and *t,* the stop is stronger than for the single consonant. Double *z* is pronounced almost the same as single *z.* Double *s* is always unvoiced—in other words, spoken as a single *s.*

TABLE 2-3

COMMON SINGLE AND DOUBLE CONSONANT WORDS			
cane	(dog)	*canne*	(canes)
casa	(house)	*cassa*	(trunk)
copia	(copy)	*coppia*	(couple)
dona	(gift)	*donna*	(woman)
nono	(ninth)	*nonno*	(grandfather)
pala	(shovel)	*palla*	(ball)
papa	(pope)	*pappa*	(bread soup)
sera	(evening)	*serra*	(greenhouse)
tufo	(tuff)	*tuffo*	(plunge)
velo	(veil)	*vello*	(pelt)

Attenzione! Yes, there is a difference in the pronunciation between *penne* and *pene.* When you order a bowl of that flavorful tube-shaped pasta, the *cameriere* (waiter) may gently nudge you and repeat PEN-neh, pronouncing the *n* longer and more emphatically, to emphasize the correct word choice. (*Penne* refers to the fact that the pasta is shaped like quills. *Pene* is the Italian word for "penis.")

I'd Like to Buy a Vowel Please

Italian vowels are short, clear cut, and are never drawn out—the "glide" with which English vowels frequently end should be avoided. It should be noted that *a, i,* and *u* are always pronounced the same way; *e* and *o,* on the other hand, have an open and a closed sound that may vary from one part of Italy to the other.

- Open *e* in *cello, lento,* and *è* sounds like the English "met."
- Closed *e* in *sete, bene, pepe,* and *vede* sounds like the English "cake."
- Open *o* in *cosa, costa,* and *donna* sounds like the English "cost."
- Closed *o* in *dopo, mondo, molto, dove,* and *sole* sounds like the English "bone."

Stressed Out?

Usually, the stress in Italian words falls on the next-to-last syllable. A few typical words that follow this general rule are listed in **TABLE 2-4**.

TABLE 2-4

COMMON SINGLE AND DOUBLE-CONSONANT WORDS			
WORDS WITH STRESS ON THE NEXT-TO-LAST SYLLABLE			
bistecca	(steak)	*campagna*	(countryside)
cervello	(brain)	*insegnare*	(to teach)
patente	(driver's license)	*pilota*	(pilot)
pizza	(pizza)	*pompelmo*	(grapefruit)
sorella	(sister)	*studiare*	(to study)

When the stress falls on the last syllable, the final vowel is accented—usually with a grave (downward-pointing) accent. The grave accent also appears in a few miscellaneous words. A few representative words with the grave accent on the last syllable are listed in **TABLE 2-5**.

TABLE 2-5

WORDS WITH STRESS ON THE LAST SYLLABLE			
cioè	(namely)	*città*	(city)
già	(already)	*però*	(however)
più	(more)	*tassì*	(taxi)
università	(university)	*venerdì*	(Friday)
virtù	(virtue)		

Grave and acute (upward-pointing) accent marks are also used with single-syllable words in order to distinguish them from others that have the same spelling but a different meaning (**SEE TABLE 2-6**).

TABLE 2-6

SINGLE-SYLLABLE WORDS			
da	(gives)	*dà*	(from)
e	(and)	*è*	(is)
la	(the; it; her)	*là*	(there)
ne	(some)	*né*	(nor)
se	(if)	*sé*	(himself, herself)
si	(oneself)	*sì*	(yes)

Traditionally, the grave (downward-pointing) accent has been used on the accented final vowels *à* and *ò*, while the acute (upward-pointing) accent was placed on all other final vowels. Today, there is a growing trend to disregard this rule, especially in nonformal publications, and only use the grave accent: for instance, *perchè* instead of *perché*, or *anzichè* instead of *anziché*.

FACTS

Here is some syllabic trivia:

Sdrucciole are words stressed on the third-to-last syllable, like *rapido*, *tavola*, and *mobile*.
Bisdrucciole are words stressed on the fourth-to-last syllable, like *litigano* and *scivolano*.
Trisdrucciole are words stressed on the fifth-to-last syllable, like *recitamelo*.

Typing Practice

When writing a document or e-mail in Italian, you will soon run into the problem of typing accented vowels. For Windows-based programs, use the Symbol menu to insert special characters into a document.

This menu will also give you shortcuts you can use:

Hit the Control key, then the ' [apostrophe], release both keys, and then type one of the vowels, to get á, é, í, ó, and ú.

Hit the Control key, then the ` [grave accent], release both keys, and then type one of the vowels, to get à, è, ì, ò, and ù.

On an Apple computer, click on the apple icon that appears in the top left of the screen, click KeyCaps, and then hold down the Option key. Click the accent you want, then the letter you want accented. For shortcuts, follow the following rules:

Hit Option + e, release, and then the correct vowel, to get á, é, í, ó, and ú.

Hit Option + `, release, and then hit the correct vowel, to get à, è, ì, ò, and ù.

No Mumbling Allowed

If you want to learn how to prepare *bruschetta* or *bistecca alla fiorentina*, you can read a cookbook—but your guests will remain hungry. You have to get in the kitchen, fire up the grill, and start slicing and dicing. Likewise, if you want to speak Italian with the correct rhythm, tone, and intonation, you have to talk. And talk and talk and talk until your mouth is numb and your brain hurts. So after you finish this chapter, make it a point to listen and repeat Italian—whether you purchase a CD or tape, rent an Italian movie, or visit Italy—because you can't eat a description of *minestrone alla milanese*, and you can't speak Italian without opening your mouth.

 **E**SSENTIALS

There are a number of tapes and CDs available to listen to and practice pronouncing Italian. Some of the most popular include the Pimsleur Foreign Language Program, the Living Language series from Random House, and Berlitz Italian. Listen and repeat often.

Did You Know?

Walk around Rome, and soon enough you'll notice the initials SPQR everywhere—stamped on street lamps, drain pipes, and manhole covers, emblazoned on workers' uniforms, and included as part of the logo for mass transit. SPQR is an acronym for the official city motto *Senatus Populusque Romanus*, a Latin phrase that means "the Senate and the People of Rome."

As a sign of the Italian spirit, many alternative meanings for the letters SPQR have been proposed. These include: *Sono Pazzi Quelli Romani* (those Romans are crazy); *Signora Prenda Questa Ricotta* (ma'am, take this ricotta); and *Solamente i Preti Regnano Qui* (only priests reign here)—a comment on the fact that Rome has been the home to the Vatican and the papacy for many centuries.

Dot, Dot, Dash

Now that you've learned your ABCs, you're probably dreaming of sitting in an olive grove, sipping *Chianti*, nibbling on *pecorino* cheese, and writing love poetry in Italian. Becoming the next Petrarca will take more than just fancy words and lots of passion. You'll need orthographic marks and punctuation too! Orthography is the representation of the sounds of a language by written or printed symbols, usually accent marks. Punctuation marks are those dots, dashes, and squiggles that denote pauses, questions, and other patterns of speech. While you may not use all of these on a regular basis, being able to refer to them in Italian will get you that much closer to captivating your Laura (Petrarca's heartthrob and the lucky recipient of his 365 love poems, one for every day of the year). Refer to **TABLE 2-7** for a list of *segni d'interpunzione* (punctuation marks).

TABLE 2-7

PUNCTUATION MARKS			
,	*la virgola*	( )	*le parentesi tonde*
.	*il punto; punto fermo*	[ ]	*le parentesi quadre*
;	*il punto e virgola*	}	*le sgraffe*

:	due punti	*	l'asterisco
...	i puntini di sospensione	´	l'accento acuto (upward-pointing accent)
!	il punto esclamativo	`	l'accento grave (downward-pointing accent)
?	il punto interrogativo	'	l'apostrofo
-	il trattino	/	la sbarretta
—	la lineetta	" "	le virgolette

Were You Paying Attention?

See if you can answer the following questions. (The answers can be found in the text. To check yourself, see the answer key in Appendix A.)

1. True/False: The Italian alphabet contains 26 letters.
2. The punctuation mark (!) is called _____ in Italian.
3. True/False: Italian word pairs like sera/serra and dona/donna are pronounced the same.
4. Usually, Italian words are stressed on the _____ -to-last syllable.
5. Italian is a _____ language, which means most words are pronounced as written.

CHAPTER 3
Surviving in Italy

Traveling to a foreign country can be a lot less stressful when you have the right words or phrases to get around. Learn how to introduce yourself and say hello to all the new friends you'll make while learning Italian, what to say when the phone rings, and how to say goodbye after that great dinner. All you need now is an updated passport and your suitcase, and it's *ciao Italia!*

Anything to Declare?

Whether you're coming or going, you'll have to make sure your *passaporto* (passport) and *visto* (visa) are in order. Although most border officials do speak English, it wouldn't hurt for you to start practicing your Italian as soon as you get to the border. For common words and phrases you might use, refer to **TABLE 3-1** and **3-2**.

TABLE 3-1

AT THE BORDER: COMMON PHRASES	
Quando arriviamo alla frontiera?	When do we get to the border?
Ecco il passaporto.	Here's my passport.
Mi fermo una settimana.	I'll be staying a week.
Sono qui per affari.	I'm here on business.
Sono qui come turista.	I'm here as a tourist (on vacation).
Sono in visita dai miei nonni.	I'm visiting my grandparents.
Posso telefonare al mio consolato?	Can I phone my consulate?
Devo riempire il modulo?	Do I have to fill in this form?

TABLE 3-2

AT THE BORDER: VOCABULARY	
color of eyes	*il colore degli occhi*
color of hair	*il colore dei capelli*
customs	*la dogana*
date of birth	*la data di nascita*
departure	*la partenza*
divorced	*divorziato* (male), *divorziata* (female)
entry visa	*il visto d'entrata*
exit visa	*il visto d'uscita*
to extend	*prolungare*
first name	*il nome di battesimo*
height	*la statura*
identity card	*la carta d'identità*
last name	*il cognome*
maiden name	*il nome da nubile*

marital status	*lo stato di famiglia*
married	*sposato* (male),
	sposata (female)
nationality	*la nazionalità*
occupation	*la professione*
place of birth	*il luogo di nascita*
place of residence	*la residenza*
to renew	*rinnovare*
signature	*la firma*
single	*celibe* (male),
	nubile (female)

ALERT

Exchanging money when traveling to Italy doesn't have to be complicated. Often the best rates are through your debit card or credit card using an ATM machine—check with your financial institution before leaving. Be aware that you'll no longer use lire in Italy. As part of the European Union, Italy now uses a common currency called the euro.

Greetings!

One of the best ways to practice your Italian is by greeting others on the street. Italians appreciate any attempt by others to speak their language, so go ahead and make the first move. Ingratiate yourself with the friendly sayings listed in **TABLE 3-3**.

TABLE 3-3

ITALIAN GREETINGS	
Salve!	Hello!
Pronto!	Hello! (when answering the phone)
Ciao!	Hi! (also: Bye!)
Buon giorno!	Good morning!
Buon pomeriggio!	Good afternoon!
Buona sera!	Good evening!

Come sta?	How are you?
Come va?	How're you doing?
Ci sentiamo bene.	We're feeling fine.
Grazie, va bene così.	Thanks, just fine.

FACTS

It's one thing to know how to say good evening in Italian, but do you know when to say it? In most of Italy, you can expect to hear a friendly *buona sera!* after 6 P.M., but it's appropriate to say "good evening" in Tuscany any time after the midday meal, or around late afternoon.

Hello, My Name Is . . .

Unless you wear a name tag (definitely *not* the fashion in Italy), you'll also have to introduce yourself. If your name has an Italian equivalent, be bold and act the part too. (See **TABLE 3-4**, which provides some common American names and their Italian counterparts.)

TABLE 3-4

COMMON ENGLISH FIRST NAMES AND THEIR ITALIAN COUNTERPARTS			
Agatha	*Agata*	Alexandra	*Alessandra*
Ann	*Anna*	Elizabeth	*Elisabeta*
Helen	*Elena*	Joan	*Giovanna*
John	*Giovann*	Joseph	*Giuseppe*
Katherine	*Caterina*	Louis	*Luigi*
Luke	*Luca*	Mark	*Marco*
Mary	*Maria*	Michael	*Michele*
Nicholas	*Nicola*	Patricia	*Patrizia*
Philip	*Filippo*	Theresa	*Teresa*
Thomas	*Tommaso*	Vincent	*Vincenzo*

For some common ways of introducing yourself, see **TABLE 3-5**.

TABLE 3-5

INTRODUCTIONS	
Mi chiamo Michele.	My name is Michael.
Piacere di conoscerla.	Pleased to meet you. (formal form)
Questa è mia moglie.	This is my wife.
Questo è mio marito.	This is my husband.
Come si chiama?	What is your name?
Di dov'è?	Where are you from?
Dove lavora?	Where do you work?
Che cosa studia?	What are you studying?
Lei abita qui?	Do you live here?

Note that in Italian—as in other Romance languages—there is a formal and an informal form of address. In Chapter 19, you'll learn more about the four ways of saying "you" in Italian and other grammatical notes on the correct forms of courtesy.

IL PRIMO GIORNO DI SCUOLA (FIRST DAY OF SCHOOL)

FABIO: *Ciao, posso sedermi vicino a te?*
(Hey, may I sit next to you?)

CHIARA: *Certo! È libero.*
(Sure! It's open.)

FABIO: *Mi chiamo Fabio e tu?*
(My name is Fabio, what's yours?)

CHIARA: *Chiara. Hai già fatto conoscenza con qualcun altro della classe?*
(Have you already met anyone in the class?)

FABIO: *No, non conosco nessuno.*
(No, I don't know anybody.)

Talking on the Phone

Speaking on the phone is one of the most difficult accomplishments for nonnative speakers of Italian. There is no body language to observe, no hand gestures to parse, and you can't read lips (you'd be surprised how often most people do—if you have poor vision, you'll be surprised at how much more difficult it is to hear when your glasses are off).

Common expressions used to make a telephone call include:

Pronto? (Hello?)
Chi parla? (Who is speaking?)
C'è [Carlo], per favore? (Is [Carlo] in?)
ArrivederLa. (Goodbye.)
Posso lasciare un messaggio? (May I leave a message?)

It is not uncommon for an Italian family to have only one telephone in the house. Most families don't need an extra phone because Italians prefer to meet one another in the town square or at the local *caffè*.

However, Italians took to *telefonini* (cell phones) a lot quicker than in many other countries, and enjoy using their phones for exchanging SMS (text) messages utilizing the phone keypad. One reason for the popularity of cell phones? The tax rate on cellular phones is one third that of landlines, so many Italians made the switch for purely economic reasons.

Stop the Thief!

Sometimes it happens. The rental car breaks down, you lose your wallet, or worse. If you find yourself in a situation like this, don't panic, and concentrate on trying to explain what happened to *la polizia* at *la stazione di polizia*. (Use vocabulary in **TABLE 3-6**.)

TABLE 3-6

VOCABULARY: POLICE STATION			
an accident	*incidente*	judge	*il giudice*
arrest, to	*arrestare*	key	*la chiave*
attorney	*l'avvocato*	money	*i soldi*
bag	*la borsa*	necklace	*la collana*
billfold	*il portafoglio*	police	*la polizia*

briefcase	la cartella	prison	la prigione
court	il tribunale	purse	il borsellino
crime	il delitto	ring	l'anello
custody	la detenzione	suitcase	la valigia
drugs	le droghe	thief	il ladro
guilt	la colpa	verdict	la sentenza
handbag	la borsetta	watch	l'orologio

When It's Time to Say Goodbye

Every party must come to an end, but don't just slouch out of the room. Use the farewells in **TABLE 3-7** to show your good manners, and you'll be invited back to the next *festa*.

TABLE 3-7

FAREWELLS	
Arrivederci!	Goodbye!
A presto!	See you soon!
A domani!	See you tomorrow!
Auguri!	All the best!
Buon viaggio!	Have a good trip!
È già tardi.	It's pretty late.
Torni presto!	Come again soon!
Ti telefono domani.	I'll call you tomorrow.
Mi è piaciuto molto.	I enjoyed myself very much.
Buonanotte!	Good night!

Partire è un po' morire. Parting is such sweet sorrow, but in Italy there's a bonus when leaving. Two kisses, one on either cheek, is the norm between friends, family, and lovers. *Che tenerezza!* (What tenderness!)

If you're waiting at the airport to board the plane or standing in line to get your passport stamped, why not practice your Italian? Here's a word search puzzle to get you in the mood for greetings, introductions, farewells, and getting along in Italy. You should recognize all of these words from this chapter. You'll find the answers in Appendix A.

```
C  I  A  O  T  S  I  V  A  C  I  N  O  M  P
V  A  L  T  D  E  R  C  I  O  T  P  Q  U  R
D  I  C  R  E  D  E  V  I  R  R  A  C  R  O
L  P  R  O  N  T  O  T  A  O  R  O  O  E  L
O  T  A  P  R  C  O  G  N  L  N  S  L  T  U
S  A  N  A  G  U  O  D  E  E  I  H  I  T  N
A  P  A  S  Z  T  E  E  S  M  T  G  M  O  G
I  S  G  S  L  D  U  O  F  G  O  A  I  N  A
Z  I  O  A  T  T  E  S  R  O  B  N  P  A  R
I  V  D  P  C  A  V  E  N  E  R  A  G  N  E
L  R  A  L  B  Z  O  L  O  I  A  S  R  O  B
O  T  A  L  O  S  N  O  C  T  A  N  O  U  C
P  A  R  R  E  S  T  A  R  E  S  R  O  B  L
R  P  I  L  O  P  G  O  C  U  B  S  R  O  B
A  I  C  R  R  A  A  R  E  I  T  N  O  R  F
```

ARRESTARE	CIAO	FRONTIERA	PROLUNGARE
ARRIVEDERCI	COGNOME	LADRO	PRONTO
BORSAIOLO	CONSOLATO	PASSAPORTO	SOLDI
BORSETTA	DOGANA	PATENTE	VALIGIA
BUONANOTTE	EURO	POLIZIA	VISTO

CHAPTER 4
Nouns and Articles

How are plurals formed in Italian? Just what are *pizze* anyway? Why are there so many ways to say "the"? Find out all about singular and plural nouns, the articles, one very important word in Italian, and why you might just want to say *che bello!*

A Person, Place, or Thing

You've heard it since grade school: What's a noun? A person, place, or thing. Nouns (*i nome*) are one of the first things that people learn, whether it's their native or second language. *Bicchiere, vino, funghi.* Glass, wine, mushrooms. And in Italian, what's noticeable almost immediately is that nouns have endings that change depending on the gender. **TABLE 4-1** includes a few nouns to start with.

TABLE 4-1

ITALIAN NOUNS	
MASCULINE	FEMININE
banco (school desk)	*cartella* (book bag)
libro (book)	*lavagna* (chalkboard)
nonno (grandfather)	*nonna* (grandmother)
ragazzo (boy)	*ragazza* (girl)
specchio (mirror)	*scuola* (school)
zaino (backpack)	*material* (subject)
zio (uncle)	*zia* (aunt)

Most Italian nouns end in a vowel—those that end in a consonant are of foreign origin—and all nouns have a gender, even those that refer to a qualities, ideas, and things. Usually, Italian singular masculine nouns end in –*o*, while feminine nouns end in –*a*. There are exceptions, of course (see **TABLE 4-2**).

TABLE 4-2

ITALIAN NOUNS ENDING IN –*E*	
MASCULINE	FEMININE
giornale (newspaper)	*frase* (sentence)
mare (sea)	*nave* (ship)
nome (name)	*notte* (night)
pane (bread)	*classe* (class)
ponte (bridge)	*canzone* (song)

All nouns ending in *–amma* are masculine, while all nouns ending in *–zione* are feminine. Almost all nouns ending in *–ore*, *–ere*, *–ame*, *–ale*, *–ile*, and a consonant + *–one* are masculine: *il pittore, il cameriere, lo sciame, l'animale, il porcile, il bastone*.

Two Pizze and a Bowl of Spaghetti

Sometimes one pizza just isn't enough—and one glass of red wine isn't sufficient to quench your thirst. When forming the plural of Italian nouns, the vowel endings change to indicate a change in number. For regular masculine nouns that end in *–o*, the ending changes to *–i* in the plural (see **TABLE 4-3**).

TABLE 4-3

PLURAL FORMS OF MASCULINE NOUNS ENDING IN *–O*		
SINGULAR	PLURAL	ENGLISH
fratello	*fratelli*	brothers
libro	*libri*	books
nonno	*nonni*	grandfather
ragazzo	*ragazzi*	boys
vino	*vini*	wine

Regular feminine nouns that end in *–a* take on *–e* endings in the plural (see **TABLE 4-4**).

TABLE 4-4

PLURAL FORMS OF FEMININE NOUNS ENDING IN *–A*		
SINGULAR	PLURAL	ENGLISH
casa	*case*	houses
penne	*penne*	pens
pizza	*pizze*	pizza
ragazza	*ragazze*	girls
sorella	*sorelle*	sisters

When forming the plural of nouns ending in a consonant, such as words of foreign origin, only the article changes: *il film/i film.* Here are some exceptions to the rule for forming feminine plurals:

Feminine-noun ending –*ea* changes to –*ee* in the plural. For example: *dea/dee* (goddess/goddesses).

Feminine-noun ending –*ca* changes to –*che* in the plural. For example: *amica/amiche* (friend/friends). Remember that –*che* is pronounced as "keh" in Italian.

Finally, recall that some nouns end in –*e.* The plural forms of these nouns will end in –*i* (regardless of gender).

TABLE 4-5

PLURAL FORMS OF NOUNS ENDING IN –*E*		
SINGULAR	PLURAL	ENGLISH
bicchiere	*bicchieri*	(wine) glass
chiave	*chiavi*	keys
fiume	*fiumi*	rivers
frase	*frasi*	phrases
padre	*padri*	fathers

Practice Pluralism

Change the following singular nouns to the plural. Check your answers in Appendix A.

1. aranciata _____
2. vitello _____
3. albicoca _____
4. torta _____
5. pesce _____
6. polpetta _____
7. gelato _____
8. bruschetta _____
9. risotto _____
10. arancino _____

LA SORELLINA (BABY SISTER)

CHIARA: *Mamma, ma quanto grande sarà la nuova sorellina?*
(Mom, how big is the new baby sister going to be?)

MAMMA: *Beh, sarà piccolina all'inizio, ma poi crescerà in fretta!*
(Well, she is going to be small at the beginning, but then she's going to grow fast!)

FABIO: *Anche noi eravamo molto piccoli una volta, non è vero mamma?*
(Even we were very little once, right mom?)

MAMMA: *Piccoli e dolcissimi!*
(Small and very sweet!)

CHIARA: *Credi che le piacerà giocare alle bambole?*
(Do you think she is going to like playing with dolls?)

FABIO: *Macché! Vorrà solo mangiare e dormire!*
(Not at all! She is just going to eat and sleep!)

MAMMA: *Beh, all'inizio, ma quando sarà un po' più grande, sono certa che adorerà giocare con te!*
(Well, at the beginning, but when she's a little older, I'm sure she'll very much like playing with you!)

CHIARA: *Allora le terrò da parte le mie.*
(Then I'm going to save mine for her!)

An Apple a Day

The English indefinite articles "a" and "an" correspond to the Italian *un, uno, un',* and *una,* which are used with singular nouns. Take a look at **TABLE 4-6** for examples.

TABLE 4-6

SINGULAR INDEFINITE ARTICLES	
MASCULINE	**FEMININE**
un amico (a friend)	*una casa* (a house)
un libro (a book)	*una lezione* (a lesson)
uno sbaglio (a mistake)	*un'automobile* (a car)
uno zio (an uncle)	*un'università* (a university)

In Italian, the form of the *l'articolo indeterminativo* (indefinite article) is dependent on the initial sound of the noun it precedes. *Uno* is used for masculine words beginning with *z, ps,* or *gn,* or with *s* + consonant; *un* is used for all other masculine words. The feminine form *una* becomes *un'* before a word that begins with a vowel (to avoid awkward pronunciation).

The Power of Articulation

Fill in the blanks with the correct indefinite article and check your answers in Appendix A.

1. _____ *agnello* (lamb)
2. _____ *cavallo* (horse)
3. _____ *elefante* (elephant)
4. _____ *aquila* (eagle)
5. _____ *orso* (bear)
6. _____ *vipera* (snake)
7. _____ *volpe* (fox)
8. _____ *sciacallo* (hyena)
9. _____ *giraffa* (giraffe)
10. _____ *tartaruga* (turtle)

The Word "The"—Seven Different Ways

In English, the definite article has only one form: "the." In Italian, *l'articolo determinativo* has different forms according to the gender, number, and first letter of the noun or adjective it precedes. Take a look at these examples:

il libro e la matita (the book and the pencil)
i ragazzi e le ragazze (the boys and girls)
la Coca-Cola e l'aranciata (the Coke and orangeade)
gli italiani e i giapponesi (the Italians and the Japanese)
le zie e gli zii (the aunts and uncles)

- *Lo* (*gli* in plural) is used before masculine nouns beginning with *s* + consonant or with *z*.

- *Il* (*i* in plural) is used before masculine nouns beginning with all other consonants.
- *L'* (*gli* in plural) is used before masculine nouns beginning with a vowel.
- *La* (*le* in plural) is used before feminine nouns beginning with a consonant.
- *L'* (*le* in plural) is used before feminine nouns beginning with a vowel.

The article agrees in gender and number with the noun it modifies and is repeated before each noun. The first letter of the word immediately following the article determines the form of the article. Compare and contrast the pairs in **TABLE 4-7**.

TABLE 4-7

USE OF DEFINITE ARTICLES WITH NOUNS AND ADJECTIVES	
il giorno (the day)	*l'altro giorno* (the other day)
lo zio (the uncle)	*il vecchio zio* (the old uncle)
i ragazzi (the boys)	*gli stessi ragazzi* (the same boys)
l'amica (the girlfriend)	*la nuova amica* (the new girlfriend)

In Italian, the definite article must always be used before the name of a language, except when the verbs *parlare* (to speak) or *studiare* (to study) directly precede the name of the language—in those cases, the use of the article is optional:

Studio l'italiano. (I study Italian.)
Parlo italiano. (I speak Italian.)
Parlo bene l'italiano. (I speak Italian well.)

The definite article is also used before the days of the week to indicate a repeated, habitual activity. For example:

Domenica studio. (I'm studying on Sunday.)
Marco non studia mai la domenica. (Marco never studies on Sundays.)

Unlike English, the Italian definite article must be used with all general or abstract nouns.

ESSENTIALS

The definite article is used before titles such as *il signor Rossi* and *la professoressa Ciampi*, and abstract nouns such as *la libertà* and *la matematica*. It is also used when referring to famous people: *il Galileo, la Loren*. In Tuscany, there is also a tendency to use *la* when referring to girls and women: *la Francesca, la Giuliana*.

Family Is Special

Mom and dad, your brothers and sisters, grandpa and your Aunt Millie. They're all special people, and so there's a rule just for them. In the plural form, the definite article will appear before the possessive adjective that refers to a family member or relative. For example, instead of saying "my brothers," you are literally saying "the my brothers." **TABLE 4-8** contains other examples.

TABLE 4-8

USE OF DEFINITE ARTICLES WITH POSSESSIVE ADJECTIVES	
Mio fratello è carino.	(My brother is cute.)
I miei fratelli sono carini.	(My brothers are cute.)
Questo è tuo zio.	(This is my uncle.)
Questi sono i tuoi zii.	(These are my uncles.)
Mia nonna è vecchia.	(My grandmother is old.)
I miei nonni sono vecchi.	(My grandmothers are old.)
Mio cugino è straordinario.	(My cousin is exceptional.)
I miei cugini sono straordinari.	(My cousins are exceptional.)

Talking about Some or Any

L'articolo partitivo (partitive article) is used to indicate imprecise or approximate quantities. It appears before singular nouns (*del miele, del caffè, del burro*) as well as before plural nouns of an unspecified amount (*dei libri, delle ragazze, degli studenti*). The partitive is expressed by the preposition *di* (of, from) combined with the definite article (see **TABLE 4-9**). For example:

Ho delle cravatte blu. (I have a few blue ties.)
Prende del caffè. (She is drinking some coffee.)
Esco con dei compagni. (I go out with some friends.)
Manca del burro. (He needs some butter.)

TABLE 4-9

PARTITIVE ARTICLES		
	SINGULAR	PLURAL
feminine	*della*	*delle*
feminine (before a vowel)	*dell'*	*delle*
masculine	*del*	*dei*
masculine (before a vowel)	*dell'*	*degli*
masculine (before the letters *z, x* +consonant, and *gn*)	*dello*	*degli*

Che belle ragazze!

What beautiful girls! Italians are profuse in their praise and description. The adjectives *bello* (beautiful, handsome, nice, fine) and *quello* (that) have shortened forms when they precede the nouns they modify (see **TABLES 4-10** and **4-11**). Note that the shortened forms are similar to those of the definite article.

TABLE 4-10

MASCULINE FORMS OF *BELLO* AND *QUELLO*		
	SINGULAR	PLURAL
before *z* + consonant or *s*	*bello/quello*	*begli/quegli*
before other consonants	*bel/quel*	*bei/quei*
before vowels	*bell'/quell'*	*begli/quegli*

TABLE 4-11

FEMININE FORMS OF *BELLO* AND *QUELLO*		
	SINGULAR	PLURAL
before consonants	*bella/quella*	*belle/quelle*
before vowels	*bell'/quell'*	*belle/quelle*

Here is how *bello* and *quello* may be used in Italian sentences:

Chi è quel bell'uomo? (Who's that handsome man?)
Che bei capelli e che begli occhi! (What beautiful hair and eyes!)
Quell'americana è di Boston. (That America woman is from Boston.)
Quelle case sono vecchie. (Those houses are old.)

Note that *bello* retains its full form when it follows the noun it modifies or the verb *essere*:

Un ragazzo bello non è sempre simpatico. (A handsome boy is not always a likable boy.)
Quel ragazzo è bello. (That boy is handsome.)

This and That

Fill in the blanks with the correct form of *quello* and then check your answers in Appendix A.

1. _____ foto è vecchia.
2. _____ automobile è una Fiat.
3. Come sono bravi _____ avvocati!
4. È irlandese _____ studente?
5. Sono facili _____ ricette?
6. _____ bambini hanno i capelli biondi.
7. _____ ospedale è grande.
8. Com'è bello _____ negozio!

CHAPTER 5

Essere and Avere: Don't Leave Home Without Them

L anguage means action, and you can't speak Italian without the verbs *essere* (to be) and *avere* (to have). These two essential verbs are used in compound verb formations, idiomatic expressions, and many other grammatical constructions. Become the maestro of these two verbs and you'll have taken a giant step toward learning Italian.

To Be or Not to Be: *Essere*

As the English verb "to be," *essere* is used in myriad grammatical and linguistic situations. Learning the many conjugations and uses of the verb is crucial to the study of the Italian language.

La bambina è piccola. (The child is small.)
Chi è? Sono io. Siamo noi. (Who is it? It's me. It's us.)
Che ore sono? Sono le quattro. (What time is it? It is four o'clock.)

Essere is an irregular verb *(un verbo irregolare)*; it does not follow a predictable pattern of conjugation (see **TABLE 5-1**). Note that the form *sono* is used with both *io* (I) and *loro* (they). The context of the sentence will usually make evident the correct meaning.

TABLE 5-1

CONJUGATING *ESSERE* (TO BE)		
PERSON	**SINGULAR**	**PLURAL**
I	*(io) sono* (I am)	*(noi) siamo* (we are)
II	*(tu) sei* (you are, familiar)	*(voi) siete* (you are, familiar)
III	*(Lei) è* (you are, formal)	*(Loro) sono* (you are, formal)
	(lui/lei) è (he/she is)	*(loro) sono* (they are)

The expression *c'è* means "there is," and *ci sono* means "there are." These expressions are used to indicate where somebody or something is located:

C'è una chiesa. (There is a church.)
Ci sono due chiese. (There are two churches.)

The word *ecco* also means "here is/here are" or "there is/there are," but is used to draw attention to or point out something. For example: *Ecco Stefano!* (Here is Stefano!)

Conjugating *Essere*

Complete each sentence with the correct form of the verb *essere*.
The answers appear in Appendix A.

1. Massimo non .... qui, ... da sua zia.
2. Ragazze, ... a scuola alle tre?
3. La sabato io .... sempre a casa.
4. Voi .... di Torino?
5. Dove .... i tuoi genitori?
6. Noi .... pronti a studiare.
7. Monica, ... italiana?
8. Luisa non .... americana: .... canadese.

The Swiss Army Knife of Verbs

You'll soon realize that the verb *essere* is an all-purpose grammatical tool that's indispensable in a variety of situations. Here are a few examples of how *essere* is used in Italian:

- *Essere* is used with *di* + name of a city to indicate city of origin (the city someone is from). To indicate country of origin, an adjective of nationality is generally used:

  Io sono di Napoli. Tu di dove sei? (I'm from Naples. Where are you from?)
  È cinese. (She is Chinese.)

- *Essere* + *di* + proper name indicates possession. Italian does not use the "apostrophe + s" constructions that English speakers rely on to signal possession.

  È di Giovanna. (It is Giovanna's. Literally: It is of Giovanna.)
  Questa chitarra è di Beppino; non è di Vittoria. (This guitar is Beppino's; it's not Vittoria's.)

- To find out who owns something, ask *Di chi è . . . ?*

  Di chi è questo libro? (Whose book is this?)
  Di chi sono questi libri? (Whose books are these?)

- *Essere* is also used as an auxiliary verb in the following cases:

  1. **Reflexive verbs:** Those verbs whose action reverts to the subject, as in the following examples: I wash myself. *Mi lavo.* They enjoy themselves. *Si divertono.* (You'll find out more about reflexive and reciprocal verbs in Chapter 16.)
  2. **Impersonal form:** As in general statements in English that rely on one of the following subjects: "one," "you," "we," "they," or "people" + verb. For example: *Si mangia bene in Italia.* (People/they eat well in Italy.)
  3. **Passive voice:** In a passive construction the subject of the verb receives the action instead of doing it, as in the sentence: Caesar was killed by Brutus. *Cesare è stato ucciso da Brutus.*

Essere is not just a verb. It can be used as a noun to mean "being," "individual," or "existence": *un essere fortunato* is a lucky fellow; *essere umano* is a human being; *essere razionale* is a rational being.

To Have and Have Not: *Avere*

Like the verb *essere*, *avere* is used in a variety of ways. After learning the conjugations and uses of the verb, you'll be that much closer to understanding the Italian language. Take a look at a few of these examples to see how *avere* works in the Italian sentence:

Ho molti amici. (I have many friends.)
Ha una villa in campagna. (He has a house in the country.)
Maria ha un vestito nuovo. (Maria has on a new dress.)

Avere is an irregular verb (*un verbo irregolare*); it does not follow a predictable pattern of conjugation. Even though most forms of *avere* begin with *h*, that letter is never pronounced. Commit to memory the present tense (*il presente*) form of *avere* (see **TABLE 5-2**)—you will see it in many Italian grammatical constructions.

TABLE 5-2	CONJUGATING *AVERE* (TO HAVE)	
PERSON	SINGULAR	PLURAL
I	*(io) ho* (I have)	*(noi) abbiamo* (we have)
II	*(tu) hai* (you have, familiar)	*(voi) avete* (you have, familiar)
IIII	*(Lei) ha* (you have, formal)	*(Loro) hanno* (you have, formal)
	(lui/lei) ha (he/she has)	*(loro) hanno* (they have)

Conjugating *Avere*

Complete each sentence with the correct form of the verb *avere*.
Check your answers in Appendix A.

1. Anna Maria _____ la penna in mano.
2. Tu _____ una bella voce.
3. Voi _____ dieci dollari.
4. Io _____ tre sorelle.
5. Alessandra _____ una macchina italiana.
6. Gli studenti _____ molti compiti da fare.
7. Oggi noi _____ ospiti in casa.
8. Stefano e Antonio _____ un cane.

What is the difference between *ho* and *o*? Between *ha* and *a*?
Ho is the first person singular form of *avere*, while *o* means "or."
Ha is the third personal singular form of *avere*, while *a* is a preposition. In both cases, the pronunciation is identical.

Idiomatic Expressions with *Avere*

Espressioni idiomatiche, or idiomatic expressions, are phrases that have a special meaning in context. The verb *avere* is used in many idiomatic expressions to convey feelings or sensations and take the form *avere* + noun. In English these expressions are usually formed with "to be" + adjective. **TABLE 5-3** contains some common idiomatic expressions using *avere*.

TABLE 5-3

IDIOMATIC EXPRESSIONS WITH *AVERE*	
avere bisogno di	to need, have need of
avere caldo	to be warm (hot)
avere fame	to be hungry
avere freddo	to be cold
avere fretta	to be in a hurry
avere paura	to be afraid
avere sete	to be thirsty
avere sonno	to be sleepy
avere voglia di	to want, to feel like
avere a che fare con	to deal with
avercela con	to have it in for
aversela a male	to feel bad

Here is how you might use these expressions in a sentence:

Michele ha sempre fretta. (Michael is always in a hurry.)
Ho caldo. Ho voglia di un gelato. (I'm hot. I feel like having ice cream.)
Non capisco proprio perché ce l'hai con me. (I really don't understand why you have it in for me.)
È inutile che io le parli; vuole avere a che fare solo con te. (It's no use my talking to her; she only wants to deal with you.)
Non avertela a male se non ti invito a quella cena. Ho già troppi invitati. (Don't feel bad if I don't invite you to that dinner. I have too many guests already.)

FACTS

Here's how to remember how many days are in each month:

*Trenta giorni ha novembre
con aprile, giugno, e settembre,
di ventotto ce n'è uno,
tutti gli altri ne hanno trentuno.*

How Old Are You?

The verb *avere* is also used in discussing age: *avere* + [number] +
anni means "to be [number] years old":

Quanti anni hai? (How old are you?)
Ho trentuno anni. (I'm thirty one.)
Questa gatta è vecchia, ha quindici anni. (This cat is old, it is fifteen
years old.)

BUON COMPLEANNO (HAPPY BIRTHDAY!)

CHIARA: *Buon compleanno, Fabio!*
(Happy birthday, Fabio!)

FABIO: *Grazie!*
(Thank you!)

CHIARA: *Ma quanti anni compi?*
(But how old are you today?)

FABIO: *Dodici, come te.*
(Twelve, like you!)

CHIARA: *Senti, ti va di aprire il mio regalo ora?*
(Listen, would you like to open my present now?)

FABIO: *Dovrei aspettare il momento della torta, ma sono curioso e se
insisti . . .*
(I should wait for the cake, but I am really curious and if you
insist . . .)

CHIARA: *Ti piace? È il nuovo CD di Eros Ramazzotti!*
(Do you like it? It's the new Eros Ramazzotti CD!)

FABIO: *Oh, sì! Grazie! Lo metto subito sù! Ecco fatto! Vieni voglio presentarti gli altri.*
(Oh, yes! Thanks! I'm going to play it right now! Done! Come on, I'm going to introduce you to the others!)

CHIARA: *Ciao a tutti!*
(Hi everybody!)

Making Verbs Interrogative

One easy way to ask questions in Italian is to add a question mark to the end of the sentence in writing. (When speaking, raise the pitch of your voice at the end of the sentence.) For example:

Hai un buon lavoro. (You have a good job.)
Hai un buon lavoro? (Do you have a good job?)

If a subject (noun or pronoun) is expressed in the interrogative, it can:

- Stay at the beginning of the sentence, before the verb.
- Move to the end of the sentence.
- Move to precede the verb (the least frequent option).

So, for instance, you can ask the question "Does Nadia have a bicycle?" in three different ways:

Nadia ha una bicicletta?
Ha una bicicletta Nadia?
Ha Nadia una bicicletta?

Compound It!

The compound tenses (*i tempi composti*) are verb tenses that consist of two words, such as the *passato prossimo* (present perfect). Both the verbs *essere* and *avere* act as helping verbs in compound tense formations. For example: *io sono stato* (I was) and *ho avuto* (I had). Now you know why *avere* and *essere* are so important!

Present Perfect with *Avere*

In general, transitive verbs (verbs that carry over an action from the sub-ject to the direct object) are conjugated with *avere* as in the following example:

Il pilota ha pilotato l'aeroplano. (The pilot flew the plane.)

When the *passato prossimo* is constructed with *avere*, the past participle does not change according to gender or number:

Io ho parlato con Giorgio ieri pomeriggio. (I spoke to George yesterday afternoon.)
Noi abbiamo comprato molte cose. (We bought many things.)

When the past participle of a verb conjugated with *avere* is preceded by the third person direct object pronouns *lo, la, le,* or *li,* the past participle agrees with the preceding direct object pronoun in gender and number. The past participle may agree with the direct object pronouns *mi, ti, ci,* and *vi* when these precede the verb, but the agreement is not mandatory.

Ho bevuto la birra. (I drank the beer.)
L'ho bevuta. (I drank it.)
Ho comprato il sale e il pepe. (I bought the salt and pepper.)
Ci hanno visto/visti. (They saw us.)

In negative sentences, *non* is placed before the auxiliary verb:

Molti non hanno pagato. (Many didn't pay.)
No, non ho ordinato una pizza. (No, I didn't order a pizza.)

For a more detailed look at past participles, see Chapter 11.

Present Perfect with *Essere*

When *essere* is used, the past participle always agrees in gender and number with the subject of the verb. In many cases, intransitive verbs (those that cannot take a direct object), especially those expressing motion, are conjugated with the auxiliary verb *essere*. The verb *essere* is also conjugated with itself as the auxiliary verb. Some of the most common verbs that form compound tenses with *essere* are listed in **TABLE 5-4**.

TABLE 5-4

INTRANSITIVE VERBS THAT APPEAR WITH *ESSERE* IN PRESENT PERFECT			
andare	to go	*arrivare*	to arrive
cadere	to fall	*dimagrire*	to diet
entrare	to enter	*immigrare*	to immigrate
morire	to die	*partire*	to depart
restare	to stay, to remain	*(ri)tornare*	to return
salpare	to weigh anchor to, to set sail	*sfuggire*	to run away, to flee
stare	to stay, to be	*uscire*	to go out
venire	to come		

It's All in the Past

Change the verbs from the singular to the plural or from the plural to the singular. The answers appear in Appendix A.

EXAMPLE: Hai un bicchiere. Avete un bicchiere.

1. Che ora è? _____
2. Non hanno amici in Italia. _____
3. Di dove sono i tuoi zii? _____
4. Voi avete molto fame? _____
5. Loro sono americane. _____
6. Hai due pizze. _____
7. Abbiamo sete? _____
8. Lui è molto occupato. _____
9. Sono italiane le tue cugine? _____
10. Ho un gatto. _____

CHAPTER 6

Big, Red, Round, and Delicious

All these words may be used to describe a pizza—and you don't need to stop here. The best in Rome, absolutely horrible, better than you'd make at home—the list of adjectives can get pretty lengthy. This chapter will cover all kinds of adjectives, including comparative and superlative forms, modifiers, and other descriptions, and how they work in Italian.

Adjectives Times Four

Italian and English differ in their usage of adjectives. Italian descriptive adjectives are usually placed after the noun they modify, and with which they agree in gender and number. (When you learn a new adjective, it will be presented to you in the masculine singular form.)

TABLE 6-1

COMMON ADJECTIVES ENDING IN –O			
allegro	cheerful, happy	*buono*	good, kind
cattivo	bad, wicked	*freddo*	cold
grasso	fat	*leggero*	light
nuovo	new	*pieno*	full
stretto	narrow	*timido*	timid, shy

Adjectives ending in –o have four forms: masculine singular, masculine plural, feminine singular, and feminine plural. Observe how the adjectives *nero* and *cattivo* change to agree with nouns they modify (**TABLE 6-2**).

TABLE 6-2

ENDINGS OF –O ADJECTIVES	
SINGULAR	**PLURAL**
il gatto nero (the black cat, masculine)	*i gatti neri* (the black cats, masculine)
la gatta nera (the black cat, feminine)	*le gatte nere* (the black cats, feminine)
il ragazzo cattivo (the bad boy)	*i ragazzi cattivoi* (the bad boys)
la ragazza cattiva (the bad girl)	*le ragazze cattive* (the bad girls)

Note that when an adjective modifies two nouns of different gender, it retains its masculine ending. For example: *i padri e le madre italiani* (Italian fathers and mothers).

Descriptions

Complete the following with the correct form of the indicated adjective, and check your answers in Appendix A.

1. La pizza è _____. (caldo)
2. La madre di Lorenza è _____. (generoso)

3. I fiori sono _____. (rosso)
4. La torta è _____. (buono)
5. Il gatto è _____. (nero)
6. Carla è _____. (magro)
7. I bambini sono _____. (cattivo)
8. Voi siete _____. (timido)
9. L'appartamento è _____. (moderno)
10. Le case non sono _____. (nuovo)

Missing in Action

Not all Italian adjectives have a singular form ending in *–o*. There are a number of adjectives that end in *–e*. The singular ending *–e* changes to *–i* in the plural, whether the noun is masculine or feminine (see **TABLE 6-3**).

TABLE 6-3

ENDINGS OF *–E* ADJECTIVES	
SINGULAR	PLURAL
il ragazzo triste (the sad boy)	*i ragazzi tristi* (the sad boys)
la ragazza triste (the sad girl)	*le ragazze tristi* (the sad girls)

FACTS

Adjectives of colors that derive from nouns do not change according to gender. For example: *Non trovo il maglione rosa.* (I can't find the pink sweater.) The adjective *blu* (blue, navy), which is monosyllabic, is also invariable. *Porto la giacca e i pantaloni blu in lavanderia.* (I'm taking the blue coat and pants to the laundry.)

TABLE 6-4

ADJECTIVES ENDING IN *–E*			
abile	able	*difficile*	difficult
facile	easy	*felice*	happy
forte	strong	*grande*	big, large, great
importante	important	*intelligente*	intelligent
interessante	interesting	*triste*	sad
veloce	fast, speedy		

There are quite a few other exceptions for forming plural adjectives. For instance, adjectives that end in *–io* (with the stress falling on that *i*) form the plural with the ending *–ii*: *addio/addii*; *leggio/leggii*; *zio/zii*.

TABLE 6-5 contains a chart of other irregular adjective endings you should know.

TABLE 6-5

FORMING PLURAL ADJECTIVES			
SINGULAR ENDING	PLURAL ENDING	SINGULAR ENDING	PLURAL ENDING
–ca	*–che*	*–gio*	*–gi*
–cia	*–ce*	*–glia*	*–glie*
–cio	*–ci*	*–glio*	*–gli*
–co	*–chi*	*–go*	*–ghi*
–ga	*–ghe*	*–scia*	*–sce*
–gia	*–ge*	*–scio*	*–sci*

AGGETTIVI (ADJECTIVES)

PAULA: *Dimmi il nome di un insetto.*
(Name an insect.)

SILVIO: *La vespa, l'ape, la mosca . . . lo scarafaggio, è un insetto?*
(A wasp, a bee, a fly . . . is a cockroach an insect?)

PAULA: *Sai dirmi il nome di qualche uccello?*
(Can you name some birds?)

SILVIO: *Pappagallo, usignolo, aquila, merlo, passero. In Italia ci sono molti piccioni.*
(Parrot, nightingale, eagle, thrush, sparrow. In Italy there are many pigeons.)

PAULA: *Quarda che bella farfalla!*
(Look at the beautiful butterfly!)

SILVIO: *Dov'è? Oh, che meraviglia! Una splendida farfalla gialla!*
(Where? Oh, how lovely! A pretty yellow butterfly!)

PAULA: *Qual è il tuo animale preferito?*
(What's your favorite animal?)

SILVIO: *Il mio animale preferito è la giraffa, ma mi piacciono anche i cavalli, i delfini, e i porcospini.*

(My favorite animal is the giraffe, but I also like horses, dolphins, and hedgehogs.)

Following the Order

As you have already seen, adjectives generally follow the noun:

È una lingua difficile. (It is a difficult language.)
Marina è una ragazza generosa. (Marina is a generous girl.)

Certain common adjectives, however, generally come before the noun:

Anna è una cara amica. (Anna is a dear friend.)
Gino è un bravo dottore. (Gino is a good doctor.)
È un brutt'affare. (It's a bad situation.)

The most common adjectives that come before the noun are listed in **TABLE 6-6.**

TABLE 6-6

ADJECTIVES THAT PRECEDE NOUNS			
bello	beautiful	*bravo*	good, able
brutto	ugly	*buono*	good
caro	dear	*cattivo*	bad
giovane	young	*grande*	large, great
lungo	long	*nuovo*	new
piccolo	small, little	*stesso*	same
vecchio	old	*vero*	true

But even these adjectives must follow the noun for emphasis or contrast, and when modified by an adverb:

Oggi non porta l'abito vecchio, porta un abito nuovo. (Today he is not wearing the old suit, he is wearing a new suit.)
Abitano in una casa molto piccola. (They live in a very small house.)

Drawing Comparisons

This tower is as tall as that one. This picture is as beautiful as that one. Maria is smarter than Guido. There are a number of ways to compare two or more things in English, and the same is true for Italian.

Equality

Comparisons of equality, in which two nouns, adjectives, or adverbs have the same characteristics, use the word pairs *così . . . come* or *tanto . . . quanto*:

Aldo è così diligente come Elena. (Aldo is as diligent as Elena.)
Luigi mangia tanto quanto Giorgio. (Luigi eats as much as Giorgio.)

When comparing nouns, only the word pair *tanto . . . quanto* is used, and *tanto* must agree in number and gender with the noun it modifies:

Ho tanto denaro quanto tu. (I have as much money as you.)
Questo parco ha tanti alberi quanto l'altro. (This park has as many trees as the other.)
Voi scrivete tante lettere quanto mia sorella. (You write as many letters as my sister.)

Inequality

Not everything is the same, and you will need to know how to make comparisons of inequality too. *Più . . . di* and *meno . . . di* are the word pairs used to describe "more than" and "less than":

Marcantonio è più alto di Leonardo. (Marcantonio is taller than Leonardo.)
Gianni non è più intelligente di Francesca. (Gianni isn't smarter than Francesca.)
Stefano ha meno amici del ragazzo. (Stefano has fewer friends than the boy.)

Relative Superlatives

The relative superlative forms of adjectives in English may be distinguished by the words "least" or "most," or the ending –*est*. In Italian, you would use the definitive article, the word *più* or *meno*, the adjective, and the preposition *di*, as follows:

Lucia è la più brava della classe. (Lucia is the best in the class.)
Quella è la pinacoteca più grande di Firenze. (That is the largest art gallery in Florence.)
Aldo è il meno svelto di questi ragazzi. (Aldo is the least quick of these boys.)

The Best of the Best

What about the most delicious pasta? The ultimate *gelato*? The absolute superlative, which expresses the concepts of very, extremely, or most? In Italian, superlatives are formed by adding the suffix –*issimo* to an adjective or adverb after dropping the final vowel. There are four forms corresponding to gender and number (see **TABLE 6-7**).

TABLE 6-7	FORMING SUPERLATIVES
alto (tall)	*altissimo, altissima, altissimi, altissime*
buono (good)	*buonissimo, buonissima, buonissimi, buonissime*
veloce (quick)	*velocissimo, velocissima, velocissimi, velocissime*

ESSENTIALS

When forming the absolute superlative of adjectives ending in –*co*, –*go*, –*ca*, and –*ga*, add an *h* to the ending before –*issimo*: *ricca/ricchissima, larga/larghissima, stanco/stanchissimo*. This is done to maintain the hard "c" or hard "g" sound.

There are several adjectives that have irregular comparative and superlative forms (see **TABLE 6-8**).

TABLE 6-8

IRREGULAR ADJECTIVES		
ADJECTIVE	COMPARATIVE	ABSOLUTE SUPERLATIVE
alto (high)	superiore (higher)	supremo/sommo (highest)
basso (low)	inferiore (lower)	infimo (lowest)
buono (good)	migliore (better)	ottimo (best)
cattivo (bad)	peggiore (worse)	pessimo (worst)
grande (big)	maggiore (big)	massimo (biggest)
piccolo (small)	minore (smaller)	minimo (smallest)

There are other ways to express the absolute superior that don't require the –*issimo* form of the adjective. For example, the terms *molto* (a lot of), *tanto* (much), *estremamente* (extremely), or *assai* (very) can be used before the unchanged adjective. It depends on how dramatic the speaker wants to be! Compare: *molto piccolo* (very small) and *piccolissimo* (smallest)—it depends on the context.

Ownership and Possession

Possessive adjectives are those that indicate possession or ownership. They correspond to the English "my," "your," "his," "her," "its," "our," and "their." The Italian possessive adjectives are also preceded by definite articles and agree in gender and number with the noun possessed, not with the possessor. **TABLE 6-9** provides a chart of possessive adjectives (*aggettivi possessivi*) in Italian.

TABLE 6-9

POSSESSIVE ADJECTIVES				
ENGLISH	MASCULINE SINGULAR	FEMININE SINGULAR	MASCULINE PLURAL	FEMININE PLURAL
my	il mio	la mia	i miei	le mie
your (of *tu*)	il tuo	la tua	i tuoi	le tue
your (of *Lei*)	il Suo	la Sua	i Suoi	le Sue
his, her, its	il suo	la sua	i suoi	le sue

our	il nostro	la nostra	i nostri	le nostre
your (of *voi*)	il vostro	la vostra	i vostri	le vostre
your (of *Loro*)	il Loro	la Loro	i Loro	le Loro
their	il loro	la loro	i loro	le loro

As a rule, Italian possessive adjectives are preceded by definite articles:

la mia camicia (my shirt)
il nostro amico (our friend)
i vostro vicini (your neighbor)
i suoi libri (his/her books)

One exception is made for idiomatic phrases such as these:

a casa mia (my house)
è colpa sua (it's his/her fault)
è merito tuo (it's your merit)
piacere mio (my pleasure)

Possession

Complete the following with the correct form of the possessive pronoun according to the cue provided. Check your answers in Appendix A.

1. _____ libri sono grossi. (noi)
2. _____ rivista è interessante. (lui)
3. _____ giacca è nera. (io)
4. _____ motociclette sono rosse. (loro)
5. _____ cravatta è bella. (tu)
6. _____ amiche sono brave. (loro)
7. _____ vicini sono italiani. (voi)
8. _____ giardino è bello. (tu)
9. _____ cappotto è leggero. (io)
10. _____ maglie sono pesante. (noi)

How would you express the phrases "of mine" (a friend of mine) and "of yours" (three friends of yours)?
Place the possessive adjective before the noun without the definite article. In Italian, there is no corresponding word for *of* in these constructions. For example: *una mia amica, tre tuoi amici, questa mia amica*.

What a Beautiful Baby!

Che bello bambino! (What a beautiful baby!) *Che bella donna!* (What a beautiful woman!) These expressions are familiar to anyone who has ever watched an Italian movie or visited Italy. The exclamation "What . . . !" is expressed in Italian with the help of the word *che*. These phrases will surely prove to be very useful in your Italian conversations:

Che bei fiori! (What beautiful flowers!)
Che belle ragazze! (What beautiful girls!)
Che buon'idea! (What a good idea!)
Che partita! (What a game!)
Che rumore! (What a noise!)

CHAPTER 7
By the Numbers

Math in another language is difficult—learning multiplication tables by rote isn't on most people's top-ten list. Nevertheless, there are times when math skills are essential, like when you buy bus tickets, pay for your meal, decide whether that leather bag at the outdoor market is really such a good deal, or need to arrive on time for an opera performance.

Three-Two-One, Count Off!

You might find cardinal (counting) numbers the most useful to know—you will need them to express time, record dates, do math, interpret recipe amounts, and, of course, count. In Italian, cardinal numbers are written as one word. Use **TABLE 7-1** to memorize numbers from 1 to 100.

TABLE 7-1

ITALIAN CARDINAL NUMBERS 1–100		
1	*uno*	OO-noh
2	*due*	DOO-eh
3	*tre*	TREH
4	*quattro*	KWAHT-troh
5	*cinque*	CHEEN-kweh
6	*sei*	SEH-ee
7	*sette*	SET-teh
8	*otto*	OHT-toh
9	*nove*	NOH-veh
10	*dieci*	dee-EH-chee
11	*undici*	OON-dee-chee
12	*dodici*	DOH-dee-chee
13	*tredici*	TREH-dee-chee
14	*quattordici*	kwaht-TOR-dee-chee
15	*quindici*	KWEEN-dee-chee
16	*sedici*	SEH-dee-chee
17	*diciassette*	dee-chahs-SET-teh
18	*diciotto*	dee-CHOHT-toh
19	*diciannove*	dee-chahn-NOH-veh
20	*venti*	VEN-tee
21	*ventuno*	ven-TOO-noh
22	*ventidue*	ven-tee-DOO-eh
23	*ventitré*	ven-tee-TREH
24	*ventiquattro*	ven-tee-KWAHT-troh
25	*venticinque*	ven-tee-CHEEN-kweh
26	*ventisei*	ven-tee-SEH-ee

ITALIAN CARDINAL NUMBERS 1–100 *(CONTINUED)*		
27	*ventisette*	ven-tee-SET-teh
28	*ventotto*	ven-TOHT-toh
29	*ventinove*	ven-tee-NOH-veh
30	*trenta*	TREN-tah
40	*quaranta*	kwah-RAHN-tah
50	*cinquanta*	cheen-KWAHN-tah
60	*sessanta*	ses-SAHN-tah
70	*settanta*	set-TAHN-ta
80	*ottanta*	oht-TAHN-ta
90	*novanta*	noh-VAHN-tah
100	*cento*	CHEN-toh

The numbers *venti*, *trenta*, *quaranta*, *cinquanta*, and so on drop the final vowel when combined with *uno* and *otto*. *Tre* is written without an accent, but *ventitré*, *trentatré*, and so on do require an accent mark.

QUESTIONS?

How can I find an address in Florence?
Be aware that the town has a dual address system. Each street has a double set of numbers: a red number indicates a shop, restaurant, or business; a blue or black number refers to a hotel or domestic residence. In addition, each set of numbers has its own sequence, so a shop at #12r (where the letter "r" not only stands for red but is also usually red in color) may be next to a hotel at #27.

Beyond 100

Do you remember those good old days before the euro's arrival in Italy when you would pay a few thousand *lire* for admission to a museum or for a *cappuccino* and *biscotti?* Tourists needed more than just the numbers up to 100 to get around.

Lire are history, but learning numbers greater than 100 might still prove useful. Though they might seem unwieldy, after a bit of practice you'll be rolling them off your tongue like a pro. (Use **TABLE 7-2** to practice.)

TABLE 7-2

ITALIAN CARDINAL NUMBERS: 100 AND GREATER		
100	*cento*	CHEN-toh
101	*centouno/centuno*	cheh-toh-OO-noh/ chehn-TOO-noh
150	*centocinquanta*	cheh-toh-cheen-KWAHN-tah
200	*duecento*	doo-eh-CHEN-toh
300	*trecento*	treh-CHEN-toh
400	*quattrocento*	kwaht-troh-CHEN-toh
500	*cinquecento*	cheen-kweh-CHEN-toh
600	*seicento*	seh-ee-CHEN-toh
700	*settecento*	set-teh-CHEN-toh
800	*ottocento*	oht-toh-CHEN-toh
900	*novecento*	noh-veh-CHEN-toh
1.000	*mille*	MEEL-leh
1.001	*milleuno*	meel-leh-OO-noh
1.200	*milleduecento*	meel-leh-doo-eh-CHEN-toh
2.000	*duemila*	doo-eh-MEE-lah
10.000	*diecimila*	dee-eh-chee-MEE-lah
15.000	*quindicimila*	kween-dee-chee-MEE-lah
100.000	*centomila*	chen-toh-mee-leh
1.000.000	*un milione*	OON mee-lee-OH-neh
2.000.000	*due milioni*	DOO-eh mee-lee-OH-neh
1.000.000.000	*un miliardo*	OON mee-lee-ARE-doh

Did you notice? When Italians write down numbers as digits, they use the period to denote breaks between thousands, and the comma to indicate the decimal point—the exact opposite of what you're used to doing in English.

The Numbers Game

A. Write out the following numbers. Check your answers in Appendix A.

EXAMPLE: 21 ventuno

1. 34 _____
2. 86 _____
3. 2.514 _____
4. 19 _____
5. 3 _____
6. 108 _____
7. 6 _____
8. 16 _____
9. 35.015 _____
10. 7 _____

B. Write the following numbers as digits.

EXAMPLE: trenta 30

1. cinquecentosessantotto _____
2. trecento _____
3. nove _____
4. milleundici _____
5. trentatré _____
6. novantanove _____
7. milleottocentododici _____
8. un milione _____
9. ventisette _____
10. quattro _____

Ordinal Numbers Aren't Ordinary

You can place items in "order" with ordinal numbers. For instance, *il primo* is the first course on a menu and *il secondo* is the second course. Vittorio Emanuele III, who ruled the unified Italian nation from 1900 to 1946, was the third king with that name. Pope Paul V (1605–1621) was the fifth pope with the name Paul. When used with the numerical succession of kings, popes, and emperors, the ordinal numbers are capitalized:

Vittorio Emanuele Secondo (Vittorio Emanuele II)
Leone Nono (Leone IX)
Carlo Quinto (Carlo V)
diciottesimo secolo (eighteenth century)

FACTS

Brush up on your Roman numerals! Remember: I = 1, V = 5, X = 10, L = 50, C = 100, D = 500, and M = 1,000. To denote numbers in between, put together numbers so that you are either adding or subtracting, depending on what will require fewer digits: VI is equivalent to 5 + 1 = 6; IX is equivalent to 10 − 1 = 9. There is no limit to the length of a Roman numeral: MCDLXXXVIII is equivalent to 1,488.

For a list of Italian ordinals, see **TABLE 7-3**.

TABLE 7-3

ITALIAN ORDINAL NUMBERS			
first	*primo*	fifteenth	*quindicesimo*
second	*secondo*	sixteenth	*sedicesimo*
third	*terzo*	seventeenth	*diciassettesimo*
fourth	*quarto*	eighteenth	*diciottesimo*
fifth	*quinto*	nineteenth	*diciannovesimo*
sixth	*sesto*	twentieth	*ventesimo*
seventh	*settimo*	twenty-first	*ventunesimo*
eighth	*ottavo*	twenty-third	*ventitreesimo*
ninth	*nono*	hundredth	*centesimo*
tenth	*decimo*	thousandth	*millesimo*
eleventh	*undicesimo*	two thousandth	*duemillesimo*
twelfth	*dodicesimo*	three thousandth	*tremillesimo*
thirteenth	*tredicesimo*	one millionth	*milionesimo*
fourteenth	*quattordicesimo*		

Notice the regularity of ordinal numbers beginning with *undicesimo*—the suffix *–esimo* is added to the cardinal numbers by dropping the final vowel of the cardinal number. The one exception includes numbers ending in *–tré*. Those numbers drop their accent and are unchanged when *–esimo* is added. Since Italian ordinal numbers function as adjectives, they must agree in gender and number with the nouns they modify: *primo, prima, primi, prime.*

All the numbers used in a date are cardinal numbers except the first day of each month: *il primo settembre* (the first of September), *il dieci settembre* (September tenth).

Do the Math

Ordinal numbers are also used to express denominations of fractions: "one third" is written as *un terzo* and "five seventh" as *cinque setimi.* "One half" may be translated as *mezzo, mezza, una metà,* or *la metà.* Take a look at how mathematical operations are described in Italian:

- *Addizione:* 2 + 3 = 5 (*due più tre fa cinque*)
- *Sottrazione:* 9 – 3 = 6 (*nove meno tre fa sei*)
- *Moltiplicazione:* 4 × 2 = 8 (*quattro per due fa otto*)
- *Divisione:* 10 ÷ 2 = 5 (*dieci diviso due fa cinque*)

Practice Counting

Complete these math problems. Write out all numbers; check your answers in Appendix A.

1. dodici + _____ = venticinque
2. sei + _____ = settantacinque
3. trenta + _____ = settantotto
4. sessantasei + _____ = cento
5. cento + _____ = trecentotrentaquattro
6. mille – _____ = tre
7. millequattrocentonovantadue – _____ = ottantotto

8. ventuno – _____ = quattro
9. novantaquattro – _____ = trentadue
10. cinque – _____ = tre

What Time Is It?

You've got to know the time if you want to see those Botticelli paintings at the *Uffizi* in Florence. Luckily, there are two ways to ask "What time is it?" in Italian: *Che ora è?* and *Che ore sono?* If the time is one o'clock, noon, or midnight, the answer is in the singular; for all other hours, it is plural. Note that the phrase "o'clock" has no direct equivalent in Italian.

Che ora è? (What time is it?)
Che ore sono? (What time is it?)
È l'una. (It's one o'clock.)
È mezzogiorno. (It's noon.)
È mezzanotte. (It's midnight.)
Sono le tre e quindici. (It's 3:15.)
È mezzo giorno e dieci. (It's 12:10.)

TABLE 7-4

COMMON TERMS RELATED TO TELLING TIME			
noon	*mezzogiorno*	midnight	*mezzanotte*
half past	*e mezzo*	a quarter	*un quarto*
a quarter to/before	*meno un quarto*	a quarter after/past	*e un quarto*
morning	*di mattino*	afternoon	*del pomeriggio*
evening	*di sera*	sharp	*in punto*

Store hours, TV timetables, performance listings, and other time references are written differently in Italy. When telling time, commas replace colons. For example, 2:00 becomes 2,00; 2:30 becomes 2,30; 2:50 becomes 2,50.

Take a look at **TABLE 7-5** to see how you would tell the time from 5:00 to 6:00.

TABLE 7-5

TELLING TIME: 5:00–6:00	
5,00	*Sono le cinque.*
5,10	*Sono le cinque e dieci.*
5,15	*Sono le cinque e un quarto.*
5,20	*Sono le cinque e venti.*
5,30	*Sono le cinque e mezzo.*
5,40	*Sono le sei meno venti.*
5,45	*Sono le sei meno un quarto.*
5,50	*Sono le sei meno dieci.*
6,00	*Sono le sei.*

As in most of Europe, Italy uses the so-called "official time" (equivalent to "military time" in the United States) in train schedules, performances, movie timetables, radio, TV, and office hours. Between friends and in other informal situations, Italians may use the numbers from 1 to 12 to indicate time, and the context of the conversation will usually be sufficient. After all, *La Scala* doesn't have performances at eight in the morning!

DATA E ORA (DATE AND TIME)

MICHELE: *Quand'è il tuo compleanno?*
(When is your birthday?)

TIMOTEO: *Non so come si dice in italiano.*
(I don't know how to say it in Italian.)

MICHELE: *È in gennaio? Febbraio? Marzo? Aprile? Maggio? Giugno?*
(Is it in January? February? March? April? May? June?)

TIMOTEO: *Che mese c'è dopo luglio?*
(What month is after July?)

MICHELE: *Agosto?*

(August?)

TIMOTEO: *Sì, il mio compleanno è in agosto.*

(Yes, my birthday is in August.)

MICHELE: *Conosci i giorni della settimana?*

(Do you know the days of the week?)

TIMOTEO: *Conosco lunedì.*

(I know Monday.)

MICHELE: *È l'unico giorno che conosci?*

(Is that the only day you know?)

TIMOTEO: *No! Conosco anche gli altri.*

(No! I also know the others.)

MICHELE: *Vado al cinema ogni sabato.*

(I go to the cinema every Saturday.)

TIMOTEO: *Veramente? Io no. Non ci vado quasi mi. Che invidia!*

(Really? I don't. I hardly ever go. Lucky you!)

MICHELE: *Oggi è mercoledì.*

(Today is Wednesday.)

TIMOTEO: *Ehi! devo andare alla mia lezione!*

(Hey! I have to go to my lesson!)

MICHELE: *Che ore sono?*

(What time is it?)

TIMOTEO: *Fammi controllare . . . le sei! Devo proprio correre!*

(Let me see . . . six o'clock! I really have to run!)

MICHELE: *Il mio orologio si è fermato.*

(My watch has stopped.)

TIMOTEO: *Guarda l'orologio a pendolo.*

(Look at the clock.)

MICHELE: *Non ci vedo, no ho i miei occhiali!*

(I can't see it, I don't have my glasses!)

TIMOTEO: *Non hai l'orologio, non hai gli occhiali . . .*

(No watch, no glasses . . .)

MICHELE: *Spero che tu abbia imparato a dire la data e l'ora!*

(I hope that you've learned to tell the time and date!)

Been Waiting Long?

In Italian, to express an action that began in the past and is still going on in the present, use the verb in the present tense + *da* + length of time. This construction does not exist in English, where you would use the present perfect tense. Here are a few examples:

Leggo questo libro da una settimana. (I've been reading this book for a week.)

Prendiamo lezioni di italiano da molti mesi. (We've been taking Italian lessons for many months.)

To ask how long something has been going on, use *da quanto tempo* + present-tense verb:

Da quanto tempo leggi questa rivista? (How long have you been reading this magazine?)

Leggo questa rivista da molto tempo. (I've been reading this magazine for a long time.)

Practice Time Phrases

Write out the following time phrases and check your answers in Appendix A.

EXAMPLE: 5,10 *Sono le cinque e dieci.*

1. 1,15 ....
2. 20,20 ....
3. 23,00 ....
4. 3,30 ....
5. 7,25 ....
6. 16,45 ....
7. 4,10 ....
8. 9,00 ....
9. 18,40 ....
10. 19,55 ....

The Metric System

Italy uses the metric system for measuring. Metric units and the English-system equivalents appear in **TABLE 7-6.**

TABLE 7-6

A CONVERSION TABLE			
1 inch	*25.4 millimetri*	1 ounce	*28.35 grammi*
1 foot	*0.30 metri*	1 pound	*0.46 kilogrammi*
1 mile	*1.61 kilometri*	1 gallon	*3.79 litri*

A Dime a Dozen

Many Italian proverbs and phrases have to do with numbers. Here are some examples:

Dare i numeri (to go mad)
Di numero (exactly)
Non c'è due senza tre. (When it rains it pours.)
Tutt'uno (all the same)

The number "four" figures prominently in many Italian proverbs:

Dirne quattro (to give a piece of one's mind)
Fare quattro chiacchiere (to chat)
Fare quattro salti (to go dancing)
Farsi in quattro (to knock oneself out)
In quattro e quattro'otto (in short order, right away)
Non dire quattro se non l'hai nel sacco! (Don't count your chickens before they're hatched!)
Quattro occhi vedono meglio di due. (Two heads are better than one.)

CHAPTER 8
First-Conjugation Verbs

Verbs are fundamental to any language, and Italian is no exception. There are three primary groups of verbs, and this chapter will deal with the first-conjugation group, those Italian verbs that end in *–are*. Most Italian verbs belong to the first-conjugation group and follow a highly uniform pattern. Once you learn how to conjugate one *–are* verb, you've essentially learned hundreds of them.

It's Time to Conjugate

The infinitives of all regular verbs in Italian end in –*are*, –*ere*, or –*ire* and are referred to as first, second, or third conjugation verbs, respectively. In English, the infinitive (*l'infinito*) consists of "to" + verb. The present tense (*il tempo presente*) is a simple tense—that is, the verb form consists of one word only.

Unlike in English, the use of the personal pronouns (*io, tu, lui, noi, voi, loro*) with the conjugated verb forms is not necessary, since the verb endings identify the mood, tense, person, number, and, in some cases, gender.

Regular Verbs

The present tense of a regular –*are* verb is formed by dropping the infinitive ending –*are* and adding the appropriate endings to the resulting stem (–*o*, –*i*, –*a*, –*iamo*, –*ate*, –*ano*). See **TABLE 8-1** for a sample conjugation of *amare* (to love).

TABLE 8-1

CONJUGATION OF THE VERB *AMARE* (TO LOVE)		
PERSON	**SINGULAR**	**PLURAL**
I	*(io) amo* (I love)	*(noi) amiamo* (we love)
II	*(tu) ami* (you love, familiar)	*(voi) amate* (you love, familiar)
III	*(Lei) ama* (you love, formal)	*(Loro) amano* (you love, formal)
	(lui/lei) ama (he/she loves)	*(loro) amano* (they love)

The infinitive of first-conjugation Italian verbs (those ending in –*are*) and the conjugated forms of the present tense are pronounced like most Italian words: The stress falls on the next-to-last syllable. The one exception is the third person plural form *amano*, which is pronounced AH-mah-noh, with stress falling on the first syllable. Other first-conjugation verbs are listed in **TABLE 8-2**.

TABLE 8-2

FIRST CONJUGATION VERBS			
arrivare	to arrive	*insegnare*	to teach
ascoltare	to listen	*lavorare*	to work
aspettare	to wait	*nuotare*	to swim
ballare	to dance	*parlare*	to speak
camminare	to walk	*pranzare*	to dine, to have lunch
cantare	to sing	*suonare*	to play (an instrument)
dimenticare	to forget	*telefonare*	to telephone
guidare	to drive	*visitare*	to visit
imparare	to learn		

First-Conjugation Regular Verbs

Complete the following sentences with the correct form of the indicated verb. Check your answers in Appendix A.

1. Loro _____ lentamente. (camminare)
2. Tu _____ la macchina. (guidare)
3. Adriana non _____ il quaderno. (trovare)
4. Marco _____ l'orologio. (guardare)
5. Io _____ i biglietti. (comprare)
6. Voi _____ ad alta voce. (cantare)
7. _____ fino a tardi voi? (lavorare)
8. Io _____ il ricevitore. (alzare)
9. Noi _____ la lezione. (imparare)
10. Loro _____ in ritardo. (arrivare)

ESSENTIALS

There are many reference guides to help study Italian verbs. Some favorites include *750 Italian Verbs and Their Uses* by Brunella Notarmarco Dutton (John Wiley & Sons); *501 Italian Verbs* by John Colaneri and Vincent Luciani (Barrons Educational Series); *Italian Skill Builder Verbs* by Renata Rosso (Living Language); and *Italian Verb Drills* by Paola Nanni-Tate (McGraw-Hill).

Spell It Again, Sam

While the endings of most Italian verbs of the first conjugation follow the regular pattern you saw in **TABLE 8-1**, there are a few exceptions with regard to spelling.

As you'll see, most of the time spelling irregularities are introduced in order to maintain the consonant sound that precedes the endings.

Verbs Ending in –*care* and –*gare*

When you conjugate verbs ending in –*care* (*giocare, caricare*) and –*gare* (*litigare, legare*), add an *h* immediately after the root in the *tu* and *noi* forms to maintain the hard *c* or hard *g* sound of the infinitive. For an example of this structure, see the conjugation of *giocare* (to play) in **TABLE 8-3**.

TABLE 8-3

CONJUGATING *GIOCARE* (TO PLAY)		
PERSON	SINGULAR	PLURAL
I	(io) gioco	(noi) giochiamo
II	(tu) giochi	(voi) giocate
III	(lui, lei, Lei) gioca	(loro, Loro) giocano

Other verbs that end in –*care* or –*gare* are listed in **TABLE 8-4**.

TABLE 8-4

VERBS ENDING IN –*CARE* AND –*GARE*			
allargare	to widen	allungare	to lengthen
attaccare	to attack, to glue	cercare	to search for
divagare	to amuse	frugare	to rummage
impaccare	are to pack	indagare	to investigate
pagare	to pay	sbarcare	to disembark
toccare	to touch	troncare	to break, to cut off

Verbs Ending in *–ciare*, *–giare*, and *–sciare*

When you conjugate verbs ending in *–ciare* (*cominciare*), *–giare* (*mangiare*), or *–sciare* (*lasciare*), drop the *i* of the root in the *tu* and *noi* forms before adding the regular endings (in order to avoid the unusual combination *ii*, which is rare in the middle of words). For an example, look at how to conjugate *mangiare* (**TABLE 8-5**).

TABLE 8-5

CONJUGATING *MANGIARE* (TO EAT)		
PERSON	SINGULAR	PLURAL
I	*(io) mangio*	*(noi) mangiamo*
II	*(tu) mangi*	*(voi) mangiate*
III	*(lui, lei, Lei) mangia*	*(loro, Loro) mangiano*

There are quite a few other verbs in this category (see **TABLE 8-6**).

TABLE 8-6

VERBS ENDING IN *–CIARE*, *–GIARE*, AND *–SCIARE*			
assaggiare	to taste	*cominciare*	to start
invecchiare	to grow old, to age	*marciare*	to march
noleggiare	to rent (a car, etc.)	*parcheggiare*	to park
racconciare	to fix, to mend	*strisciare*	to creep, to crawl
viaggiare	to travel		

Verbs Ending in *–iare*

With verbs ending in *–iare* (*inviare, studiare, gonfiare*), the i of the root is dropped when the accent is on the next-to-last syllable in the first person singular of the present indicative (*io invio*)—see **TABLE 8-7** for a complete conjugation of *avviare* (to direct, to send).

TABLE 8-7

CONJUGATING *AVVIARE* (TO DIRECT, TO SEND)		
PERSON	SINGULAR	PLURAL
I	*(io) avvio*	*(noi) avviamo*
II	*(tu) avvii*	*(voi) avviate*
III	*(lui, lei, Lei) avvia*	*(loro, Loro) avviano*

Other verbs that may be included in this category appear in **TABLE 8-8**.

TABLE 8-8	VERBS ENDING IN –IARE		
cambiare	to change	*espiare*	to atone for
gonfiare	to inflate	*inviare*	to dispatch, to forward
rinviare	to send back, to return	*spiare*	to spy on, to watch
studiare	to study		

Verbs Ending in –gliare and –gnare

Verbs ending in *–gliare* (*tagliare*, *pigliare*) drop the *i* of the root only before the vowel *i*. To see a sample conjugation, refer to **TABLE 8-9**.

TABLE 8-9	CONJUGATING *TAGLIARE* (TO CUT)	
PERSON	**SINGULAR**	**PLURAL**
I	*(io) taglio*	*(noi) tagliamo*
II	*(tu) tagli*	*(voi) tagliate*
III	*(lui, lei, Lei) taglia*	*(loro, Loro) tagliono*

Other verbs that belong to this category are listed in **TABLE 8-10**.

TABLE 8-10	VERBS ENDING IN –GLIARE AND –GNARE		
aggrovigliare	to entangle	*agognare*	to long for, to crave
avvinghiare	to clutch, to grip	*pigliare*	to take
regnare	to rule, to reign	*sbagliare*	to mistake, to err
sognare	to dream		

First-Conjugation Irregular Verbs

Complete each sentence with the present tense form of the indicated verbs. Check your answers in Appendix A.

1. La regina _____. (regnare)
2. Io e Marco _____ per molte ore. (marciare)

3. Io _____ la zuppa. (assaggiare)
4. Tu _____ forte. (avvinghiare)
5. Lei _____ molto. (invecchiare)
6. Voi _____ la macchina. (noleggiare)
7. Marco _____ la motocicletta. (parcheggiare)
8. Loro _____ i pantaloni. (racconciare)

Three's a Crowd

So far, you've learned irregular verbs that undergo spelling changes for reasons of pronunciation. However, there are three first-conjugation verbs that are irregular in their stem as well as some of the endings. They include *dare* (to give), *stare* (to stay), and *andare* (to go)—**TABLES 8-11**, **8-12**, and **8-13** will help you conjugate these verbs.

TABLE 8-11

CONJUGATING *DARE* (TO GIVE)		
PERSON	SINGULAR	PLURAL
I	*(io) do*	*(noi) diamo*
II	*(tu) dai*	*(voi) date*
III	*(lui, lei, Lei) dà*	*(loro, Loro) danno*

TABLE 8-12

CONJUGATING *STARE* (TO STAY)		
PERSON	SINGULAR	PLURAL
I	*(io) sto*	*(noi) stiamo*
II	*(tu) stai*	*(voi) state*
III	*(lui, lei, Lei) sta*	*(loro, Loro) stanno*

TABLE 8-13

CONJUGATING *ANDARE* (TO GO)		
PERSON	SINGULAR	PLURAL
I	*(io) vado*	*(noi) andiamo*
II	*(tu) vai*	*(voi) andate*
III	*(lui, lei, Lei) va*	*(loro, Loro) vanno*

You might think that the irregular verb *fare* (to do, to make) should also belong here, but it belongs to the second-conjugation category, because it is derived from the Latin verb *facere*, a second-conjugation verb.

Idiomatic Expressions

The verbs *stare* and *andare* are used in many idiomatic expressions. *Stare* has different English equivalents according to the adjective or adverb that accompanies it. See if you can memorize the following expressions:

stare attento/a/i/e (to be on one's guard)
stare bene/male (to be well/not well)
stare zitto/a/i/e (to keep quiet)
stare fresco (to be mistaken/to kid oneself)
stare fuori (to be outside)
starsene da parte (to stand aside, to be on one side)
stare su (to stand/sit up straight)
stare a cuore (to matter, to have at heart)
stare con (to live with)
stare in piedi (to be standing)
stare in guardia (to pay attention)

The following are some examples of idiomatic expressions with *stare*:

Ciao, Alessandra, come stai? (Hi Alessandra, how are you?)
Sto bene, grazie. (I'm fine, thanks.)
Molti studenti non stanno attenti. (Many students don't pay attention.)

ALERT

There are many types of domestic railpasses that can save you money while traveling in Italy. These include the Cartaverde, Eurailpass, Europass, and Interrail Pass. Shop around and compare to see which type best suits your travel plans.

The Scoop on *Andare*

In Italian, the sequence of *andare* + *a* + infinitive is equivalent to the English "to go" + infinitive (to go dancing, to go eat, and so on). Note that it is necessary to use *a* even if the infinitive is separated from the form of *andare*. For example:

Quando andiamo a ballare? (When are we going dancing?)
Chi va in Italia a studiare? (Who's going to Italy to study?)

Andare also works with various means of transportation—for instance, *andare in aeroplano* is literally "to go by airplane" (to fly). Note that in all of these expressions *andare* is followed by *in*, except in the expression *andare a piedi* (to walk). Here are a few additional examples:

andare in bicicletta (to ride a bicycle)
andare in treno (to go by train)
andare in automobile/in macchina (to drive, to go by car)

Here is an interesting rule: The phrase "go to" will translate as *andare in* when referring to countries, and *andare a* when referring to cities, so you would say *vado in Italia, a Roma* (I'm going to Italy, to Rome).

Like the verb *stare*, *andare* may be combined with other words to take on new meanings. **TABLE 8-14** contains the most frequently used expressions with *andare*.

TABLE 8-14	EXPRESSIONS WITH *ANDARE*
andare avanti	to proceed, to go on
andare con	to accompany, to take, to go with
andare dentro	to enter, to go in
andare fuori	to go out
andare indietro	to back up
andare lontano	to go far away
andare per terra	to fall
andarsene	to go away, to leave

Conjugating *Dare*, *Stare*, and *Andare*

Complete each sentence with the present tense form of *dare, stare,* or *andare*. Check your answers in Appendix A.

1. Voi quando _____ a trovare vostro padre all'ospedale?
2. Ciao, Silvio, come _____?
3. Bambini, perché non _____ ziti?
4. Noi _____ in treno a Pisa.
5. _____ un film di Fellini.
6. Io _____ per uscire.
7. Chi _____ a Bologna?
8. Lei _____ in aeroplano a Roma.
9. Monica _____ una festa.
10. Noi _____ per mangiare.

CHAPTER 9

Second- and Third-Conjugation Verbs

What about all those Italian verbs that don't end in *–are*? In this chapter, you will learn about the other two verb classifications, the second- and third-conjugation verbs, find out more about the continuing Latin influence on Italian, and discover how to dramatically improve your vocabulary with just a few prefixes.

I'll Second That

Italian verbs with infinitives ending in *–ere* are called second-conjugation (*seconda coniugazione*) or *–ere* verbs. The present tense of a regular *–ere* verb is formed by dropping the infinitive ending and adding the appropriate endings (*–o, –i, –e, –iamo, –ete, –ono*) to the stem. For an example on how to conjugate a regular second-conjugation verb, take a look at **TABLE 9-1**.

TABLE 9-1

CONJUGATING *SCRIVERE* (TO WRITE)		
PERSON	SINGULAR	PLURAL
I	*(io) scrivo*	*(noi) scriviamo*
II	*(tu) scrivi*	*(voi) scrivete*
III	*(lui, lei, Lei) scrive*	*(loro, Loro) scrivono*

Second-conjugation (*–ere*) verbs account for approximately one quarter of all Italian verbs. Although many have some sort of irregular structure, there are also many regular verbs (see **TABLE 9-2**) that are conjugated in the same way as *scrivere*.

TABLE 9-2

SECOND-CONJUGATION REGULAR VERBS			
accendere	to put out, extinguish	*battere*	to beat, to hit
cadere	to fall	*chiedere*	to ask
conoscere	to know	*correre*	to run
credere	to believe	*descrivere*	to describe
eleggere	to elect	*leggere*	to read
mettere	to put, to place	*mordere*	to bite
nascere	to be born	*offendere*	to offend
perdere	to lose	*vendere*	to remain, to stay
ridere	to laugh	*rompere*	to sell
rimanere	to break	*sopravvivere*	to survive

Second-Conjugation Regular Verbs

Complete the following sentences with the correct form of the indicated verb. Check your answers in Appendix A.

1. Il professore non _____. (rispondere)
2. Noi _____ un caffé. (bere)
3. Loro _____ un film. (vedere)
4. Io _____ la macchina. (vendere)
5. Tu _____ i giornali. (leggere)
6. Io _____ due aspirine. (prendere)
7. Noi non _____ la storia. (credere)
8. Voi _____ ogni sera. (correre)
9. Anna Maria _____ sempre le chiavi! (perdere)
10. Roberta e Fabrizio _____ volentieri delle lettere. (scrivere)

Highly Irregular Behavior

Second-conjugation Italian verbs can give your mental spellchecker a vigorous workout. Here are just some of the many phonetic rules to be aware of. (See Appendix B for a complete listing of irregular verbs.)

Verbs Ending in –*gnere*

TABLE 9-3 contains a conjugation of the verb *spegnere* (to turn off, to put out). Can you see what's irregular about it?

TABLE 9-3

CONJUGATING *SPEGNERE* (TO TURN OFF, TO PUT OUT)		
PERSON	SINGULAR	PLURAL
I	*(io) spengo*	*(noi) spegniamo*
II	*(tu) spegni*	*(voi) spegnete*
III	*(lui, lei, Lei) spegne*	*(loro, Loro) spengono*

As you might have noticed, *spegnere* has two irregular forms: in the *io* and *loro/Loro* forms, where the soft *gn* switches to the hard *ng*.

While the infinitive forms of both first- and third-conjugation Italian verbs always have the accent on the final *–are* or *–ire*, second-conjugation verbs are often pronounced with the accent on the third-to-last syllable, as in *prendere* (PREHN-deh-ray).

Verbs Ending in *–cere*

Another verb group that undergoes a spelling modification includes verbs that end in *–cere*, like *dispiacere* (to displease). To see how this verb is conjugated, refer to **TABLE 9-4**.

TABLE 9-4	CONJUGATING *DISPIACERE* (TO DISPLEASE)	
PERSON	**SINGULAR**	**PLURAL**
I	*(io) dispiaccio*	*(noi) dispiacciamo*
II	*(tu) dispiaci*	*(voi) dispiacete*
III	*(lui, lei, Lei) dispiace*	*(loro, Loro) dispiacciono*

Other verbs that belong to this category are listed in **TABLE 9-5**.

TABLE 9-5	VERBS ENDING IN *–CERE*
compiacere	to gratify, to please
giacere	to lie down
nuocere	to harm, to injure
piacere	to please
tacere	to be quiet

Verbs Ending in *–gliere*

Verbs in this category are very similar to verbs that end in *–gnere* (refer to **TABLE 9-3**). That is, they undergo a spelling change in the *io* and *loro/Loro* forms, where two consonants switch places—in this case, from *gl* to *lg*. For example, take a look at the conjugation of *cogliere* (to pick, to pluck) in **TABLE 9-6**.

TABLE 9-6

CONJUGATING *COGLIERE* (TO PICK, TO PLUCK)		
PERSON	SINGULAR	PLURAL
I	*(io) colgo*	*(noi) cogliamo*
II	*(tu) cogli*	*(voi) cogliete*
III	*(lui, lei, Lei) coglie*	*(loro, Loro) colgono*

Other verbs conjugated like *cogliere* are listed in **TABLE 9-7**.

TABLE 9-7

VERBS ENDING IN *–GLIERE*	
accogliere	to give hospitality to, to welcome
raccogliere	to harvest, to gather
sciogliere	to undo, to untie, to loosen
togliere	to take off, to remove

FACTS

Knowing a few common prefixes will enable you to rapidly build up your vocabulary. The prefix *ri–*, for example, can mean "to do again, to repeat": *ribollire* (to boil again, to reboil), *rileggere* (to reread), *riparlare* (to speak again). *Stra–* often conveys the meaning of overdoing to excess: *strafare* (to do too much), *stralodare* (to overpraise), *strapagare* (to overpay). The prefix *dis–* implies undoing or the opposite of doing: *disfare* (to undo), *disobbedire* (to disobey), *disorganizzare* (to disorganize).

Lingering Latin Lovers

As you may recall from Chapter 1, Italian is the direct offspring of Latin and retains much of its grammar, usage, and vocabulary. The verbs *fare* (to do, to make) and *dire* (to say, to tell) are considered second-conjugation verbs because they are derived from two Latin verbs of the second conjugation—*facere* and *dicere*, and do not follow the regular pattern of conjugation (infinitive stem + endings). See **TABLE 9-8** and **TABLE 9-9**, which conjugate *fare* and *dire* in the present tense. (For idiomatic expressions using *fare*, see Chapter 17.)

TABLE 9-8	CONJUGATING *FARE* (TO DO, TO MAKE)		
PERSON		**SINGULAR**	**PLURAL**
I		*(io) faccio*	*(noi) facciamo*
II		*(tu) fai*	*(voi) fate*
III		*(lui, lei, Lei) fa*	*(loro, Loro) fanno*

TABLE 9-9	CONJUGATING *DIRE* (TO SAY, TO TELL)		
PERSON		**SINGULAR**	**PLURAL**
I		*(io) dico*	*(noi) diciamo*
II		*(tu) dici*	*(voi) dite*
III		*(lui, lei, Lei) dice*	*(loro, Loro) dicono*

TABLE 9-10 lists other verbs conjugated like *dire*.

TABLE 9-10	VERBS THAT CONJUGATE LIKE *DIRE*	
benedire		to bless
contraddire		to contradict
disdire		to retract, to cancel
indire		to announce publicly, to declare
interdire		to prohibit
maledire		to curse

Verbs Ending in *–arre*, *–orre*, and *–urre*

Like *fare* and *dire*, verbs ending in *–arre* (*trarre*), *–orre* (*porre*), and *–urre* (*tradurre*) are considered second-conjugation verbs because they also derive from the contractions of Latin verbs (*trahere*, *ponere*, *traducere*). For the conjugation of *trarre* (to pull, to draw out), see **TABLE 9-11**.

TABLE 9-11	CONJUGATING *TRARRE* (TO PULL, TO DRAW OUT)		
PERSON		**SINGULAR**	**PLURAL**
I		*(io) traggo*	*(noi) traiamo*
II		*(tu) trai*	*(voi) traete*
III		*(lui, lei, Lei) trae*	*(loro, Loro) traggono*

Other verbs conjugated like *trarre* include *distrarre* (to distract), *contrarre* (to contract), and *sottrarre* (to subtract).

There are also quite a few verbs that end in –*orre*, the most common of which is, of course, *porre* (to place, to set down). **TABLE 9-12** illustrates how to conjugate *porre* in the present tense.

TABLE 9-12

CONJUGATING *PORRE* (TO PLACE, TO SET DOWN)		
PERSON	SINGULAR	PLURAL
I	*(io) pongo*	*(noi) poniamo*
II	*(tu) poni*	*(voi) ponete*
III	*(lui, lei, Lei) pone*	*(loro, Loro) pongono*

TABLE 9-13 includes other verbs that end in –*orre*.

TABLE 9-13

VERBS THAT CONJUGATE LIKE *PORRE*			
disporre	to arrange, to set out	*posporre*	to place or put after
esporre	to exhibit, to display	*proporre*	to propose, to put
imporre	to impose	*riporre*	to put back, to replace
opporre	to oppose	*supporre*	to suppose

Finally, you need to remember verbs that end in –*urre*, like *tradurre* (**TABLE 9-14**).

TABLE 9-14

CONJUGATING *TRADURRE* (TO TRANSLATE)		
PERSON	SINGULAR	PLURAL
I	*(io) traduco*	*(noi) traduciamo*
II	*(tu) traduci*	*(voi) traducete*
III	*(lui, lei, Lei) traduce*	*(loro, Loro) traducono*

Other verbs conjugated like *tradurre* are listed in **TABLE 9-15**.

TABLE 9-15

VERBS THAT CONJUGATE LIKE *TRADURRE*			
condurre	to take, to lead	*produrre*	to produce, to yield
introdurre	to introduce, to show	*ridurre*	to reduce, to curtail

Third Time's a Charm

If there are first-conjugation and second-conjugation verbs, then it stands to reason there are third-conjugation verbs (*terza coniugazione*)! This final group contains verbs that end in *–ire* in the infinitive. The present tense of a regular *–ire* verb is formed by dropping the infinitive ending and adding the appropriate endings (*–o, –i, –e, –iamo, –ite, –ono*) to the resulting stem. Note that, except for the *voi* form, these endings are the same as for regular second-conjugation (*–ere*) verbs. For an example of how to conjugate a regular *–ire* verb, see **TABLE 9-16**, which conjugates *sentire* (to hear, to feel, to smell).

TABLE 9-16

CONJUGATING *SENTIRE* (TO HEAR, TO FEEL, TO SMELL)		
PERSON	SINGULAR	PLURAL
I	(io) sento	(noi) sentiamo
II	(tu) senti	(voi) sentite
III	(lui, lei, Lei) sente	(loro, Loro) sentono

TABLE 9-17 contains other *–ire* third-conjugation regular verbs.

TABLE 9-17

THIRD-CONJUGATION REGULAR VERBS			
acconsentire	to agree, to acquiesce	offrire	to offer
assorbire	to soak	partire	to leave
aprire	to open	riaprire	to reopen
bollire	to boil	scoprire	to discover, to uncover
coprire	to cover	sequire	to follow
cucire	to sew	sentire	to hear, to feel, to smell
dormire	to sleep	servire	to serve
fuggire	to flee	sfuggire	to escape
mentire	to lie	soffrire	to suffer
morire	to die	vestire	to dress, to wear

Third-Conjugation Regular Verbs

Complete the following sentences with the correct form of the indicated verb. Check your answers in Appendix A.

1. Loro _____ il campanello. (sentire)
2. Il cuoco _____ le patate. (bollire)
3. Franco _____ la scatola. (aprire)
4. Io _____ il caffé alle amiche. (offrire)
5. Voi _____ la verità. (scoprire)
6. Noi _____ la finestra. (aprire)
7. Marcantonio _____ bene. (vestire)
8. Tu _____ il pericolo. (sfuggire)
9. Voi _____ oggi. (partire)
10. Io _____ le bevande. (servire)

A Special Case: *–isc–* Verbs

There is a special group of third-conjugation verbs that needs the suffix *–isc–* to be added to the stem of all three singular and the third-person plural forms. One good example of such verbs is *finire* (to finish). For a conjugation of *finire*, see **TABLE 9-18**.

TABLE 9-18	CONJUGATING *FINIRE* (TO FINISH)		
PERSON		**SINGULAR**	**PLURAL**
I		*(io) finisco*	*(noi) finiamo*
II		*(tu) finisci*	*(voi) finite*
III		*(lui, lei, Lei) finisce*	*(loro, Loro) finiscono*

Other verbs that need the *–isc–* suffix and are conjugated similar to *finire* are listed in **TABLE 9-19**. Unfortunately, there is no way to know which third-conjugation verbs are "isc" verbs. Your only option is to commit these verbs to memory.

TABLE 9-19

VERBS WITH –*ISC*– SUFFIX			
capire	to understand	*proibire*	to forbid, to prohibit
compatire	to commiserate with	*pulire*	to clean
condire	to season, to flavor	*reagire*	to react
conferire	to confer, to bestow	*restituire*	to return, to give back
contribuire	to contribute, to share in	*ricostruire*	to rebuild, to reconstruct
dimagrire	to lose weight	*riferire*	to relate, to refer
impazzire	to go mad	*ristabilire*	to re-establish, to restore
inghiottire	to swallow up	*svanire*	to disappear, to vanish
istruire	to teach, to instruct	*tossire*	to cough
partire	to leave, to depart	*tradire*	to betray, to be disloyal to
preferire	to prefer	*ubbidire*	to obey

Using –*isc*– Verbs

Complete the following sentences with the correct form of the –*isc*–
verb. Check your answers in Appendix A.

1. I fratelli _____ ai genitori. (ubbidire)
2. Loro _____ la case. (pulire)
3. Io _____ rimanere qui. (preferire)
4. Noi _____ la professoressa. (capire)
5. Gianfranco _____ il suo messaggio. (riferire)
6. Beatrice _____ durante l'estate. (dimagrire)
7. I pronomi _____ i nome. (sostituire)
8. Noi _____ tutto. (capire)
9. Tu _____ gli esami. (finire)
10. Le studentesse _____ la lezione. (capire)

Adverbs—Finally!

An adverb (*avverbio*) is a word that modifies a verb, an adjective, or
another adverb. In English, adverbs are often formed by adding the suffix
"–ly" to adjectives: slowly, softly, surely. Adverbs often answer the question
come? (how?), *quando?* (when?), or *dove?* (where?):

Luciano agisce lentamente. (Luciano acts slowly.)
Leonardo viene tardi. (Leonardo comes late.)
Usciamo adesso. (We're leaving now.)
Ci andiamo a giugno. (We are going there in June.)

In Italian, many adverbs are formed by adding the ending –*mente* to the singular feminine form of the adjective (see **TABLE 9-20**).

TABLE 9-20

FORMING ADVERBS IN ITALIAN		
ADJECTIVE (GENERAL OR MASCULINE)	ADJECTIVE (FEMININE SINGULAR)	ADVERB
felice	*felice*	*felicemente* (happily)
lento	*lenta*	*lentamente* (slowly)
stanco	*stanca*	*stancamente* (tiredly)

If an adjective ends in –*ale*, –*ile*, or –*are*, the adverb is formed with the root of the adjective plus the ending –*mente* (see **TABLE 9-21**).

TABLE 9-21

FORMING ADVERBS FROM ADJECTIVES THAT END IN –*ALE, –ILE,* OR –*ARE*		
ADJECTIVE (GENERAL OR MASCULINE)	ADJECTIVAL ROOT	ADVERB
esemplare	*esemplari–*	*esemplarmente*
gentile	*gentil–*	*gentilmente*
speciale	*special–*	*specialmente*

Not all adjectives can be formed into adverbs; for example, the words "postalmente" and "malatamente" do not exist. On the other hand, not all Italian adverbs are formed from adjectives (adverbs that are not derived from adjectives are listed in **TABLE 9-22**). When in doubt, check the dictionary.

TABLE 9-22

ADVERBS THAT DON'T DERIVE ADJECTIVES			
ancora	still	*attorno*	around, about
bene	well	*contro*	against

dentro	in, inside	*dietro*	behind, at the back of
dopo	then, afterwards	*fuori*	outside
già	already	*inoltre*	moreover
insieme	together	*male*	badly
(non) . . . mai	never	*(non) . . . più*	no longer, not anymore
oltre	beyond	*presto*	soon, before long
sempre	always	*sopra*	above, on top
sotto	underneath, below	*vicino*	nearby, close by

Adverbs always precede the adjective or adverb that they modify, and they generally follow a simple verb form. For example: *Beve sempre la birra.* (He always drinks beer.) In sentences with compound tenses, most adverbs are placed after the participle. For example: *Sono arrivato tardi al museo.* (I arrived late at the museum.) However, certain common adverbs such as *già, ancora, sempre, (non) . . . mai,* and *(non) . . . più* are inserted between the auxiliary verb and the past participle of the compound form:

Non ci sei più andata. (You don't go there anymore.)
Enzo è sempre venuto in orario. (Enzo always came on time.)
Non ho ancora finito i miei compiti. (I still hadn't finished my homework.)

Making Adverbs

Convert the following adjectives into adverbs. Check your answers in Appendix A.

1. vero ....
2. certo ....
3. felice ....
4. veloce ....
5. triste ....
6. leggero ....
7. speciale ....
8. preciso ....
9. forte ....
10. largo ....

UNA CENA TRA AMICI (A DINNER AMONG FRIENDS)

Alba ha deciso di telefonare alla sua amica Marina per invitare lei e il marito a cena. Marina risponde al telefono. (Alba has decided to call her friend Marina to have her and her husband over for dinner. Marina answers the phone.)

ALBA: *Ciao, Marina. Sono io. Volevo invitarvi a cena questa sera.*
(Hi, Marina, it's me. I wanted to invite you over for dinner this evening.)

MARINA: *Devo chiedere a Roberto . . . allora, verremo molto volentieri!*
(I must ask Robert . . . all right, we'll come with pleasure.)

ALBA: *A questa sera, allora!*
(See you tonight, then!)

MARCO: *Bene, allora dovremmo cominciare a cucinare.*
(Good, we'd better start cooking then.)

ALBA: *Perfetto. Ma che cosa cuciniamo?*
(Perfect. But what shall we cook?)

MARCO: *Non abbiamo della carne?*
(Don't we have some meat?)

ALBA: *Sì, cuciniamo quella. Potremmo fare un bel brasato.*
(Yes, we'll cook that. We could make a great stew.)

MARCO: *Pensi che lo gradiranno?*
(Do you think they will enjoy it?)

ALBA: *Sono sicuro di sì!*
(I'm sure they will!)

MARCO: *Posso aiutarti?*
(Can I help you?)

ALBA: *Sì potresti pelare le potate?*
(Yes, could you peel the potatoes?)

MARCO: *Non abbiamo un pelapatate elettrico?*
(Don't we have an electric potato peeler?)

ALBA: *Sì, ma non funziona molto bene.*
(Yes, but it doesn't work very well.)

MARCO: *Basta che tu non mi chieda di sbucciare le cipolle.*
(As long as you don't ask me to peel the onions.)

ALBA: *Non, solo un po' di patate.*
(No, just a few potatoes.)

MARCO: *E chi prepara la tavola? Io non posso fare tutto.*
(And who's going to set the table? I can't do everything.)

ALBA: *Chiedi a Matteo di darti una mano.*
(Ask Matteo to give you a hand.)

MARCO: *Matteo? Matteo? Dove sei?*
(Matteo? Matteo? Where are you?)

MATTEO: *Mi avete chiamato?*
(Did you call me?)

MARCO: *Sì, potresti preparare la tavola per favore?*
(Yes, could you set the table, please?)

MATTEO: *Perché?*
(Why?)

MARCO: *Ci serve il tuo aiuto. Abbiamo invitato alcuni amici a cena.*
(We need your help. We've invited some friends over for dinner.)

MATTEO: *Perché io?*
(Why me?)

ALBA: *Perché tuo padre ed io abbiamo altre cose da fare.*
(Because your father and I have other things to do.)

MATTEO: *Dov'è la tovaglia?*
(Where's the tablecloth?)

ALBA: *Nell'armadio.*
(In the cupboard.)

MATTEO: *Quali piatti usiamo?*
(Which plates shall we use?)

ALBA: *Quelli bianchi.*
(The white ones.)

MATTEO: *E quali bicchieri metto?*
(And which glasses shall I use?)

ALBA: *I soliti.*
(The usual ones.)

MATTEO: *E quali tovagioli?*
(And which napkins?)

ALBA: *Vanno bene i tovaglioli blu.*

	(The blue ones are fine.)
MATTEO:	*Non li trovo!*
	(I can't find them!)
ALBA:	*Hai guardato nella stanza di pranzo?*
	(Have you looked in the dining room?)
MATTEO:	*Dov'è il vino?*
	(Where's the wine?)
ALBA:	*Qui. Prendi anche il cavatappi.*
	(Here. Take the corkscrew as well.)
MATTEO:	*Ho sistemato tutto?*
	(Have I got everything?)
ALBA:	*Sì, va benissimo. Grazie, Matteo.*
	(Yes, it's fine. Thank you, Matteo.)
MARCO:	*Abbassa un po' la fiamma!*
	(Turn the gas down a little.)
ALBA:	*Hai ragione! Sta bruciando tutto!*
	(You're right! Everything's burning.)
MARCO:	*È tutto pronto?*
	(Is everything ready?)
ALBA:	*Abbiamo qualche problema.*
	(We've got some problems.)
MARCO:	*Che cosa c'è che non va?*
	(What's wrong?)
ALBA:	*La carne è troppo cotta! Le patate sono bruciate!*
	(The meat's overcooked! The potatoes are burnt!)
MARCO:	*Ecco, stanno arrivando. Che cosa facciamo?*
	(Here they come! What shall we do?)
ALBA:	*Offri loro qualcosa da bere, intanto che sistemo un po'.*
	(Offer them something to drink while I sort it out a little.)
MARCO:	*E se andassimi al ristorante?*
	(What if we went to a restaurant?)
ALBA:	*Non mi sembra gentile. Li abbiamo invitati qui! Dobbiamo trovare una scusa.*
	(That's not nice. We invited them here. We've got to find an excuse.)

CHAPTER 10

Negative Words and Constructions

Non *sapete nulla di nulla sulla negazione?* (Don't know anything about the use of the negative?) *Non fa niente!* (It doesn't matter!) There are plenty of ways to say "no" in Italian, turn down an offer, or refer to nothing or nobody. Hopefully you'll learn something very positive in this chapter on negativity.

Non Means No

A sentence is usually made negative in Italian by placing the word *non* in front of the verb:

Francesca voule dormire. (Francesca wants to sleep.)
Francesca non voule dormire. (Francesca doesn't want to sleep.)
Loro parlano cinese. (They speak Chinese.)
Loro non parlano cinese. (They don't speak Chinese.)

Only object pronouns may be placed between *non* and the verb:

Lo conosciamo. (We know him.)
Non lo conosciamo. (We don't know him.)
Lo hanno fatto. (They did it.)
Non lo hanno fatto. (They did not do it.)

Practice Saying "No"

Rewrite the following sentences in the negative. Then check your answers in Appendix A.

1. Loro mangiano troppo.

   ----

2. Hanno visto Roberta ieri sera.

   ----

3. Mi sono svegliato alle sette.

   ----

4. Patrizia vuole venire adesso.

   ----

5. Voglio andare al cinema.

   ----

6. Lo avete dimenticato.

----

7. I suoi amici mi visitano.

----

8. Il facchino porta i bagagli.

----

9. Conosciamo quelle ragazze.

----

10. Vado alle Alpi ogni inverno.

Two Negatives Make a Negative

Your grade school English teacher told you repeatedly that you couldn't use more than one negative word in the same sentence. In Italian, though, the double negative is the acceptable format, and even three negative words can be used in a sentence:

Non viene nessuno. (No one is coming.)
Non vogliamo niente/nulla. (We don't want anything.)
Non ho mai visto nessuno in quella stanza. (I didn't see anyone in that room.)

In fact, there is a whole host of phrases made up of double (and triple) negatives. **TABLE 10-1** includes most of them.

TABLE 10-1	DOUBLE AND TRIPLE NEGATIVE PHRASES			
non . . . nessuno	no one, nobody	*non . . . affatto*	not at all
non . . . niente	nothing	*non . . . mica*	not at all (in the least)
non . . . nulla	nothing	*non . . . punto*	not at all
on . . . né . . . né	neither . . . nor	*non . . . neanche*	not even
non . . . mai	never	*non . . . nemmeno*	not even
non . . . ancora	not yet	*non . . . neppure*	not even
non . . . più	no longer	*non . . . che*	only

Here are some examples of how these phrases may be used in Italian:

Non ha mai letto niente. (She read nothing.)
Non ho visto nessuna carta stradale. (I didn't see any street signs.)
Non abbiamo trovato né le chiavi né il portafoglio. (We found neither
the keys nor the wallet.)

Note that in the case of the negative expressions *non . . . nessuno,
non . . . niente, non . . . né . . . né,* and *non . . . che,* the second
part of the expression always follows the past participle. Observe the
following examples:

Non ho trovato nessuno. (I haven't found anyone.)
Non abbiamo detto niente. (We haven't said anything.)
Non ha letto che due libri. (She has read only two books.)
Non ho visto niente di interessante al cinema. (I didn't see anything of
interest at the cinema.)

When using the combinations *non . . . mica* and *non . . . punto,*
mica and *punto* always come between the auxiliary verb and the past
participle:

Non avete mica parlato. (They haven't spoken at all.)
Non è punto arrivata. (She hasn't arrived at all.)

When using the expressions *non . . . affatto* (not at all), *non . . . ancora* (not yet), and *non . . . più* (no more, no longer), the words *affatto, ancora,* or *più* can be placed either between the auxiliary verb and the past participle or after the past participle:

Non è stato affatto vero. Non è affatto stato vero. (It wasn't true at all.)

Non mi sono svegliato ancora. Non mi sono ancora svegliato.
   (I hadn't woken yet.)

Non ho letto più. Non ho più letto. (I no longer read.)

FESTA DI BENVENUTO (WELCOME PARTY)

FRANCO: *Non potresti presentarci?*
            (Could you introduce us?)

ANGELO: *Teresa, questo è Franco. Franco, questo è Teresa.*
            (Teresa, this is Franco. Franco, this is Teresa.)

FRANCO: *E quella ragazza, come si chiama?*
            (And that girl, what's her name?)

ANGELO: *Si chiama Gina. Chiediglielo! Te lo dirà la stessa!*
            (Her name's Gina. Ask her! She'll tell you herself!)

FRANCO: *Hai mai visto questa persona prima d'ora?*
            (Have you ever seen this person before?)

ANGELO: *Non mi ricordo.*
            (I don't remember.)

FRANCO: *Non era sul treno con te?*
            (Wasn't she on the train with you?)

ANGELO: *Sì, era seduta vicino a me.*
            (Yes, she was sitting next to me.)

FRANCO: *Tu dovresti essere Mauro.*
            (You must be Mauro.)

CARLO: *No, ti confondi con qualcun altro: non sono Mauro.*
            (No, you're mistaking me for someone else. I'm not Mauro.)

FRANCO:	*Il tuo italiano è molto buono, lo sai?*
	(Your Italian is pretty good, you know?)
CARLO:	*Sei molto gentile. Ho fatto solo un corso intensivo.*
	(You're very kind. I've only had an intensive course.)
FRANCO:	*Capisci bene quello che diciamo?*
	(Do you understand everything we are saying?)
CARLO:	*Mi sembra di capire abbastanza bene.*
	(I think I understand well enough.)
FRANCO:	*Quanto ti fermerai?*
	(How long are you staying?)
CARLO:	*Due settimane.*
	(Two weeks.)
FRANCO:	*Bene, spero che tu ti diverta!*
	(Well, I hope you'll have fun!)
CARLO:	*Lo spero proprio.*
	(I hope so.)

Nattering Nabobs of Negativism

Not in a very agreeable mood today? There are a number of negative expressions to counteract all those smiley, happy people. Some very common negative expressions include the following:

non cambiare una virgola (not to change a single word)
non dire una sillaba (not to say a word)
non per la quale (not to be trusted)
Non vale! (That's not fair/that's cheating!)
fuori dal nulla (out of the blue)
buono a nulla (good for nothing)

Other common phrases that rely on the negatives are listed in **TABLE 10-2**.

TABLE 10-2

NEGATIVE PHRASES	
da niente	not important
mai	never
nessuno	no one, nobody
niente (nulla)	nothing
né . . . né	neither . . . nor
nessun	no, not . . . any
neanche, nemmeno, neppure	not even
per niente	at all

Note that *nessun* is used as an adjective, and must agree in gender and number with the thing that it describes. Moreover, *nessun* and *niente* usually follow the verb when they act as the object. When one of these words is the subject of the sentence, its position can vary:

Nessuno parla. (No one speaks.)
Niente ci piace. (We like nothing at all.)
Non parla nessuno. (No one speaks.)

To review the negatives, compare the two sets of phrases in **TABLE 10-3**.

TABLE 10-3

POSITIVE AND NEGATIVE PHRASES
Ha fame. (She is hungry.)
Non ha fame. (She isn't hungry.)
Ho comprato qualcosa. (I bought something.)
Non ho comprato niente. (I didn't buy anything.)
Ride sempre. (He always laughs.)
Non ride mai. (He never laughs.)
Vediamo qualcuno. (We see someone.)
Non vediamo nessuno. (We don't see anyone.)

Give Me a Negative

Rewrite the following sentences, adding the Italian equivalents of the English words provided. Then check your answers in Appendix A.

EXAMPLE: Hai scritto la lettera. (only)   *Non hai scritto che la lettera.*

1. Abbiamo chiamato. (not at all)

_____

2. È arrivato. (not yet)

_____

3. Voi siete entrati. (not even)

_____

4. Avete visto quel film. (never)

_____

5. Loro hanno sciato. (not at all)

_____

6. Siete andati a nuotare. (never)

_____

7. Hai visto uno spettacolo. (not any)

_____

8. Ho visto. (no one)

_____

9. Mi sono svegliato. (not yet)

_____

What Part of No Don't You Understand?

The negative words *neanche*, *nemmeno*, and *neppure* are used to replace *anche* (too, also, as well) in negative sentences. Please note that these three words can be used interchangeably, as in the following examples:

Non ha preso neanche il dolce. (He didn't even take the dessert.)
Nemmeno io ho visto nessuno. (I didn't see anyone either.)
Non leggiamo neppure i fumetti. (We don't even read the comic strips.)
Neanche loro lo so. (They don't know it either.)

We Don't Know It Either

Replace *anche* with *neanche*, *nemmeno*, or *neppure* in the following sentences and make the necessary changes. Then check your answers in Appendix A.

1. Anche le mie cugine hanno molto denaro.

   ---

2. Viviana lo sa e anch'io lo so.

   ---

3. Anche Luisa viene.

   ---

4. Anche noi lo abbiamo fatto.

   ---

5. Anche loro sono ricco.

In a negative mood? Swimming in a soup of negation? *Non venite niente in tasca alla lezione?* (Not getting anything out of the lesson?) Here's a word search puzzle that's sure to combat the negative vibes. You'll find the answers in Appendix A.

```
M  O  N  I  C  A  L  Ù  N  F  A  G  N  O  N
A  E  T  N  E  I  N  A  D  H  F  B  E  B  C
I  R  T  H  O  N  O  U  B  D  F  L  S  U  N
D  Z  E  N  P  E  D  A  M  F  A  P  S  O  A
A  F  I  N  E  M  T  G  U  U  T  I  U  N  N
O  F  M  R  I  I  É  N  Q  O  T  M  N  U  E
B  A  A  R  O  C  N  A  E  R  O  I  O  T  A
O  N  O  N  V  A  L  E  M  I  Ù  A  N  T  N
N  Ù  I  E  V  R  C  M  R  D  N  E  U  E  C
E  P  A  P  E  B  S  M  C  A  I  R  N  I  H
M  E  B  P  I  Ù  T  E  N  N  F  Z  E  A  E
M  N  N  U  L  L  A  N  A  U  U  N  A  P  F
E  O  C  R  B  N  E  S  S  L  O  V  O  M  F
N  U  L  E  L  A  U  Q  A  L  R  É  L  N  A
N  E  S  A  A  L  L  U  N  A  O  N  O  U  B
```

AFFATTO	MAI	NEPPURE	NON PER LA QUALE
ANCORA	MICA	NESSUNO	NON VALE
BUONO A NULLA	NÉ	NIENTE	NULLA
DA NIENTE	NEANCHE	NON	PER NIENTE
FUORI DA NULLA	NEMMENO	NON FARE NIENTE	PIÙ

CHAPTER 11

Tense about Tenses?
Don't Be!

If only the present existed and there were no past and no future, learning verb tenses would be superfluous. But you can't talk about that great Caravaggio painting you saw last year at the *Museo di Capodimonte* in Naples or make plans to take part in the *Carnevale* celebration in Venice next February without a temporal point of reference.

It Seems Like Just Yesterday

The *passato prossimo*—referred to as the present perfect—is a compound tense (*tempo composto*) that expresses a fact or action that happened in the recent past or that occurred long ago but still has ties to the present.

In southern Italy, the *passato remoto* (historical past tense) is often substituted for the *passato prossimo* (conversational past), even to describe events of the recent past.

Here are a few examples of how the *passato prossimo* appears in Italian:

Ho appena chiamato. (I just called.)
Mi sono iscritto all'università quattro anni fa. (I entered the university four years ago.)
Questa mattina sono uscito presto. (This morning I left early.)
Il Petrarca ha scritto sonetti immortali. (Petrarca wrote enduring sonnets.)

TABLE 11-1 lists some adverbial expressions that are often used with the *passato prossimo*.

TABLE 11-1	COMMON ADVERBIAL EXPRESSIONS		
ieri	yesterday	*ieri pomeriggio*	yesterday afternoon
ieri sera	last night	*il mese scorso*	last month
l'altro giorno	the other day	*stamani*	this morning
tre giorni fa	three days ago		

Past Parcels? Past Particles? Past Participles!

Compound tenses such as the *passato prossimo* are formed with the present indicative of the auxiliary verb *avere* or *essere* and the past participle (*participio passato*). The past participle of regular verbs is formed by dropping the infinitive ending –*are*, –*ere*, or –*ire* and adding the appropriate final ending: –*ato*, –*uto*, or –*ito* (see **TABLES 11-2, 11-3,** and **11-4**).

TABLE 11-2	REGULAR PAST PARTICIPLES OF *–ARE* VERBS	
INFINITIVE FORM	**PAST PARTICIPLE**	
camminare (to walk)	*camminato*	
imparare (to learn)	*imparato*	
lavare (to wash)	*lavato*	
telefonare (to telephone)	*telefonato*	

TABLE 11-3	REGULAR PAST PARTICIPLES OF *–ERE* VERBS	
battere (to beat)	*battuto*	
credere (to believe)	*creduto*	
sapere (to know)	*saputo*	
tenere (to keep)	*tenuto*	

TABLE 11-4	REGULAR PAST PARTICIPLES OF *–IRE* VERBS	
capire (to understand)	*capito*	
finire (to finish)	*finito*	
gradire (to accept)	*gradito*	
sentire (to feel, to smell)	*sentito*	

The *passato prossimo* is formed with a conjugated form of *avere*. To review, refer to **TABLE 11-5**.

TABLE 11-5	*PASSATO PROSSIMO* WITH REGULAR VERBS		
PERSON	***IMPARARE* (TO LEARN)**	***CREDERE* (TO BELIEVE)**	***CAPIRE* (TO UNDERSTAND)**
(io)	*ho imparato*	*ho creduto*	*ho capito*
(tu)	*hai imparato*	*hai creduto*	*hai capito*
(lui, lei, Lei)	*ha imparato*	*ha creduto*	*ha capito*
(noi)	*abbiamo imparato*	*abbiamo creduto*	*abbiamo capito*
(voi)	*avete imparato*	*avete creduto*	*avete capito*
(loro, Loro)	*hanno imparato*	*hanno creduto*	*hanno capito*

Going Back in Time

Complete the following with the appropriate *passato prossimo* (present perfect) forms of the indicated verbs. Check your answers in Appendix A.

1. Nino _____ tutto il giorno. (lavorare)
2. Ieri mia madre _____ un piatto tipico toscano. (cucinare)
3. Loro _____ tutte le vecchie case. (demolire)
4. Il professore _____ molto chiaramente l'uso degli ausiliari. (spiegare)
5. Conosco bene Firenze perché ci _____ per dieci anni. (abitare)
6. Qualcuno _____ alla porta. (bussare)
7. Noi _____ molte cose. (comprare)
8. Loro _____ tutta la notte. (ballare)
9. Io _____ un terribile raffreddore. (avere)
10. Noi _____ tutta la pizza! (mangiare)

QUESTIONS?

How many tenses in Italian are compound?
Including the *passato prossimo*, there are seven compound tenses, including *trapassato remoto* (past perfect), *futuro anteriore* (future perfect), and *congiuntivo trapassato* (pluperfect subjunctive).

Irregular Past Participles

Many verbs in Italian, especially the *–ere* verbs, have irregular past participles. A list of some of the most common infinitives, along with a sample variation, as well as their past participle forms, appears in **TABLE 11-6**.

TABLE 11-6

IRREGULAR PAST PARTICIPLES			
INFINITIVE	PAST PARTICIPLE	VARIATION ON THE INFINITIVE	PAST PARTICIPLE
accendere	*acceso*	*riaccendere*	*riacceso*
chiedere	*chiesto*	*richiedere*	*richiesto*
chiudere	*chiuso*	*racchiudere*	*racchiuso*

	IRREGULAR PAST PARTICIPLES *(CONTINUED)*		
INFINITIVE	PAST PARTICIPLE	VARIATION ON THE INFINITIVE	PAST PARTICIPLE
cogliere	*colto*	*raccogliere*	*raccolto*
cuocere	*cotto*	*stracuocere*	*stracotto*
dire	*detto*	*predire*	*predetto*
dividere	*diviso*	*condividere*	*condiviso*
fare	*fatto*	*strafare*	*strafatto*
leggere	*letto*	*rlleggere*	*rlletto*
porre	*posto*	*fraporre*	*fraposto*
reggere	*retto*	*correggere*	*corretto*
rispondere	*risposto*	*corrispondere*	*corrisposto*
rompere	*rotto*	*corrompere*	*corrotto*
scegliere	*scelto*	*prescegliere*	*prescelto*
scrivere	*scritto*	*riscrivere*	*riscritto*
trarre	*tratto*	*ritrarre*	*ritratto*
vincere	*vinto*	*convincere*	*convinto*
volgere	*volto*	*rivolgere*	*rivolto*

Build Your Vocabulary!

The irregular past participles of many groups of verbs have repeating patterns. For example, the past participle of any verb that ends in *–mettere* will also end in *–messo*:

- *ammettere* (to admit, to allow in, to let in)   *ammesso*
- *commettere* (to commit, to commission)   *commesso*
- *dimettere* (to dismiss, to remove)   *dimesso*
- *omettere* (to omit, to leave out)   *omesso*
- *rimettere* (to remit, to refer)   *rimesso*

Once you recognize the patterns, you'll be on your way to rapidly becoming an *esperto* of Italian verbs!

How to Choose the Auxiliary Verb

When forming the *passato prossimo*, which auxiliary verb should be used—*avere* or *essere*? How do you decide? As mentioned earlier in this chapter, compound tenses such as the *passato prossimo* are formed with the present indicative of the auxiliary verb *avere* or *essere* and the past participle (*participio passato*).

The majority of Italian verbs call for the auxiliary verb *avere* when forming the *passato prossimo* and other compound tenses. There are only a very small number of verbs that can be conjugated with either *avere* or *essere*, depending on the sentence structure.

Transitive Verbs Take *Avere*

As you might remember from Chapter 5, transitive verbs are those that take a direct object. For instance:

Io ho mangiato una pera. (I ate a pear.)
Loro hanno già studiato la lezione. (They already studied the lesson.)
Non ho mai visto Genoa. (I've never visited Genova.)

The compound tense of a transitive verb is formed with the present indicative of the auxiliary verb *avere* and the past participle (*participio passato*). The past participle is invariable and ends in *–ato*, *–uto*, or *–ito*. In phrases with a transitive verb, the direct object of the verb may be expressed explicitly or implied. For example: *Io ho mangiato tardi.* (I ate late.)

Intransitive Verbs Take *Essere*

Simply put, intransitive verbs are those that do not take a direct object. These verbs usually express movement or a state of being. The auxiliary verb *essere* plus the past participle is used to form the *passato prossimo* and other compounds of almost all intransitive verbs (and the

past participle must agree in number and gender with the subject.)
TABLE 11-7 contains conjugations of *arrivare*, *crescere*, and *partire* in the *passato prossimo*.

TABLE 11-7

	PASSATO PROSSIMO WITH ESSERE		
PERSON	***ARRIVARE*** (TO ARRIVE)	***CRESCERE*** (TO GROW)	***PARTIRE*** (TO LEAVE, TO DEPART)
(io)	*sono arrivato(–a)*	*sono cresciuto(–a)*	*sono partito(–a)*
(tu)	*sei arrivato(–a)*	*sei cresciuto(–a)*	*sei partito(–a)*
(lui, lei, Lei)	*è arrivato(–a)*	*è cresciuto(–a)*	*è partito(–a)*
(noi)	*siamo arrivati(–e)*	*siamo cresciuti(–e)*	*siamo partiti(–e)*
(voi)	*siete arrivati(–e)*	*siete cresciuti(–e)*	*siete partiti(–e)*
(loro, Loro)	*sono arrivati(–e)*	*sono cresciuti(–e)*	*sono partiti(–e)*

Notice that each of the past participles conjugated with *essere* has two possible endings, depending on the gender of its subject. Take a look at these examples:

La zia è andata a casa. (The aunt went home.)
Le zie sono andate a casa. (The aunts went home.)
Lo zio è andato a casa. (The uncle went home.)
Gli zii sono andati a casa. (The uncles went home.)

When the gender of the subject consists of both males and females, or is unstated, use the masculine form (think of it as a "generic" or "standard" form):

Lo zio e la zia sono andati a casa. (The uncle and aunt went home.)
Noi siami andati a casa. (We went home.)

TABLE 11-8 contains a list of other most commonly used intransitive verbs and their past-participle forms.

TABLE 11-8

INTRANSITIVE VERBS: PAST PARTICIPLES			
andare (to go)	*andato*	*entrare* (to enter)	*entrato*
arrivare (to arrive, to reach)	*arrivato*	*essere* (to be)	*stato*
cadere (to fall, to drop)	*caduto*	*morire* (to die)	*morto*
costare (to cost)	*costato*	*nascere* (to be born)	*nato*
crescere (to grow)	*crescuito*	*partire* (to leave)	*partito*
diventare (to become)	*diventato*	*uscire* (to exit)	*uscito*
durare (to last, to continue)	*durato*	*venire* (to come)	*venuto*

EXERCISE

Practice Past Participle Endings

Complete the following with the appropriate *passato prossimo* (present perfect) forms of the indicated verbs. Check your answers in Appendix A.

1. Le ragazze _____ a Modena. (essere)
2. Luca _____ in ritardo. (arrivare)
3. L'opera _____ due ore. (durare)
4. Noi _____ in montagna. (andare)
5. Quei vini _____ a tutti. (piacere)
6. Le ragazze _____ alle undici. (uscire)
7. Paola _____ tarde. (ritornare)
8. Loro _____ a casa di Vincenzo. (restare)

Some Verbs Take Either!

How could it be that some verbs take EITHER *essere* or *avere* as the auxiliary verb in compound tenses? It depends on the context of the sentence. Here are a few examples of verbs functioning both transitively and intransitively:

• *bruciare* (to burn)

Hai bruciato la torta? (Did you burn the cake?)
Durante la notte scorsa la cascina è bruciata. (During the night, the dairy burned.)

- *diminuire* (to reduce, decrease)

  Abbiamo diminuito il consumo d'energia in casa. (We reduced energy consumption at home.)

  I prezzi della carne sono diminuiti questa settimana. (The price of meat has decreased this week.)

- *finire* (to finish)

  Il professore ha finito la conferenza alle tre. (The professor finished the conference at three o'clock.)

  La conferenza è finita alle tre. (The conference finished at three o'clock.)

For a complete listing of verbs that can be conjugated with both *avere* and *essere*, see Appendix B.

Are We All in Agreement on This?

Italians are all one big happy family, right? Maybe it's because there is so much cooperation in the Italian language. Plural nouns take plural articles, adjectives reflect the nouns they describe in both number and gender, and the past participles of verbs have a similar grammatical rule.

When using the conversational past or other compound tenses, the past participle of the acting verb must agree in gender and number with the direct-object pronoun preceding the verb *avere*. For example:

Hanno visitato il nonno. (They have visited their grandfather.)
BUT: *Lo hanno visitato.* (They have visited him. Also: *L'hanno visitato.*)

Ho comprato i pantaloni. (I have bought the pants.)
BUT: *Li ho comprati.* (I have bought them.)

Abbiamo veduto Teresa. (We have seen Theresa.)
BUT: *L'abbiamo veduta.* (We have seen her.)

Ha ricevuto le lettere. (He has received the letters.)
BUT: *Le hai ricevute.* (He has received them.)

IN VISITA AI NONNI (VISITING GRANDMA AND GRANDPA)

MAMMA: *Bene ragazzi, siete pronti? I nonni ci stanno aspettando!*
(Well guys, are you ready? Your grandparents are waiting for us!)

FABIO: *Sì. È un'ora che sto aspettando!*
(Yes, I am. I have been waiting for over an hour!)

CHIARA: *Metto le scarpe e ci sono anch'io!*
(I put on my shoes and I'm ready too!)

MAMMA: *OK, ricordatevi che non vi fa bene mangiare troppi dolci!*
(All right! Remember that eating too many cookies is not good for you!)

FABIO: *Speriamo comunque che la nonna abbia fatto la sua torta di mele!*
(Anyway I hope grandma made her apple cake!)

CHIARA: *Non vedo l'ora di abbracciare il nonno!*
(I can't wait to hug grandpa!)

FABIO: *Quant'è che non li vediamo? Quasi un mese oramai?*
(How long that we haven't see them? Almost a month already?)

MAMMA: Sì, era prima dell'inizio dell'estate.
(Yes, it was before the beginning of the summer.)

CHIARA: Ciao, siamo arrivati!
(Hello, we're here!)

Verbs with Big Shiny Reflectors

You've already had a brief introduction to reflexive verbs, verbs that reflect upon themselves because their subject and object is one and the same person. When conjugating reflexive verbs in the *passato prossimo* or any other compound tense, you would use the auxiliary verb *essere* plus the past participle.

Chapter 16 explains reflexive verbs in much greater detail. For the purposes of this chapter, observe the following examples:

La ragazza si è guardata allo specchio. (The girl looked at herself in the mirror.)

Il bambino si è addormentato. (The baby fell asleep.)

Oggi mi sono alzato alle sei. (Today I got up at six.)

CHAPTER 12

Asking Questions in Italian

When is *il Colosseo* open? What ingredients are in *ribollito*? Where is *la stazione centrale*? Why is it called *olio extra vergine di oliva*? How much do those Ferragamo shoes cost? Who painted the *frescos* in the Sistine Chapel? If you want the answers, you'll need to know how to ask the questions!

Where Were You the Night of . . . ?

Interrogatives are words used to form questions. One of the easiest ways to *fare una domanda* (ask a question) in Italian is to place a question mark at the end of a statement. When speaking, the intonation of the voice rises at the end of the sentence. For example:

Il treno è arrivato. (The train has arrived.)
Il treno è arrivato? (Has the train arrived?)
È arrivato il treno. (The train has arrived.)
È arrivato il treno? (Has the train arrived?)

In questions beginning with an interrogative word, the subject is usually placed at the end of the sentence or after the verb:

Dove sta Luigi? (Where is Luigi?)
Quando usciamo? (When do we go out?)

Furthermore, adding the words or phrases *no?, non è vero?, è vero?,* or *vero?* to the end of a statement will change into a question:

Il tuo fratello ha avuto un incidente, non è vero? (Your brother had an accident, didn't he?)
Sono i padroni, vero? (They are the owners, right?)

Turn It into a Question

Rewrite the following statements into questions, using the same words. Check your answers in Appendix A.

1. Noi abbiamo paura.

----

2. Francesca viene a casa.

----

3. La squadra ha perso la partita.

---

4. Noi ci siamo alzati presto.

---

5. Gli studenti sono tornati.

---

6. I ragazzi vanno a casa.

---

7. Voi vi sedete qui.

---

8. La mamma prepara la cena.

---

9. Il vino costa molto.

---

10. Luigi ha tradotto quel libro.

Interrogative Adjectives

Interrogative adjectives indicate a quality or indefinite quantity and come with specific nouns. The most common forms are *che* (what? what kind of?), *quale* (which?), and *quanto* (how much? how many?). For example:

Quali parole ricordi? (Which words do you remember?)
Che libri leggete? (What books do you read?)
Quante ragazze vengono? (How many girls are coming?)
Che ora è? (What time is it?)
Quanto pane vuoi? (How much bread do you want?)

ESSENTIALS

Note that *che* does not change according to number or gender, while *quale* varies only in number (becoming *quali* in the plural). Furthermore, *quale* loses its final *–e* before vowels and consonant sounds such as *gn, pn, x,* and *z.*

Notice the difference in meaning between *che* and *quale*. The question *Quali film hai visto?* asks "Which films have you seen?" (For example, *Il postino, Ciao professore!* or *La vita è bella.*) The question *Che film hai visto?* asks "What types of films have you seen?" (For example, comedy, romance, or thriller.)

The interrogative adjective *quanto* (how many, how much) agrees in number and gender with the noun it modifies and has four forms (see **TABLE 12-1**).

TABLE 12-1

FOUR FORMS OF *QUANTO?* (HOW MUCH?/HOW MANY?)			
masculine/singular	*quanto*	*Quanto tempo fa?*	(How long ago?)
masculine/plural	*quanti*	*Quanti anni hai?*	(How old are you?)
feminine/singular	*quanta*	*Quanta farina c'è?*	(How much flour is there?)
feminine/plural	*quante*	*Quante studentesse ci sono?* (How many students are there?)		

LA VITA QUOTIDIANA (EVERYDAY LIFE)

UMBERTO: *Ciao! Che cosa fai? Lavori?*
(Hello! What are you doing? Are you working?)

CATERINA: *No. Sto leggendo.*
(No, I'm reading.)

UMBERTO: *Che cosa stai leggendo?*
(What are you reading?)

CATERINA: *Tu che dici? Un libro. E che cosa stai facendo allora?*
(What do you think? A book. And what are you doing now?)

UMBERTO: *Scrivo.*
(I'm writing.)

CATERINA:	*Che cosa stai scrivendo?*
	(What are you writing?)
UMBERTO:	*Sto scrivendo una lettera ai miei genitori.*
	(I'm writing a letter to my parents.)
CATERINA:	*Che cos'è quale rumore?*
	(What's that noise?)
UMBERTO:	*Non so.*
	(I don't know.)

What's Happening?

Sometimes interrogatives replace nouns altogether, and act as interrogative pronouns that introduce a question. They are:

TABLE 12-2

INTERROGATIVE PRONOUNS		
ITALIAN	**ENGLISH**	**EXAMPLE**
Chi?	(Who? Whom?)	*Chi sei?*
Che/Che cosa/Cosa?	(What?)	*Cosa dici?*
Quale?	(Which (one/s)?)	*Quale giornali vuoi?*

Chi is invariable and used exclusively when referring to people: *Chi ha parlato? Di chi stai ridendo?* The gender of the pronoun *chi* is usually recognized in context or by the agreement of the adjective or participle. *Chi hai salutato per prima/primo?*

Che or *che cosa* refers only to a thing and has the significance of *quale/i cose? Che (che cosa) vuoi? Che cosa desideri di più dalla vita?*

Che often appears in the interrogative phrase *che cosa* (what/which thing), though sometimes one of these two words may be dropped. The following three phrases are all equally correct:

Che cosa bevi? (What are you drinking?)
Che dici? (What are you saying?)
Cosa fanno i bambini? (What are the children doing?)

Quale is used to indicate people, animals, or things. It expresses "What is . . . ?" when the answer involves a choice, or when one requests information such as a name, telephone number, or address. *Quale* is invariable in gender. For example: *Quale di voi ha studiato a Parigi? Quale vuoi conservare di queste due fotografie?*

Interrogative Prepositions—Never at the End!

In Italian, a question never ends with a preposition. Prepositions such as *a, di, con,* and *per* always precede the interrogative *chi* (who).

A chi scrivi? (To whom are you writing?)
Di chi sono queste chiavi? (Whose keys are these?)
Con chi escono stasera? (Who(m) are they going out with tonight?)

Where, Oh Where, Are They?

One other group of words is also used in the formation of questions—the interrogative adverbs *come?* (how), *dove?* (where), *perché?* (why), and *quando?* (when).

TABLE 12-3

INTERROGATIVE ADVERBS		
Come (KOH-meh)?	(How?)	*Come sta Giancarlo?*
Dove (DOH-vay)?	(Where?)	*Dov'è la biblioteca?*
Perché (pair-KEH)?	(Why?)	*Perché non dormono?*
Quando (KWAN-doh)?	(When?)	*Quando parte Pietro?*

The following interrogative words are the most commonly used to introduce a question:

A che ora? (At what time?)
Come? (How?)
Come mai? (How come? Why [on earth]? Why ever?)
Dove? (Where?)

Perché? (Why?)
Quando? (When?)
Quanto? (How much?)

Two common contractions are *com'è?* (a contraction of *come è?* meaning "how is?") and *dov'è?* (a contraction of *dove è?* meaning "where is?"). Again, note that in Italian the subject and verb are inverted in interrogative sentences:

A che ora partono i tuoi amici? (When are your friends leaving?)
Come sta Luigi? (How is Louis?)
Dove sono i bambini? (Where are the children?)
Dov'è il bambino? (Where is the child?)
Perché fumi tanto? (Why do you smoke so much?)
Quanto fa due più tre? (How much is two plus three?)

The subject and verb are not inverted with *come mai: Come mai Umberto non è qui?* (How come Umberto is not here?/Why ever isn't Umberto here?)

Interesting Interrogatives

Complete the following sentences with the correct interrogative. Check your answers in Appendix A.

1. _____ preferisci: la birra o il vino?
2. _____ caffè bevi al giorno?
3. _____ ti chiami?
4. _____ è il tuo compleanno?
5. _____ anni hai?
6. _____ è l'autore dell'*Orlando Furioso?*
7. _____ temi hai scritto quest'anno?
8. _____ è la capitale d'Italia?
9. _____ non mi aiuti?
10. _____ è stato abbattuto il muro di Berlino?

Just the Facts, Ma'am

One of the first lessons in journalism is to write crisp, clear sentences that answer the questions who? what? where? when? why? and how? There are many newspapers and magazines published in Italy, some of the most well-known being *Il Corriere della Sera, La Repubblica, Il Sole 24 Ore, L'Espresso,* and *Panorama.* Often they can be found online or at newsstands that sell foreign publications. One of the best ways to improve your Italian reading skills is to pick an article of interest—for example, sports, fashion, or politics—and read for overall content. Don't get frustrated by those words you don't understand at first; instead, focus on the essential points. Gradually your knowledge of the vocabulary and grammar will improve. For some vocabulary to get you started, see **TABLE 12-4**.

TABLE 12-4

VOCABULARY: THE NEWSSTAND			
articolo	article	*cruciverba*	crossword puzzle
edicola	newsstand	*fumetti*	comic strips
giornale	newspaper	*interrogare*	to interrogate
intervista	interview	*oroscopo*	horoscope
redatto capo	editor in chief	*rivista*	magazine
rivista letteraria	literary magazine	*rubrica sportiva*	sports column

Make That a Question!

Given the following responses, formulate an appropriate question using an interrogative adjective, adverb, or pronoun. Check your answers in Appendix A.

1. Ho due sorelle.

_____

2. Perché non mi piacciono!

_____

3. Sono alle tre.

---

4. Abbiamo una Fiat.

---

5. È in Sicilia.

---

6. Non avete mangiato niente.

---

7. Parto domani.

---

8. Ne avete tre.

---

9. Sono di Trieste.

---

10. Vogliamo quelle!

FACTS

Many Italian idiomatic expressions begin with interrogative phrases or are stated as questions:

Che razza di . . . ? (What kind of . . . ?)
Che ti prende? (What's the matter with you?)
Come la mettiamo? (What are we going to do about it?)
Dove voi arrivare? (What are you getting at?)

WORD SEARCH: THE FIVE W'S

Want to be an interrogation expert in Italian? Are you a *ficcanaso* (busybody)? To answer who? what? where? when? and why? Try solving this word search puzzle. You'll find the answers in Appendix A.

```
H  E  I  N  T  E  R  V  I  S  T  A  M  O  C
I  L  V  L  C  R  U  C  I  V  E  R  B  A  E
L  E  O  I  P  O  M  A  L  O  C  I  D  E  A
P  H  V  C  C  E  S  R  R  E  T  N  I  C  C
É  C  Ò  I  I  R  R  A  E  R  A  F  I  O  É
R  I  D  N  T  D  C  C  M  E  N  S  H  N
C  N  N  N  A  A  E  V  O  D  O  U  C  R  A
H  T  A  E  T  V  G  D  M  M  Z  R  O  I  I
E  E  U  G  N  O  A  O  E  É  E  I  R  T  L
C  R  Q  U  A  N  T  E  R  P  G  L  G  N  A
O  D  N  A  U  Q  U  N  L  R  E  S  A  A  U
S  D  A  E  Q  O  E  I  A  Z  E  B  A  U  Q
A  B  R  U  H  B  R  U  N  U  H  T  C  Q  Q
H  A  A  C  Q  U  A  N  T  U  Q  R  N  E  P
F  N  D  V  I  D  F  E  L  A  N  R  O  I  G
```

CHE	EDICOLA	INTERROGATIVE	QUANTE
CHE COSA	FARE UNA	INTERVISTA	QUANTI
COME	DOMANDA	QUALE	QUANTO
COSA	GIORNALE	QUALI	
CRUCIVERBA	IL PERCHÉ	QUANDO	
DOVE	IL PERCOME	QUANTA	

CHAPTER 13

Making Sense of the la-di-das

The beat goes on with those stubborn prepositions like *a, con, da, di, in, per,* and *su.* They stand for many different words and are used in a variety of grammatical constructions. This chapter also covers *piacere* and similar verbs.

What Are These Pre-Positioning Words?

In English, you know them as "to," "in," "by," "on," "from," "for," and "since." In Italian, they are known as *a, in, da, di, con, in, per,* and *su,* among others. They are prepositions, those words that usually precede a noun or pronoun and express a relation to another word, as in the following simple sentences:

The woman *on* the platform.
They came *after* lunch.
Why not go *by* bus?

Although there are general rules for the use of Italian prepositions, there's only one sure way to learn the correct usage: practice, practice, practice.

Mix and Match

When the prepositions *a, da, di, in,* and *su* are followed by a definite article, they are combined to form one word. The prepositional articles (*le preposizioni articolate*) take the forms listed in **TABLE 13-1**.

TABLE 13-1

PREPOSITIONAL ARTICLES					
DEFINITE ARTICLE	A	DA	DI	IN	SU
il	al	dal	del	nel	sul
lo	allo	dallo	dello	nello	sullo
l'	all'	dall'	dell'	nell'	sull'
i	ai	dai	dei	nei	sui
gli	agli	dagli	degli	negli	sugli
la	alla	dalla	della	nella	sulla
l'	all'	dall'	dell'	nell'	sull'
le	alle	dalle	delle	nelle	sulle

There are only two contracted forms of *con: col (con + il)* and *coi (con + i)* and their use is optional:

Vedete la ragazza col cane (con il cane)?
(Do you see the girl with the dog?)

A: the All-Purpose Preposition

The preposition *a* can mean "to," "at," or "in," depending on how you use it in context. You will need the preposition *a* in the following cases:

1. To express the idea of going somewhere or staying somewhere (with names of cities):

   Vado a Milano. (I go to Milan.)
   Vado al mercato ogni lunedì. (I go to the market every Monday.)
   Si trova a Venezia. (It can be found in Venice.)
   Si trova alla piazza. (It can be found in the plaza.)

2. Before direct objects:

   Scriva a Rita. (He/she writes to Rita.)
   Scriviamo alla zia. (We write to our aunt.)
   Telefono agli amici. (They call their friends.)

3. The preposition *a* is also used with several verbs. Often those are verbs of motion, but in other instances it's a case of usage. That means either you'll have to commit them to memory, or, more likely, you'll grow accustomed to the usage over time as you listen and read Italian:

   andare a . . . (to go to)
   fermarsi a . . . (to stop)
   incoraggiare a . . . (to encourage)
   invitare a . . . (to invite to)
   insegnare a . . . (to teach)
   riuscire a . . . (to be careful)
   venire a . . . (to come to)

4. To form several grammatical constructions with particular significance:

a mezzogiorno (at noontime)
alle tre (at three)
barca a vela (sailboat)
sedia a rotelle (wheelchair)

ESSENTIALS

The preposition *a* changes to *ad* before infinitives that begin with *a–* for ease of pronunciation: *imparare ad altalenare* (to learn to seesaw). The preposition *di* often becomes *d'* before infinitives beginning with *i–*: *dimenticare d'imburrare* (to forget to butter).

Saying "Aah"

Complete the following with the correct form of the preposition *a*. Then check your answers in Appendix A.

1. La lezione comincia _____ dieci.
2. Scriviamo spesso _____ zii.
3. Vive _____ Bologna, ma lavora _____ Milano.
4. Finalmente comincio _____ capire la grammatica italiana!
5. A che ora torni _____ casa? _____ sei?
6. Andiamo _____ Napoli ogni anno.
7. Giovanna studia _____ Bologna ogni estate.
8. È nata _____ Palermo.

In Means In

Usually the Italian preposition *in* means "in" in English, but it can also mean "to" or "by"! The preposition *in* is used in the following cases.

1. To express the idea of going somewhere or staying somewhere (with countries, continents, regions, large islands, and addresses):

Vado in Italia. (I am going to Italy.)
Vado nella Sicilia. (I am going to Sicily.)
Abita in Germania. (He/she lives in Germany.)
Roma è in Italia. (Rome is in Italy.)

2. In describing a method of transportation:

Andiamo in macchina. (We are going by car.)
Andiamo in autobus. (We are going by bus.)
Viaggiamo in aereo. (We are traveling by plane.)
Viaggiamo in barca. (We are traveling by boat.)

3. In dates, as a contraction *nel (in + il)*:

Cristoforo Colombo è nato nel 1451. (Christopher Columbus was born
    in 1451.)
Caravaggio è morto nel 1570. (Caravaggio died in 1570.)

SSENTIALS   With nouns that refer to rooms of the house, such as *salotto*,
cucina, and *sala da pranzo*, an article is usually not used with the
preposition *in*. For example: *Mangiano in sala da pranzo, non in
cucina*. (They eat in the dining room, not in the kitchen.)

Da: from Sea to Shining Sea

The Italian preposition *da* means "from" in English. This preposition is
used in time expressions, in which case you may translate it as "since" or
"for." Italian uses the construction of present tense + *da* + time
expressions to indicate an action that began in the past and is still going
on in the present. For example:

Da quanto tempo leggi questa rivista? (How long have you been reading
    this magazine?)
Leggo questa rivista da molto tempo. (I've been reading this magazine
    for a long time.)

Da is also used in the following instances:

1. To express the equivalent of the English phrase "at the house of":

    Vado dal fratello. (I'm going to my brother's house.)
    Vado da Filippo. (I'm going to Filippo's house.)
    Andiamo dai signori Rossi. (We're going to the Rossi's house.)
    Andiamo da Gino. (We're going to Gino's house.)

2. To indicate origin or source:

    Vengo da Torino. (I come from Torino.)
    Vengo dalla Francia. (I come from France.)
    È tornato dalle vacanze. (He is back from vacation.)
    È tornato dagli zii. (He is back from his aunt and uncle's house.)

3. To indicate the worth or price of something:

    Voglio un francobollo da cento lire. (I want a 100 lire stamp.)
    È una casa da poco prezzo. (It's a house of little worth.)

Di: of the People

The Italian preposition *di* means "of" in English. It is used in the following cases:

1. To indicate possession:

    il libro di Maria (Maria's book)
    la padella del cuoco (the cook's pan)
    la casa dello zio (the uncle's house)

2. To indicate what an object is made of:

    il tavolo di legno (wooden table)
    la spada di metallo (metal knife)
    la medaglia di bronzo (bronze medal)

3. To indicate origin using the verb *essere* + *di* + *nome di città* (name of the city):
   Elisa è di Napoli. (Elisa is from Napoli.)
   Maurizio è di Prato. (Maurizio is from Prato.)
   I Rossi sono di Catania. (The Rossis are from Catania.)

FACTS

With the seasons *primavera* (spring), *estate* (summer), *autunno* (fall), and *inverno* (winter), the Italian prepositions *in* and *di* are interchangeable:

d'inverno/in inverno (in winter)
di primavera/in primavera (in spring)

4. The preposition *di* is used with certain verbs and adjectives:

   accorgersi di qualcosa (to notice something)
   innamorarsi di qualcuno (to be in love with someone)
   malato di una malattia (ill with a sickness)
   vergognarsi di qualcosa (to be ashamed by something)

5. The preposition *di* is found in many particular grammatical constructions:

   di sera (during the evening)
   di notte (at night)
   d'estate (during the summer)
   un uomo di mezza età (a man of middle age)

ALERT

In a phrase with the indefinite pronouns *qualcosa, niente,* or *nulla,* the preposition *di* is placed before the adjective but after the pronoun. For example:

Ho visto qualcosa di bello. (I saw something beautiful.)

A Fearsome Foursome

The fearsome foursome of Italian prepositions are *per, su, con,* and *fra/tra*. The preposition *per* ("for" in English) is used to indicate the following:

1. Movement through space:

   Sono passati per Roma. (They passed through Rome.)
   Sono passati per Londra. (They passed through London.)

2. Duration of time:

   Ho lavorato per un anno intero. (I worked for an entire year.)
   Ho lavorato per due giorni senza una pausa. (I worked for two days without a break.)

3. Destination:

   Questa lettera è per il direttore. (This letter is for the director.)

Another useful preposition to know is *su* (on). *Su* is used in Italian to indicate location or a topic of discourse. For example:

Il libro è sul tavolo. (The book is on the table.)
Il cuscino è sul divano. (The cushion is on the couch.)
È una conferenze sull'inquinamento industriale. (It is a conference on industrial pollution.)

The Italian preposition *con* is similar to the English "with":

È uscito con la cugina. (He left with his cousin.)
Sono andato con la mia famiglia. (I left with my family.)
Taglia il pane con quel coltello. (He cuts the bread with that knife.)
Apre la porta con questa chiave. (She opens the door with this key.)
Ha risposto con gentilezza. (He/she responded with gentleness.)
Lei ha gridato con gioa. (She screamed with joy.)

Finally, there is the preposition *tra* or *fra* (these words are fraternal twins and interchangeable in all cases), which may be used in the sense of "between" (whether between two locations, things, or people), or to indicate a time in the future with respect to the speaker. For example:

Livorno è fra Roma e Genova. (Livorno is between Rome and Genoa.)
Silvano è fra Maria e Davide. (Silvano is between Maria and David.)
Fra qualche giorno arriverà la primavera. (In a few days spring will arrive.)
Tra alcuni ore arriveremo. (In a few hours we'll arrive.)

Introduction to *Piacere*

Indirect object + verb + subject. Not your usual sentence structure, but in the case of *piacere* (to please, to like) that's the way it works in Italian, and here's why: In English, you say that A likes B. In Italian, though, the same meaning is understood in different terms: B pleases A. Here are some examples:

Agli italiani piace il calcio. (Italians like soccer. Literally: Soccer is pleasing to Italians.)
Ai professori piace insegnare. (Professors like teaching. Literally: Teaching is pleasing to professors.)
Mi piacciono le carote. (I like carrots. Literally: Carrots are pleasing to me.)

Note that in these examples, *piacere* is conjugated to match the subject of the sentence; in the first example, *agli italiani piace il calcio*, *piacere* is conjugated in the third person singular form, to match with *calcio* (soccer) and not with *agli italiani* (all Italians). Other verbs that follow this construction of inversion and behave similarly to *piacere* are listed in **TABLE 13-2**.

TABLE 13-2

VERBS THAT ACT LIKE *PIACERE*	
bastare	to be sufficient, to suffice
dispiacere	to displease, to upset
mancare	to be lacking, to miss
occorrere	to require, to need
servire	to serve, to be of use

Subject/Object Inversion

Complete the following with the correct form of the italicized verb.
Then check your answers in Appendix A.

1. Mi _____ dieci dollari. Puoi prestarmeli? (servire)
2. Ti _____ quel ragazzo? (piacere)
3. Mi _____ le forbice. (occorrere)
4. _____ dopo dieci pagine per un saggio. (bastare)
5. Quanti fogli vuoi? Me ne _____ due. (occorrere)
6. Ci _____ il tuo aiuto. (servire)
7. Ci _____ molto che tu non sia potuto venire.
   (dispiacere)
8. Ai Rossi _____ molto la figlia. (mancare)
9. Non mi _____ il pesce. (piacere)
10. Mi _____ molto i miei genitori. (mancare)

ALLO ZOO (AT THE ZOO)

FABIO: *Per prima cosa vorrei vedere le scimmie!*
(First I'd like to look at the monkeys!)

CHIARA: *Guarda! I delfini . . . si stanno divertendo a schizzare il pubblico!*
(Look! Dolphins . . . they are having fun splashing the audience!)

FABIO: *Sì, ho visto. Poverino quel signore in prima fila è tutto bagnato!*
(Yes, I saw. That poor man sitting in the first row is all wet!)

CHIARA: *Presto, vieni! Voglio vedere i coccodrilli.*
(Hurry up, come on! I want to see the crocodiles.)

FABIO: *Allora dobbiamo andare da questa parte.*
(Then we have to go this way.)

CHAPTER 14

I Command You!

Without the imperative, it would be difficult to advise your friends about what Italian towns to visit, the *forze armate* (armed forces) would cease to exist, and, most important, you'd no longer hear that famous phrase uttered by Italian mothers at the dinner table everywhere: *Mangia!* (Eat!)

Do Your Homework!

One of the most familiar figures in Mafia movies is that of *consigliere* (advisor, counselor). His role is to give advice to the head of the clan. And then, of course, the godfather gives the command to commit various nefarious acts—in the imperative, of course. The imperative verb forms are used to give orders or advice, to urge strongly, and to exhort. It is a simple tense—in the sense that it isn't compound—and has only one form, the present. Furthermore, you can address your command only to an informal form of "you": *tu* or *voi*, depending on whether you are talking to one or more people.

When conjugating a first-conjugation verb, the familiar singular (*tu*) command is the same as the third-person singular (*Lei*) form of the present indicative, and the plural *voi* command is the same as the *voi* form of the present indicative (see **TABLE 14-1**).

TABLE 14-1

FIRST-CONJUGATION VERB IMPERATIVES		
INFINITIVE	TU	VOI
cantare	Canta!	Cantate!
mangiare	Mangia!	Mangiate!
parlare	Parla!	Parlate!

The familiar commands for regular *–ere* and *–ire* verbs are the same as the *tu* and *voi* forms of the present indicative (see **TABLE 14-2**).

TABLE 14-2

SECOND- AND THIRD-CONJUGATION VERB IMPERATIVES		
INFINITIVE	TU	VOI
dormire	Dormi!	Dormite!
finire	Finisci!	Finite!
pulire	Pulisci!	Pulite!
salire	Sali!	Salite!
scrivere	Scrivi!	Scrivete!
vendere	Vendi!	Vendete!

Listen to Me!

Although the imperative conjugation has a form you're already familiar with, there are some Italian verbs that have irregular forms for the familiar commands in the *tu* and *voi* forms (see **TABLE 14-3**).

TABLE 14-3

IRREGULAR IMPERATIVES		
INFINITIVE	TU	VOI
andare (to walk)	*Va'!*	*Andate!*
avere (to have)	*Abbi!*	*Abbiate!*
dare (to give)	*Da'!*	*Date!*
dire (to say, to tell)	*Di'!*	*Dite!*
essere (to be)	*Sii!*	*Siate!*
fare (to make)	*Fa'!*	*Fate!*
sapere (to know)	*Sappi!*	*Sappiate!*
stare (to stay)	*Sta'!*	*State!*

EXERCISE

Are You Talking to Me?

Complete the following imperative sentences using the forms as indicated. Check your answers in Appendix A.

1. (voi) _____ (mangiare) la minestra!
2. (tu) _____ (telefonare) a Gino!
3. (tu) _____ (dire) questo a tuo padre!
4. (voi) _____ (fare) questo favore!
5. (tu) _____ (guardare) allo specchio!
6. (tu) _____ (uscire) subito!
7. (voi) _____ (girare) a destra!
8. (voi) _____ (bere) il latte!
9. (tu) _____ (sbrigarsi), è tardi!
10. (voi) _____ (spegnere) la radio!

Don't Touch That Dial!

We grew up hearing negative commands: Don't bother your brother!
Don't scream! Don't forget to do your homework! The negative *tu*
command forms of all verbs are formed by the infinitive of the verb
preceded by *non*: *Non andare! Non fare!*

The negative *voi* command forms of all verbs are formed simply by
placing *non* before the affirmative *voi* form: *Non credete! Non finite!*

It's a Negative!

Complete the following sentences with a negative command.
Then check your answers in Appendix A.

1. Fabio, _____ addesso; ceneremo presto! (mangiare)
2. Pierino, _____ parolacce! (dire)
3. Mamma, _____ la cena per me: sono invitata a cena
   fuori. (preparare)
4. Aspettate ragazzi; _____ sempre così impazienti!
   (essere)
5. Bambini, _____ sulle pareti! (scrivere)
6. Roberta, _____ così cattiva con la sorellina! (essere)
7. Monica, _____ la pentola; è piena di acqua calda!
   (toccare)
8. Davide, _____ con la bocca piena! (parlare)
9. Ragazzi, _____ a pallone in questa strada; è
   pericoloso! (giocare)
10. Gianna, _____ così pessimista! La vita è troppo bella!
    (essere)

Let's! Let's Not!

The imperative tense is used in other ways as well. For instance, in
order to express the idea of "let's . . . ," the imperative of *noi* is used
(that would make sense, if you consider that "let's" is the contraction for
"let us"). Fortunately, the imperative form of *noi* is identical to its

present-indicative form, except that an exclamation mark is used for the imperative. For the negative "let's not," simply place *non* before the verb. Some examples appear in **TABLE 14-4**.

TABLE 14-4

IMPERATIVES IN THE *NOI* FORM			
INFINITIVE	PRESENT-INDICATIVE FORM OF *NOI*	IMPERATIVE FORM OF *NOI*	NEGATIVE COMMAND
andare	andiamo (we go)	Andiamo! (Let's go!)	Non andiamo! (Let's not go!)
credere	crediamo (we believe)	Crediamo! (Let's believe!)	Non crediamo! (Let's not believe!)
dormire	dormiamo (we sleep)	Dormiamo! (Let's sleep!)	Non dormiamo! (Let's not sleep!)
stare	stiamo (we stay)	Stiamo! (Let's stay!)	Non stiamo! (Let's not stay!)

AL LUNA PARK (AT THE CARNIVAL)

FABIO: *Vieni con me sulle montagne russe?*
(Would you come with me on the roller coaster?)

CHIARA: *OK, ma dopo devi venire con me nella casa dei fantasmi!*
(Okay, but then you have to come with me into the haunted house!)

FABIO: *Ti piace il mio pupazzo di peluche? L'ho vinto al tiro a segno.*
(Do you like my stuffed animal? I won it playing target shooting.)

CHIARA: *Carino! Che dici di comprarci dello zucchero filato?*
(Nice! What do you say we buy some cotton candy to eat?)

FABIO: *Sì, bella idea!*
(Yes, great idea!)

Stand up Straight—Please!

Need to tell your teacher, supervisor, or the Italian prime minister to do something? Use the subjunctive form of the verb to form the formal commands.

For more on the subjunctive tense, see Chapter 20. **TABLE 14-5** contains some examples of formal commands.

TABLE 14-5

FORMAL COMMANDS		
INFINITIVE	*LEI*	*LORO*
cantare	*Canti!*	*Cantino!*
dormire	*Dorma!*	*Dormano!*
finire	*Finisca!*	*Finiscano!*
vendere	*Venda!*	*Vendano!*

If you remember, some of the verbs have irregular stem changes in the *io* form. Sometimes, this form is used to construct the imperatives of *Lei* and *Loro* (see **TABLE 14-6**).

TABLE 14-6

FORMAL COMMANDS: VERBS WITH STEM CHANGES			
INFINITIVE	PRESENT-INDICATIVE FORM OF *IO*	IMPERATIVE FORM OF *LEI*	IMPERATIVE FORM OF *LORO*
andare (to walk)	*vado*	*Vada!*	*Vadano!*
apparire (to appear)	*appaio*	*Appaia!*	*Appaiano!*
bere (to drink)	*bevo*	*Beva!*	*Bevano!*
cogliere (to pick, to pluck)	*colgo*	*Colga!*	*Colgano!*
dire (to say, to tell)	*dico*	*Dica!*	*Dicano!*
fare (to make)	*faccio*	*Faccia!*	*Facciano!*
porre (to place, to put down)	*pongo*	*Ponga!*	*Pongano!*
rimanere (to stay, to remain)	*rimango*	*Rimanga!*	*Rimangano!*
salire (to climb)	*salgo*	*Salga!*	*Salgano!*
scegliere (to choose, to pick)	*scelgo*	*Scelga!*	*Scelgano!*
sedere (to sit down)	*siedo*	*Sieda!*	*Siedano!*

suonare (to play an instrument)	suono	Suoni!	Suonino!
tradurre (to translate)	traduco	Traduca!	Traducano!
trarre (to draw, to pull)	traggo	Tragga!	Traggano!
udire (to listen)	odo	Oda!	Odano!
uscire (to exit)	esco	Esca!	Escano!
venire (to come)	vengo	Venga!	Vengano!

SSENTIALS

Attenzione! The vowel of the subjunctive ending is *–i* for *–are* verbs and *–a* for *–ere* and *–ire* verbs (the reverse of the present-tense forms). Also note that the formal pronouns *Lei* and *Loro* are usually omitted with the commands; as with all other commands, an exclamation mark follows the order or request.

Finally, some verbs have irregular formal command forms that are not based on any present-indicative forms, and which you will have to memorize. These verbs are listed in **TABLE 14-7**.

TABLE 14-7

FORMAL COMMANDS: IRREGULAR VERBS		
INFINITIVE	LEI	LORO
avere	Abbia!	Abbiano!
dare	Dia!	Diano!
essere	Sia!	Siano!
sapere	Sappia!	Sappiano!
stare	Stia!	Stiano

Note that the same form of the verb is used for the negative formal commands.

Count Off, Soldier!

Had enough ordering around? Imagine how those recruits feel in boot camp. From Roman soldiers in chariots to da Vinci's drawings for armored vehicles, from papal armies to the wars for a united Italy in the 1800s, Italy has been the scene for many pitched battles. Today, both men and women serve in *la forza armata* (the Italian armed forces). Some military vocabulary appears in **TABLE 14-8**.

TABLE 14-8

VOCABULARY: THE MILITARY			
aircraft carrier	*portaerei*	general	*generale*
army	*esercito*	navy	*marina*
battering ram	*ariete*	pistol	*pistola*
battle	*battaglia*	recruit	*ricluta*
bayonet	*baionetta*	rifle	*carabina*
bomb	*bomba*	Second World War	*seconda guerra mondiale*
cavalry	*cavalleria*	sentry	*sentinella*
conscription	*leva*	soldier	*soldata*
defense	*difesa*	war	*Guerra*
fort	*fortezza*	weapon	*arma*

CHAPTER 15

Pasta, Pronouns, and Porcini

Mention Italian food, and the heady aroma of pizza, fresh olive oil, and garlic come to mind immediately. The Italian culinary tradition is one reason so many people want to visit Italy, and every region has its own specialty. Learn how to decipher a menu and offer a toast in Italian, then sample a *minestra* (vegetable soup) of pronouns to whet your grammatical appetite.

Three Meals a Day

Breakfast (*la prima colazione*) in Italy typically consists of coffee and a bun. Large calorie-heavy dishes such as pancakes, eggs, and sausage links are served almost exclusively in hotels that cater to American tourists. For some vocabulary you might find useful as you sit down to breakfast, see **TABLE 15-1**.

TABLE 15-1

VOCABULARY: BREAKFAST			
bread	*il pane*	honey	*il miele*
breakfast	*la prima colazione*	hot chocolate	*la cioccolata*
butter	*il burro*	jam	*la marmellata*
cereal	*i fiocchi di cereale*	milk	*il latte*
coffee	*il caffè*	orange juice	*succo d'arancia*
croissant	*il cornetto*	tea	*il tè*

Like many southern Mediterranean countries, the midday meal in Italy is traditionally the largest of the day. In fact, according to a recent poll by the national statistics institute Istat, 75 percent of Italians go home for lunch. That number has decreased in recent years because business hours conform to the nine-to-five schedule familiar in the United States and many other European countries, and more women are now working outside of the home. *Il pranzo* is traditionally the meal served at midday, while *la cena* is the evening meal.

In Italy, those milky concoctions—*cappuccino* and *caffé latte*—are drunk only at breakfast. During the day, Italians may stop for an *espresso* (not to be confused with *expresso*, which is a fast train).

For possible dinner menu items you might encounter, see **TABLE 15-2**.

TABLE 15-2

VOCABULARY: DINNER (MIDDAY MEAL)			
angel hair pasta	*i capellini*	rabbit	*il coniglio*
beef	*il manzo*	ring-shaped cake	*la ciambella*
butterfly-shaped pasta	*le farfalle*	sausage	*la salsiccia*

chestnut fritters	*le castagnole*	spicy tomato sauce	*all'arrabbiata*
chicken	*il pollo*	steak	*la bistecca*
filled ring-shaped pasta	*i tortellini*	vegetable soup	*il minestrone*
fried squid	*i calamari fritti*	thin ribbon noodles	*le fettuccine*
ice cream	*il gelato*	almond cookies	*i biscotti*
lamb	*l'agnello*	whipped cream	*la panna montata*
pork	*il maiale*	wild boar	*il cinghiale*

FACTS

Cacciucco alla livornese, the traditional fish stew from Livorno, has five kinds of seafood, one for each *c* in its name. The dish can include prawns, octopus, monkfish, clams, and mussels.

Deciphering the Menu

If spaghetti and meatballs with a glass of red wine from a straw-covered flask is the closest you've come to authentic Italian cuisine, then a refresher course is in order. In Italy, dishes are usually served on separate plates in a specific order. Here are the main components of a typical menu, in the order they are served:

- *L'antipasto*, which literally means "before the meal," includes hot and cold appetizers such as *crostini* (small, thin slices of toasted bread with toppings such as pâté or cheese), *bruschetta* (bread dipped in olive oil, toasted, and covered with diced tomatoes and basil), and *mozzarella in carrozza* (fried mozzarella squares).
- *Il primo*, or "first course," usually consists of *pasta*, *minestrone*, *risotto*, or *zuppa* (soup).
- *Il secondo*, or "second course," is the main course—meat, poultry, game, or fish.
- *Il contorno*, or "side dish," may consist of vegetables such as *melanzane* (eggplant), *spinaci* (spinach), or *insalata mista* (mixed salad).

- *Il dolce*, or "dessert," includes such favorite sweets as *tiramisù*, *torta della nonna* (custard shortbread pie), or *zabaglione* (custard of egg yolks with wine and brandy).

ESSENTIALS

Italians often say *Buon appetito!* or "Enjoy your meal!" when the first course is served, and *Salute!* or "To your health!" when toasting with a drink.

We Don't Take Reservations

Restaurants in Italy include the *autogrill*, or roadside snack bar; the *osteria*, an informal place; the *trattoria*, which is a medium-priced, often family-run eating establishment; and the *paninoteca*, a place where sandwiches and salads are often available.

You need to make reservations only if you are planning to go to one of the most expensive restaurants. If that is the case, use the expression *vorrei fare una prenotazione* (I would like to make a reservation). If, for example, it's a reservation for two people at 8:00 P.M., the complete phrase would be: *Vorrei fare una prenotazione per due alle otto.*

E

FACTS

Both *il servizio* (service charge/tip) and *il coperto* (cover charge for bread and water) are usually included in *il conto* (the bill). By Italian law, the gratuity is included in the bill, and extra tipping isn't necessary. If the service warrants it, leave your waiter a little extra.

What else do you need to know? Well, to ask for the bill, say: *Il conto, per favore.* And if you want the waiter to keep the change, say: *Tenga pure il resto.* For other vocabulary you might find useful when you find yourself at an Italian restaurant, see **TABLE 15-3**.

TABLE 15-3	VOCABULARY: TABLE SERVICE			
bottle	*la bottiglia*		napkin	*il tovagliolo*
bottle opener	*l'apribottiglia*		pepper shaker	*il portapepe*

bowl	*la scodella*	plate	*il piatto*
bread basket	*il cestino del pane*	salt shaker	*il portasale*
carafe	*la caraffa*	spoon	*il cucchiaio*
cutlery	*le posate*	sugar bowl	*la zuccheriera*
decanter	*la caraffa*	tablecloth	*la tovaglia*
fork	*la forchetta*	table service	*le stoviglie*
glass	*il bicchiere*	teaspoon	*il cucchiaino*
knife	*il coltello*	toothpick	*lo stuzzicadente*

AL RISTORANTE (AT THE RESTAURANT)

LUCA: *Ho telefonato qualche qiorno fa per prenotare un tavolo.*
(I phoned a few days ago to book a table.)

CAMERIERE: *A quale nome?*
(What name, please?)

LUCA: *Il mio nome: Marchetti.*
(My name's Marchetti.)

CAMERIERE: *Per quante persone?*
(How many people is it for?)

LUCA: *Noi siamo in quattro, ma sta arrivando un'altra coppia.*
(Four of us, with another couple coming.)

CAMERIERE: *Prego, da questa parte. Vi piace qui, vicino alla finestra?*
(Come this way please. Is it all right here, by the window?)

LUCA: *Va benissimo, così ci godiamo anche questa bella vista.*
(That's fine, that way we can also enjoy the beautiful view.)

CAMERIERE: *Datemi pure i vostri cappotti.*
(Let me take your coats.)

LUCA: *Posso lasciarle anche la sciarpa?*
(Can I also give you my scarf?)

CAMERIERE: *Oh! Ecco i vostri amici! Vi porto subito il menu e la lista dei vini. Gradite un aperitivo?*
(Oh! Here are your friends! I'll bring you the menu and the wine list right away. Would you like an aperitif?)

LUCA: *Sì, prenderei un martini. Ne vuoi uno anche tu, Susanna?*
(Yes, I'll have a martini. Do you also want one, Susanna?)

CAMERIERE: *Avete già scelto?*
(Have you decided yet?)

LUCA: *Qual è il piatto del giorno?*
(What's today's special?)

CAMERIERE: *Tagliatelle ai funghi porcini.*
(Tagliatelle and porcini mushrooms.)

LUCA: *Molto allettante. Ma non riesco a decidermi.*
(Very appealing. But I can't make up my mind.)

CAMERIERE: *E come secondo, preferite carne o pesce?*
(Do you prefer fish or meat for your main course?)

LUCA: *Non so. Sicuramente vorrei assaggiare un piatto tipico.*
(I don't know. I'd really like to try a local dish.)

CAMERIERE: *Che cosa ne dite di un piatto di salmone fresco alla piastra, o di un buonissimo caciucco? È un piatto tipico toscano: una zuppa di pesce con pomodoro, servita con pane casareccio.*
(What would you say to grilled fresh salmon, or a very good fish soup? It's a typical Tuscan dish: a fish soup with tomatoes served with home-baked bread.)

LUCA: *No, preferisco una bella costata con patatine.*
(No, I prefer a nice big chop with potatoes.)

CAMERIERE: *Volete dell'insalata come contorno? Abbiamo dell'insalata mista o semplice. L'insalata mista è con lattuga, pomodoro, pepperoni, cetrioli, carote, e, se volete, cipolle rosse. Oppure abbiamo un'insalata di sedano, funghi, e grana.*
(Would you like it served with salad? We have mixed or plain salad. The mixed salad comes with lettuce, tomato, green peppers, cucumbers, carrots, and, if you like, red onions. Otherwise, we have a salad with celery, mushrooms, and grana cheese.)

LUCA: *Per me senza contorno, grazie.*
(No side dish, thank you.)

CAMERIERE: *Eccomi a voi. Questo è per Lei, e questo è per Lei. Tutto a posto?*
(Here I am now. This is for you, and this one is for you.

Is everything all right?)

LUCA: *Tutto benissimo. Posso avere un'altra forchetta, per favore?*
(Everything's fine. May I also have another fork, please?)

CAMERIERE: *Per i dolci abbiamo una torta al cioccolato e pere, torta di mele, panna cotta, macedonia, gelati, sorbetto e la specialità del nostro cuoco: la pastiera napoletana.*
(We have a chocolate and pear cake, apple tart, crème caramel, fruit salad, ice cream, sorbet, and our chef's specialty, *pastiera napoletana*.)

LUCA: *Ha un nome invitante. Com'è fatta?*
(It's got an appealing name. What's it made of?)

CAMERIERE: *È un dolce tipico napolitano, fatto di pasta frolla, grano, ricotta, e frutta candita.*
(It's a typical Neapolitan dessert, made of short-crust pastry, wheat germ, ricotta cheese, and candied fruit.)

LUCA: *E che cosa sono i cantucci?*
(And what are the cantucci?)

CAMERIERE: *Sono dei biscottini alle mandorle. Vengono servite con un vino dolce tipico: il Vin Santo.*
(They're almond biscuits and are served with a local sweet wine: Vin Santo.)

LUCA: *Preferisco quel dolce napoletano!*
(I prefer that Neapolitan dessert!)

CAMERIERE: *Desiderano altro?*
(Would you like anything else?)

LUCA: *No, grazie, va bene così.*
(No thank you. That'll be fine.)

CAMERIERE: *Prendete il caffè?*
(Will you have coffee?)

LUCA: *Certo, caffè per tutti.*
(Of course, coffee for everybody.)

CAMERIERE: *Ecco il conto. Spero che siate stati bene.*
(Here's the bill. I hope everything was all right.)

LUCA: *Siamo stati molto bene, grazie.*
(We've been fine, thank you.)

Subject Pronouns—Now You See Them, Now You Don't

I, you, he, she, we, they. These are what grammarians call the subject pronouns—they stand in for the subject: "she" instead of "Teresa," or "they" instead of "the children." Observe the following examples in Italian:

Noi non facciamo così! (We don't do it like that.)
Domani io farò un esame. (Tomorrow I'm taking an exam.)
Voi studiate per l'esame? (Are you studying for the exam?)
Domain vieni a lezione tu? (Tomorrow are you going to the lesson?)

Oftentimes, the subject pronouns are implied in Italian since the form of the verb already indicates the number, gender, and case of the subject. The same sentences in the previous list have the same meaning even with the subject pronouns omitted.

To review the subject pronouns, see **TABLE 15-4**.

TABLE 15-4

SUBJECT PRONOUNS		
PERSON	SINGULAR	PLURAL
I	*io* (I)	*noi* (we)
II	*tu* (you, informal)	*voi* (you)
III	*lui, lei* (he, she)	*loro* (they)
	Lui (you, formal)	*Loro* (you, formal)

Points of Requirement

There are a few cases in which subject pronouns are required in Italian.

- For contrast: *Noi lavoriamo e tu ti diverti.* (We work and you amuse yourself.)
- For emphasis: *Lo pago io.* (I'll pay for it.)

- After the words *almeno, anche, magari, neanche, nemmeno, neppure:*
  Neanche noi andiamo al cinema. (We aren't going to the cinema either.)
- When the subject pronoun stands by itself: *Chi voule giocare? Io!*
  (Who wants to play? I do!)

Name Your Pronoun

Provide the correct subject pronoun for each of the following nouns or pronouns. Then check your answers in Appendix A.

1. Io e tu: ....
2. Marco: ....
3. Giorgio e Maria: ....
4. Tu e lei: ....
5. Gli studenti: ....
6. Cinzia: ....

The Lowdown on Direct Objects

Remember transitive verbs from Chapter 11? They take direct objects, which may be direct object pronouns (*i pronomi diretti*). These pronouns are the person or thing affected by the action of the transitive verb and answer the question what? or whom? For example:

She invites the girls. Whom does she invite? The girls.
I read the book. What do I read? The book.

The nouns "girls" and "book" are direct objects. Direct object pronouns replace direct object nouns:

She invites the girls. She invites them.
I read the book. I read it.

The forms of Italian direct object pronouns appear in **TABLE 15-5**.

TABLE 15-5	DIRECT OBJECT PRONOUNS	
PERSON	**SINGULAR**	**PLURAL**
I	*mi* (me)	*ci* (us)
II	*ti* (you, informal)	*vi* (you, informal)
III	*lo, la* (him, her, it)	*li, le* (them, masculine/feminine)
	La (you, formal)	*Li, Le* (you, formal, masculine/feminine)

In Italian, a direct object pronoun is placed immediately before a conjugated verb:

Se vediamo i ragazzi, li invitiamo. (If we see the boys, we'll invite them.)
Compra la frutta e la mangia. (He buys the fruit and eats it.)

The only exception to this is when a sentence contains an infinitive. In this case, the object pronoun is attached to the end of it (note that the final *–e* of the infinitive is dropped):

È importante mangiarla ogni giorno. (It is important to eat it every day.)
È una buon'idea invitarli. (It's a good idea to invite them.)

In a negative sentence, the word *non* must come before the object pronoun:

Non la mangiano. (They don't eat it.)
Perché non li inviti? (Why don't you invite them?)

It is possible (but not necessary) to omit singular direct object pronouns in front of verbs that begin with a vowel or forms of *avere* that begin with an *h*. However, the plural forms *li* and *le* are never omitted:

M'ama, non m'ama. [Mi ama, non mi ama.] (He loves me, he loves me not.)
Il passaporto? Loro non l'hanno [lo hanno]. (The passport? They don't have it.)

A few Italian verbs that take a direct object, such as *ascoltare, aspettare, cercare*, and *guardare*, correspond to English verbs that are used with prepositions (to listen to, to wait for, to look for, to look at). Compare the following:

Chi cerchi? (Who are you looking for?)
Cerco il mio ragazzo. (I'm looking for my boyfriend.)
Lo cerco già da mezz'ora! (I've been looking for him for half an hour!)

Object pronouns are attached to *ecco* (here) to express the phrases "here I am," "here you are," "here he is," and so on:

Dov'è la signorina? Eccola! (Where is the young woman? Here she is!)
Hai trovato le chiavi? Sì, eccole! (Have you found the keys? Yes, here they are!)

Indirect Object Pronouns

Indirect object nouns and pronouns (*i pronomi indiretti*) answer the question to whom? or for whom? In English, the word "to" is sometimes omitted:

We gave a cookbook to Uncle John.
We gave Uncle John a cookbook.

In Italian, the preposition *a* is always used before an indirect object noun:

Ho regalato un libro di cucina allo zio Giovanni. (I gave a cookbook to Uncle John.)
Perché non regali un profumo alla mamma? (Why don't you give Mother some perfume?)
Puoi spiegare questa ricetta a Paolo? (Can you explain this recipe to Paul?)

Indirect object pronouns replace indirect object nouns. They are identical in form to direct object pronouns, except for the third-person forms *gli, le,* and *loro*. For all the forms, see **TABLE 15-6**.

TABLE 15-6	INDIRECT OBJECT PRONOUNS		
PERSON	**SINGULAR**		**PLURAL**
I	*mi* (to/for me)		*ci* (to/for us)
II	*ti* (to/for you, informal)		*vi* (to/for you, informal)
III	*gli, le* (to, for him/her)		*loro* (to/for them)
	Le (to/for you, formal)		*Loro* (to/for you, formal)

All indirect object pronouns except *loro* and *Loro* precede a conjugated verb, just like the direct object pronouns (*loro* and *Loro* follow the verb):

Le ho dato tre ricette. (I gave her three recipes.)
Ci offrono un caffè. (They offer us a cup of coffee.)
Parliamo loro domani. (We'll talk to them tomorrow.)

Similarly, indirect object pronouns attach to infinitives, which lose their final *–e*:

Non ho tempo di parlargli. (I have no time to talk to him.)

If the infinitive is preceded by a conjugated form of *dovere*, *potere*, or *volere*, the indirect object pronoun may also precede the conjugated verb:

Voglio parlargli./Gli voglio parlare. (I want to talk to him.)

Also note that *le* and *gli* are never omitted before a verb beginning with a vowel or an *h*:

Le offro un caffè. (I offer her a cup of coffee.)
Gli hanno detto "Ciao!". (They said *"Ciao!"* to him.)

TABLE 15-7 provides a few common Italian verbs that are often used with indirect object nouns or pronouns.

VERBS THAT TAKE ON INDIRECT OBJECTS			
dare	to give	*portare*	to bring
dire	to say	*preparare*	to prepare
domandare	to ask	*regalare*	to give (as a gift)
(im)prestare	to lend	*rendere*	to return, give back
insegnare	to teach	*riportare*	to bring back
mandare	to send	*scrivere*	to write
mostrare	to show	*telefonare*	to telephone
offrire	to offer		

An Indirect Question?

Complete each sentence with the appropriate indirect object pronoun. Then check your answers in Appendix A.

1. Professore, per favore, vorrei parlar _____.
2. Tuo figlio _____ assomiglia molto: è il tuo ritratto.
3. Io sono affezionatissima a mia nonna: _____ voglio molto bene.
4. Massimo guardava la ragazza e _____ sorrideva.
5. È maleducato: quando _____ parlo, lui non _____ risponde mai.
6. Devi imparare a non toccare le cose che non _____ appartengono.

ALERT

You might encounter a few other pronouns in formal contexts and literature. *Egli* and *esso* (he) are alternative forms of *lui*. *Ella* and *essa* (she) are alternative forms of *lei*. *Essi* (they, masculine plural) and *esse* (they, femininine plural) are alternate forms of *loro* and show gender; they are used when gender needs to be signaled.

Nay? Neigh? No, *Ne!*

In Italian, the pronoun *ne* can mean "about," "any," "some," "of it," "of them," from it," "from them," or "from there." It can also replace a prepositional phrase beginning with *da* or *di.* Here are a few examples:

Parliamo di Mario. (We talk about Mario.)
Ne parliamo. (We talk about him.)
Hai bisogno di due francobolli. (You need two stamps.)
Ne hai bisogno di tre. (You need two of them.)
Avete molti amici. (You have many friends.)
Ne avete molti amici. (You have many of them.)
Ho due fratelli. (I have two brothers.)
Ne ho due. (I have two of them.)

Combining Direct and Indirect Pronouns

There are many times when the same verb has both a direct object pronoun and an indirect object pronoun. Usually, the indirect object pronoun precedes the direct object pronoun and the indirect object pronouns *mi, ti, ci,* and *vi* change to *me, te, ce,* and *ve*:

Renato porta il libro a me. (Renato brings the book to me.)
Renato me lo porta. (Renato brings it to me.)
Il professore insegna la lezione a voi. (The professor teaches the lesson to you.)
Il professore vi l'insegna. (The professor teaches you the lesson.)

For a complete chart of all the double object pronouns, see **TABLE 15-8**. Note the economy in words: *gli, le,* and *Le* become *glie–* before direct object pronouns and before *ne,* and combine with them to become one word.

TABLE 15-8

INDIRECT OBJECT PRONOUN	LO	LA	LI	LE	NE
	DOUBLE OBJECT PRONOUNS				
mi	me lo	me la	me li	me le	me ne
ti	te lo	te la	te li	te le	te ne
gli, le, Le	glielo	gliela	glieli	gliele	gliene
ci	ce lo	ce la	ce li	ce le	ce ne
vi	ve lo	ve la	ve li	ve le	ve ne
. . . loro	lo . . . loro	la . . . loro	li . . . loro	le . . . loro	ne . . . loro

EXERCISE

In Combination

Rewrite each sentence, replacing the direct and indirect object nouns with the correct pronouns. Then check your answers in Appendix A.

1. Riportiamo il libro a lei.

   _____

2. Restituisci il quaderno a lui.

   _____

3. Presto la macchina a Paolo.

   _____

4. Mandate i regali ai bambini.

   _____

5. Mi zio porta i documenti ai signori.

   _____

6. Date la palla alle ragazze.

   _____

7. Do il libro agli studenti.

    ----

8. Inviano i pacchi a lui.

    ----

9. Prestiamo le fotografie a Luisa.

    ----

10. Do la penna a Martina.

CHAPTER 16

Your Body and Your Self

id you eat too much *linguini alle vongole* and now have a stomachache? Did you stare up at the ceiling of the Sistine Chapel too long to gaze at Michelangelo's masterpiece and now have a crick in your neck? Learn how to talk about what ails you and find out more about reflexive and reciprocal verbs.

What a Body!

From the classical sculptures in the Vatican museums to Botticelli's *The Birth of Venus*, from Michelangelo's *David* to the bronzed beauties on Rimini's beaches, Italians have revered the human form for millennia. Here are a few of the ways to refer to all those parts that make up our wonderful physical form (see **TABLE 16-1**).

TABLE 16-1

VOCABULARY: PARTS OF THE BODY			
ankle	*la caviglia*	heart	*il cuore*
arm	*il braccio*	heel	*il calcagno*
body	*il corpo*	hip	*l'anca*
bone	*l'osso*	knee	*il ginocchio*
brain	*il cervello*	leg	*la gamba*
calf	*il polpaccio*	muscle	*il muscolo*
elbow	*il gomito*	nail	*l'unghia*
finger	*il dito*	shoulder	*la spalla*
foot	*il piede*	skin	*la pelle*
hand	*la mano*	stomach	*lo stomaco*

Two Arms, Two Legs

There are several words in Italian that have two plural forms—a masculine and a feminine. Many of these are related to parts of the body and have diverse meanings (see **TABLE 16-2**).

TABLE 16-2

VOCABULARY: IRREGULAR PLURAL FORMS		
SINGULAR	MASCULINE PLURAL	FEMININE PLURAL
braccio	*i bracci* (arms of a lamp or cross)	*le braccia* (arms)
budello	*i budelli* (streets, alleyways)	*le budella* (intestines)
calcagno	*i calcagni* (ankles)	*stare alle calcagna* (to follow someone closely)
ciglio	*i cigli* (edge, rim)	*le ciglia* (eyelashes)

dito	*i diti* (used when followed by the finger's name)	*le dita* (fingers)
labbro	*i labbri* (border, brim)	*le labbra* (lips)
osso	*gli ossi* (bones for dogs to eat)	*le ossa* (bones)

There are also body parts with masculine and feminine plurals that have the same meaning. One such example is *ginocchio. I ginocchio* and *le ginocchia* both refer to "the knees."

ESSENTIALS

There are many Italian idiomatic expressions referring to the body:

- *avere polso* (to be firm)
- *avere le spalle larghe* (to have broad shoulders)
- *non aver sangue nelle vene* (to have no guts)

Is There a Doctor in the House?

When referring to a medical doctor, the words *dottore, dottoressa,* or *medico* are all used interchangeably. When speaking directly to a doctor, *dottore* or *dottoressa* may be used. *Avere mal di . . .* is a phrase you would begin with to describe pain or soreness. For all other vocabulary, see **TABLE 16-3**.

TABLE 16-3

VOCABULARY: AT THE DOCTOR'S OFFICE			
allergy	*l'allergia*	German measles	*la rosolia*
appendicitis	*l'appendicite*	heartburn	*il bruciore di stomaco*
arthritis	*l'artrite*	hypertension	*l'ipertensione*
chicken pox	*la varicella*	insomnia	*l'insonnia*
cold	*il raffreddore*	mumps	*gli orecchioni*
cough	*la tosse*	pain	*il dolore*
diabetes	*il diabete*	pneumonia	*la polmonite*
dizziness	*il capogiro*	seasickness	*il mal di mare*
fever	*la febbre*	sore throat	*la faringite*
frostbite	*il congelamento*	wound	*la ferita*

Oh, My Aching Tooth!

Did you bite down too hard on that *panforte di Siena* (a hard, flat, honey-sweetened cake that's a specialty of Siena) and now can't even chew on *spaghetti*? It might be time to visit *il dentista* and have it looked at. When you get there, here are a few words you might find handy (**TABLE 16-4**).

TABLE 16-4

VOCABULARY: AT THE DENTIST'S OFFICE			
anesthesia	*l'anestesia*	gums	*le gengive*
braces	*l'apparecchio*	jaw	*la mascella*
bridge	*il ponte*	nerve	*il nervo*
cavities	*le carie*	oral surgeon	*l'odontoiatra*
crown	*la corona*	orthodontist	*l'ortodontista*
cuspid	*il canino*	root	*la radice*
dentist	*il dentista*	temporary filling	*l'otturazione provvisoria*
denture	*la dentiera*	tooth	*il dente*
extract	*estrarre*	toothache	*il mal di denti*
filling	*l'otturazione*	wisdom tooth	*il dente del guidizio*

Teeth also have a fair amount of Italian expressions associated with them. Here are a few:

a denti stretti (with clenched teeth)
armato fino ai denti (armed to the teeth)
avere i denti lunghi (to be greedy)

ESSENTIALS

In Italy, pasta is usually served *al dente* (to the tooth). Instead of that unidentifiable, overcooked glob of carbohydrates that you may remember in school cafeterias, *spaghetti*, *penne*, *rigatoni*, and rice are all cooked only until they are slightly chewy and still somewhat firm. The inside should be a bit crisp and tender.

Mirror, Mirror, on the Wall

What is a reflexive verb (*verbo riflessivo*)? A verb is reflexive when the action carried out by the subject is performed on the same subject. Not all verbs are reflexive. In order to make a verb reflexive, drop the –*e* of its infinitive ending and add the pronoun *si*.

For example, *pettinare* (to comb) becomes *pettinarsi* (to comb oneself) in the reflexive. *Si* is an additional pronoun, known as the reflexive pronoun, which is needed when conjugating reflexive verbs.

The reflexive pronouns (*i pronomi reflessivi*), *mi, ti, si, ci, vi, si*, are identical in form to direct object pronouns, except for the third-person form *si* (which is the same in the singular and in the plural). **TABLE 16-5** includes the reflexive pronouns in Italian.

TABLE 16-5

REFLEXIVE PRONOUNS		
PERSON	SINGULAR	PLURAL
I	*mi* (myself)	*ci* (ourselves)
II	*ti* (yourself)	*vi* (yourselves)
III	*si* (himself; herself; itself; yourself, formal)	*si* (themselves; yourselves, formal)

To see how reflexive pronouns work with verbs, see a sample conjugation of *lavarsi* (to wash oneself) in **TABLE 16-6**.

TABLE 16-6

CONJUGATION OF THE VERB *LAVARSI* (TO WASH ONESELF)		
PERSON	SINGULAR	PLURAL
I	(*io*) *mi lavo*	(*noi*) *ci laviamo*
II	(*tu*) *ti lavi*	(*voi*) *vi lavate*
III	(*lui, lei, Lei*) *si lava*	(*loro, Loro*) *si lavano*

Just like direct object pronouns, reflexive pronouns are placed before a conjugated verb or attached to the infinitive. Note that the reflexive pronoun agrees with the subject even when attached to the infinitive:

Mi alzo. (I'm getting up.)
Voglio alzarmi./Mi voglio alzare. (I want to get up.)

Mi, *ti*, *si*, and *vi* may drop the *i* before another vowel or an *h* and replace it with an apostrophe. *Ci* may drop the *i* only before another *i* or an *e*:

Voi v'arrabbiate facilmente. (You get angry easily.)
I ragazzi s'alzano alle sette. (The boys woke up at seven o'clock.)
A casa, m'annoio. (At home, I get bored.)

For a list of common reflexive verbs in Italian, see **TABLE 16-7**.

TABLE 16-7

COMMON REFLEXIVE VERBS			
accorgersi (di)	to notice	*laurearsi*	to graduate
addormentarsi	to fall asleep	*mettersi*	to put (clothing) on
alzarsi	to get up	*pettinarsi*	to comb one's hair
arrabbiarsi	to get angry	*radersi*	to shave
chiamarsi	to be named	*sbarbarsi*	to shave
coprirsi	to cover oneself	*sedersi*	to sit down
divertirsi	to have fun, to enjoy oneself	*sentirsi*	to feel
farsi il bagno	to bathe oneself	*spogliarsi*	to undress
farsi la doccia	to take a shower	*sposarsi (con)*	to get married
farsi male	to get hurt, hurt oneself	*svegliarsi*	to wake up
innamorarsi (di)	to fall in love with	*vestirsi*	to get dressed
lavarsi	to wash oneself		

Remember that some reflexive verbs can be used nonreflexively—without the reflexive pronouns. In this case, their meaning changes:

Tu ti alzi. (You get up.)
Tu alzi la sedia. (You lift the chair.)

Reflexive Healing

Complete the following with the appropriate present-tense forms of the indicated reflexive verbs. Check your answers in Appendix A.

1. Il signor Rossi _____ in medicina. (laurearsi)
2. Massimo _____ vicino alla porta. (sedersi)
3. Io _____ Anna Grazia. (chiamarsi)
4. Mia madre non lavora: _____ interamente alla famiglia. (dedicarsi)
5. Perché tu non _____ una vacanza? (prendersi)
6. Giorgio _____ la vita lavorando in un bar. (guadagnarsi)
7. Cinzia _____ una gonna per la festa. (comprarsi)
8. Il ghiaccio, col calore, _____. (sciogliersi)
9. Il cristallo è fragile: _____ facilmente. (rompersi)
10. Io e mio fratello _____ una lettera alla settimana. (scriversi)

ESSENTIALS

When forming compound tenses, all reflexive verbs use the appropriate conjugated tenses of *essere* and the past participles of the acting verbs. Remember that the past participle of reflexive verbs must agree in gender and number with the subject.

Vi siete preparati bene per l'esame? (Did you prepare yourselves well for the exam?)
Si sono salutati con freddezza. (They saluted each other coldly.)
Ti sei trovato nel mezzo della manifestazione. (You found yourself in the middle of the demonstration.)

It Takes Two

Romeo and Juliet meet, hug, kiss, and fall in love. They comfort each other, admire each other, and get married—but not without some help from reciprocal reflexive verbs! These verbs express a reciprocal action that involves more than one person. The plural reflexive pronouns *ci, vi,* and *si* are used when conjugating reciprocal reflexive verbs:

Si abbracciarono affettuosamente. (They embraced each other affectionately.)
Vi scriveste frequentemente, dopo quell'estate. (They frequently wrote to each other after that summer.)

Other reciprocal verbs are listed in **TABLE 16-8**.

TABLE 16-8

COMMON RECIPROCAL VERBS	
abbracciarsi	to embrace each other (one another)
aiutarsi	to help each other (one another)
amarsi	to love each other (one another)
ammirarsi	to admire each other (one another)
baciarsi	to kiss each other (one another)
conoscersi	to know each other (also: to meet)
consolarsi	to comfort each other (one another)
contrarsi	to meet (each other)
innamorarsi	to fall in love (with each other)
insultarsi	to insult each other (one another)
riconoscersi	to recognize each other (one another)
rispettarsi	to respect each other (one another)
rivedersi	to see each other again (one another)
salutarsi	to greet each other (one another)
scriversi	to write to each other (one another)
sposarsi	to get married (to each other)
vedersi	to see each other (one another)
visitarsi	to visit each other (one another)

In Return

Complete the following sentences with the present indicative of the indicated verbs. Check your answers in Appendix A.

1. I miei parenti _____ spesso. (visitarsi)
2. _____ molto bene, noi due! (conosersi)
3. Purtroppo Giuseppe e Lidia non _____ più. (capirsi)
4. Voi _____ tutti i giorni? (vedersi)
5. Gli spagnoli e i portoghese, quando parlano _____ fra loro. (capirsi)
6. A questo incrocio _____ sempre tante macchini. (scontrarsi)
7. Alberto e Caterina _____ sul serio: vogliono sposarsi. (amarsi)
8. Anna e Angela _____ al museo. (incontrarsi)
9. Voi _____ ogni giorno. (salutarsi)
10. I signori _____ molto. (rispettarsi)

WORD SEARCH: WHERE DOES IT HURT?

You spent all afternoon walking the ruins of Pompeii, and now you're aching all over. From the top of your head to the bottom of your *piedi*, there's an Italian word to describe every part of the body. Now you can identify those sore muscles and bones with this word search puzzle. Check your answers in Appendix A.

```
A  I  G  R  E  L  L  A  A  R  O  T  T  O  D
V  D  A  I  S  R  A  I  C  C  A  R  B  B  A
E  M  E  R  O  D  D  E  R  F  F  A  R  S  D
R  E  É  N  R  I  T  R  E  I  C  C  A  R  E
E  D  T  A  T  I  R  R  E  F  D  È  D  A  N
O  D  I  T  A  I  B  A  A  E  R  O  R  M  T
S  C  D  V  S  B  S  R  N  R  L  O  E  A  I
L  A  S  S  E  R  O  T  T  O  D  P  V  I  O
O  P  C  F  L  R  I  S  R  A  M  A  I  H  C
P  O  C  L  R  S  T  E  E  E  C  C  D  C  I
E  G  A  G  T  S  É  I  E  R  T  O  T  I  D
R  I  R  A  R  T  S  E  R  S  F  T  R  O  E
E  R  B  A  C  I  N  O  M  S  S  F  I  P  M
V  O  S  S  E  B  R  A  C  C  I  O  A  A  O
A  I  D  O  L  L  E  V  R  E  C  T  T  R  D
```

A DENTI STRETTI	CAPOGIRO	DITA	FEBBRE
ABBRACCIARSI	CERVELLO	DIVERTIRSI	FERRITA
ALLERGIA	CHIAMARSI	DOLORE	MEDICO
AVERE POLSO	CORPO	DOTTORESSA	RAFFREDDORE
BRACCIO	DENTISTA	ESTRARRE	TOSSE

CHAPTER 17

More Fun with Verbs

Understanding Italian verbs is like learning to kick a soccer ball. Both of these skills are cornerstones to the greater task at hand, whether it's speaking a language or playing Italy's national sport. Here is a season pass to helper verbs, verbs used in many idiomatic expressions, and verbs that share a definition but have different usage.

Coulda, Woulda, Shoulda

The helper verbs *potere* (to be able to, can), *volere* (to want), and *dovere* (to have to, must) take on different meanings in different tenses. *Potere*, for example, can mean "to be able to," "can," "to succeed," "could," or "would be able to," depending on the context and tense. *Dovere* can mean "to owe," "to have to," "must," or "to be supposed to," according to the tense.

Potere

In the present indicative tense, *potere* means "to be able to" or "can." For example:

Posso uscire? (May I go out?)
Posso suonare il trombone. (I can/am able to play the trombone.)

In the present perfect, *potere* means "to be able to, to succeed":

Ho potuto spedire il pacco. (I was able to mail the package.)
Non sono potuti venire più presto. (They could not come earlier, but they tried.)

In the conditional tenses (*condizionale presente* and *condizionale passato*), this verb may be translated as "could," "would be able to," "could have," or "could have been able to":

Potrei arrivare alle tre. (I was able to arrive at three o'clock—I would be able to arrive at three o'clock.)
Avrei potuto farlo facilmente. (I could have done it easily—I would have been able to do it easily.)

Volere

In the present indicative, *volere* means "want":

Voglio quell'automobile. (I want that car.)

In the present perfect (conversational past), *volere* is used in the sense of "decided, refused to":

Ho voluto farlo. (I wanted to do it—I decided to do it.)
Marco non ha voluto finirlo. (Mark didn't want to do it—Mark refused to do it.)

In the conditional, *volere* means "would like":

Vorrei un bicchiere di latte. (I would like a glass of milk.)
Vorrei visitare i nonni. (I would like to visit my grandparents.)

Dovere

The present indicative forms of *dovere* translate as "owe":

Gli devo la mia gratitudine. (I owe him my gratitude.)
Ti devo venti dollari. (I owe you twenty dollars.)

In the conditional tenses, however, *dovere* carries the meaning "should" or "ought to." For example:

Dovrei finire i compiti di scuola a tempo. (I should/ought to finish my homework on time.)
Avrei dovuto telefonarle immediatamente. (I should have/ought to have telephoned her immediately.)

A Wealth of Proverbs

The Italian language is rich with proverbs! Here are a few proverbs and expressions in which *potere*, *volere*, and *dovere* make their appearances:

Volere è potere. (Where there's a will there's a way.)
Volere o volare! (There's no getting away from it.)
Quello che ci vuole (just what the doctor ordered)
Volerne a qualcuno (to hold it against someone)
Non poterne più (to have had it)

Come si deve (decent)
Chi di dovere (the person responsible)
A dovere (properly)

Should You, Can You, Must You Know?

Complete the following phrases, using the appropriate verb form of *potere*, *volere*, or *dovere*. Then check your answers in Appendix A.

1. Come, tu non _____ nemmeno assaggiarlo?
2. Ragazzi, questa sera _____ andare a mangiare una pizza?
3. Tu _____ accompagnarmi dal parrucchiere oggi alle due?
4. In casa nostra, noi figli sia maschi che femmine, _____ aiutare nostra madre.
5. Hanno bisogno di una seconda macchina, ma non _____ permettersela.
6. Vi accompagno io. A che ora _____ essere all'aeroporto?
7. L'aereo parte alle sette, ma i passeggeri _____ presentarsi un'ora prima.
8. Perché tu non _____ venire alla festa?

I Know You Know

The verbs *sapere* and *conoscere* both mean "to know," but have different implications. *Sapere* means "to know," "to be able to," or "to know how to." Take a look at these examples with the *io* form of *sapere*:

So la lezione. (I know the lesson.)
So cantare. (I know how to sing—I am able to sing.)

Conoscere means "to know, to be acquainted with, or to make the acquaintance of":

Io conosco Francesca a casa di Giuseppe. (I met Francesca at
   Giuseppe's house.)
Non conosciamo la città. (We don't know the city.)

QUESTIONS?

Ever heard the saying that somebody is acquainted with every Tom, Dick, and Harry?
In Italian, these triplets are well known: They are *Tizio*, *Caio*, and *Sempronio*.

What to Do about *Fare*

If essere is the Swiss army knife of verbs (see Chapter 5), then fare is the all-in-one, handy-dandy kitchen appliance. The verb fare expresses the basic idea of doing or making, as in fare gli esercizi (to do the exercises) and fare il letto (to make the bed), but it is also used in many idioms (see **TABLE 17-1**).

TABLE 17-1

IDIOMATIC EXPRESSIONS WITH *FARE*	
fare alla romana	to split the check
fare castelli in aria	to daydream
fare colazione	to have breakfast
fare del proprio meglio	to do one's best
fare di tutto	to do everything possible
fare fingere	to pretend, make believe
fare forca	to play hooky
fare i compiti	to do one's homework
fare il biglietto	to purchase a ticket
fare il pieno	to fill up the gas tank
fare la fila/la coda	stand in line/wait in line
fare la spesa	to go grocery shopping
fare le spese	to go shopping
fare male	to be painful, to ache
fare passare	to let through

IDIOMATIC EXPRESSIONS WITH *FARE* (CONTINUED)	
fare un capello in quattro	to split hairs
fare un viaggio	to take a trip
fare una domanda	to ask a question
fare una fotografia	to take a picture
fare una passeggiata	to take a walk
fare vedere	to show someone something
farsi coraggio	to take heart
farsi degli amici	to make friends
farsi in la	to step to one side
farsi la barba	to shave

Note that the infinitive *fare* is frequently abbreviated to *far* before a consonant. For example, you may say *far colazione, far male, far torto. Fare* is also used in many expressions relating to the weather (note that in the following translations, "it" is an impersonal subject and does not have an equivalent in Italian):

Che tempo fa? (How is the weather?)
Fa bel tempo. (The weather is nice.)
Fa cattivo tempo. (The weather is bad.)
Ha fatto caldo. (It has been warm.)
Qui fa sempre freddo. (It's always cold here.)
In primavera fa sempre fresco. (In spring it's always cool.)

Besides idiomatic expressions, and expressions relating to the weather, the verb *fare* is used in a number of proverbs:

Chi la fa l'aspetti. (You will get as good as you gave.)
Chi fa da sé fa per tre. (If you want something done, do it yourself.)
Non fare agli altri ciò che non vorresti fosse fatto a te. (Do as you
    would be done by.)
Tutto fa brodo. (Every little bit helps.)
Chi non sa fare, non sa comandare. (A bad worker is a bad master.)

AL LAVORO (AT WORK)

ANNA MARIA: *Che cosa ci fai qui?*
(What are you doing here?)

GIULIANA: *Imparo ad usare la nuova macchina.*
(I'm learning to use the new machine.)

ANNA MARIA: *Ma non dovevi scrivere una relazione?*
(Shouldn't you be writing a report?)

GIULIANA: *Infatti, la sto scrivendo.*
(Actually, I am writing it.)

ANNA MARIA: *Ma mi stai ascoltando o stai scrivendo?*
(Are you listening to me or are you writing?)

GIULIANA: *Riesco a fare contemporaneamente entrambe le cose.*
(I can do both at the same time.)

ANNA MARIA: *Mi stai prendendo in giro?*
(Are you pulling my leg?)

GIULIANA: *No, figurati! Non potrei mai prenderti in giro.*
(No, of course not. I could never pull your leg.)

ANNA MARIA: *Potresti tornare al tuo lavoro?*
(Could you get back to your work?)

GIULIANA: *Benissimo.*
(All right.)

Brushing up on *Idioma*

Complete the following statements with the appropriate idiomatic expressions listed in **TABLE 17-2**. Then check your answers in Appendix A.

1. Oggi vado a _____ in campagna.
2. La tua casa è molto lontana, prima ho preso l'autobus e poi _____ a piedi.
3. Per mantenersi in forma e in buona salute è bene _____.
4. C'è molta gente allo sportello dei biglietti, devi _____ per una mezz'oretta.
5. Ogni mattina, prima di uscire, io _____ con la mia famiglia.

6. Prendo il treno dell 12,40 per Milano e devo ancora

   _____.

7. Oggi vado in centro a _____, devo comprare diverse
   cose.

8. Maria va al mercato ogni mattina e _____, dopo
   torna a casa e _____ per tutta la famiglia.

9. Il serbatoio della macchina è vuoto, se voglio partire devo
   _____ al distributore.

10. Ho comprato un dolce, posso _____ con te se lo vuoi.

11. Oggi tu _____ al tuo amico che è ammalato.

TABLE 17-2	IDIOMATIC EXPRESSIONS WITH *FARE*		
fare a metà	*fare a pezzi*	*fare colazione*
fare la spesa	*fare il biglietto*	*fare una gita*
fare il viaggio	*fare il pieno*	*fare una domanda*
fare le spese	*fare la coda*	*fare presto/fare tardi*
fare la valigia	*fare un pezzo di strada*	*fare dello sport*
fare da mangiare	*fare vedere qualcosa a qualcuno*	*fare una visita*

At Your Service

In Italian there are several ways to express the concept of serving or
helping oneself. The verb *servire* means "to serve":

Il cameriere serve il caffè ai clienti. (The waiter serves coffee to the customers.)

The phrase *servirsi da*, which literally means "to serve oneself" refers
to the concept of helping oneself:

Grazie lo stesso; ci serviamo do soli. (Thank you anyway; we'll serve
(help) ourselves.)

The phrase *servirsi di* means "to use" or "to avail oneself of":

Per adesso mi servo di questi libri. (For now I use these books.)

And finally, the phrase *non servire a nulla* means "to be of no use":

Queste cose non servono a nulla. (These things are useless.)

A Few Other Verbs to Know

Have you had enough verbs yet? Well, there are more on the way! How about *giocare, suonare, pensare, tornare, restituire, riportare,* and *mettersi*? This section will dispel the confusion and present these verbs one by one.

It's Play Time

The verb *giocare* means "to play," in the sense of playing a game or a sport. When referring to sports, it is usually followed by the preposition *a*:

I bambini giocano sull spiaggia. (The children play on the beach.)
Mario e Carlo giocano a carte. (Mario and Carlo play cards.)
Paola gioca molto bene a tennis. (Paola plays tennis very well.)

The phrase *giocare d'azzardo* means "to gamble":

Pietro gioca d'azzardo e perde sempre. (Pietro gambles and always loses.)

FACTS

Italians love gambling and card games. There are several types of lotteries, and *Totocalcio* (soccer pool) is followed by millions of people. Italian card games include *briscolla, tresette, scopa, madrasso, coteccio,* and *calabresella*.

Another verb that means "to play" is *suonare*, which is used in the sense of playing a musical instrument. For example:

Teresa suona il pianoforte. (Teresa plays the piano.)

However, *suonare* has an additional meaning: It may also mean "to ring" or "to sound a doorbell":

Marcello suona il campanello. (Marcello rings the doorbell.)

I've Been Thinking of You

Have an opinion about something or someone? Use the term *pensare a* or *pensare di*, which both mean "to think about." Take a look at a few examples in Italian:

In questi giorni penso a mia nonna perché è malata. (Nowadays I think about my grandmother because she is ill.)

Che cosa pensi di quella macchina sportive? (What do you think about the sportscar? (What is your opinion about that sportscar?)

Spesso pensiamo ai nostri cugini che vivono in Italia. (We often think about our cousins who live in Italy.)

Giovanna, dimmi la verità! Cosa pensi dell'esame? (Giovanna, tell me the truth! What do you think about the exam?)

Return to Sender

Sometimes the only way to tell the difference between two words with the same literal meaning is to observe how they are used in practice. *Tornare*, *restituire*, and *riportare* all mean "to return," but each has a slightly different shade of meaning.

Tornare means "to return" in the sense of coming back from somewhere. It is interchangeable with *ritornare*:

Torno dall'Italia. (I'm returning from Italy.)
Le ragazze ritornano stasera. (The girls are coming back tonight.)

Restituire means "to return" in the sense of giving something back:

Mi ha restituito il denaro che mi doveva. (He returned the money he owed me.)

And *riportare* means "to return" in the sense of bringing or taking something back:

Mi hanno riportato i libri. (They returned my books.)
Hai riportato i libri in biblioteca. (Did you return the books to the library?)

Put It Here, Put It There

Mettersi (to put or place) is another versatile verb that's used in a variety of idiomatic expressions. Increase your word power by using the phrases listed in **TABLE 17-3** in daily conversation.

TABLE 17-3

IDIOMATIC EXPRESSIONS USING *METTERSI*	
mettercela tutto	to do one's best
mettersi a confronto	to compare
mettersi a sedere	to seat oneself
mettersi al brutto	to turn nasty
mettersi giù	to put (or lay) down
mettersi innanzi	to produce
mettersi insieme	to put together
mettersi sotto	to put underneath
mettersi su casa	to set up house
mettersi via	to put away

The verb *mettersi* can also be used for activities: *mettersi a mangiare* (start/begin to eat), *mettersi a dormire* (go to sleep), *mettersi a gridare* (start/begin to shout), *mettersi a piangere* (start/begin to cry).

Zing! Zing!

I am eating, you are drinking, the soprano is singing. In Italian, the gerund (*il gerundio*) is equivalent to the "–ing" verb form in English. To form the simple gerund in Italian, add *–ando* to the stem of *–are* verbs and *–endo* to the stem of *–ere* and *–ire* verbs. There is also another form of the gerund, the compound gerund (*il gerundio composto*). It is formed with the gerund form of either *avere* or *essere* + past participle of the action verb (see **TABLE 17-4**).

TABLE 17-4

FORMING GERUNDS	
GERUNDIO	*GERUNDIO COMPOSTO*
cadendo (falling)	*essendo caduto/a/i/e* (having fallen)
leggendo (reading)	*avendo letto* (having read)
mangiando (eating)	*avendo mangiato* (having eaten)

The imperfect stems are used to form the gerunds of verbs such as *dire* (*dicendo*), *fare* (*facendo*), *porre* (*ponendo*), and *tradurre* (*traducendo*). The reflexive verbs attach the reflexive pronoun to the end of the word: *lavandosi, sedendosi, divertendosi*.

ALERT

Some constructions that rely on the gerunds in English use the infinitives in the Italian. For example: "Do you prefer dancing or singing?" translates to *Preferisci ballare o cantare?* In Italian, the gerund cannot act as either the subject or direct object of a sentence.

CHAPTER 18

Back to the Future

Enter the professor's time machine and set the thingamajig to 2045. Or set it back to the time of Caesar, the medieval era, or the Renaissance. You're about to take a trip into the remote past and the distant future—and you'll have all the verb forms you'll need to talk about them!

Che Sarà, Sarà

Tomorrow you will prepare *pasta puttanesca*. Saturday you will buy that Italian leather jacket you've been thinking about. Next year you will learn the future tense. *Che sarà, sarà*—what will be, will be! The future tense in Italian expresses an action that will take place in the future. Although in English the future is expressed with the helping verb "will" or the phrase "to be going to," in Italian a verb ending marks it as being set in the future tense. For example:

Alla fine di settembre partirò per Roma. (At the end of September I will leave for Rome.)

First-Conjugation Verbs

The future tense (*futuro semplice*) of first-conjugation regular (*–are*) verbs is formed first by changing the infinitive ending *–are* into *–er* to obtain the root for the future tense. The following future endings are then added to the root: *–ò, –ai, à, –emo, –ete, –anno.* (**TABLE 18-1** includes a sample conjugation of the verb *cantare.*)

TABLE 18-1

FUTURE TENSE CONJUGATION OF *CANTARE*		
PERSON	SINGULAR	PLURAL
I	*(io) canterò*	*(noi) canteremo*
II	*tu canterai*	*(voi) canterete*
III	*(lui, lei, Lei) canterà*	*(loro, Loro) canteranno*

Future Course of Action

Complete the following with the appropriate forms of the future of the indicated regular *–are* verbs. Then check your answers in Appendix A.

1. Quanto tempo tu _____ in Italia? (restare)
2. Noi _____ al nuovo concorso. (partecipare)
3. I genitori _____ il mese prossimo. (arrivare)
4. Io _____ tardi domani. (alzarsi)
5. Daniele _____ una macchina. (noleggiare)

6. Sabato voi _____. (arrivare)
7. Tu e Luca _____ di calcio. (parlare)
8. Gli studenti _____ la matematica. (imparare)
9. Noi _____ la settimana prossima. (prenotare)
10. Loro _____ in autobus. (viaggiare)

Second- and Third-Conjugation Verbs

The future tense of regular second- and third-conjugation (*–ere* and *–ire*) verbs is formed by simply dropping the final *–e* of the infinitive to obtain the stem and adding to the stem the following future endings: *–ò, –ai, –à, –emo, –ete, –anno* (the same endings, in fact, as those added to the first-conjugation group). For a sample conjugation, see **TABLE 18-2**, which conjugates the verbs *credere* and *partire*.

TABLE 18-2

FUTURE TENSE CONJUGATIONS OF *CREDERE* AND *PARTIRE*		
PERSON	SINGULAR	PLURAL
I	*(io) crederò, partirò*	*(noi) crederemo, partiremo*
II	*tu crederai, partirai*	*voi crederete, partirete*
III	*(lui, lei, Lei) crederà, partirà*	*loro, Loro crederanno, partiranno*

Future Course of Action II

Complete the following with the appropriate forms of the future of the indicated regular *–ere* and *–ire* verbs. Check your answers in Appendix A.

1. Noi _____ per l'Italia il mese prossimo. (partire)
2. Gli studenti _____ molti libri. (leggere)
3. Tu e Carlo _____ la lezione. (ripetere)
4. Il negoziante _____ tutta la merce. (vendere)
5. Noi _____ le nuove regole. (capire)
6. Gli atleti _____ per un'ora. (correre)
7. Il bambino _____ la mancanza dei genitori. (sentire)
8. La professoressa _____ i compiti domani. (correggere)
9. Tu _____ i compiti domani mattina. (finire)
10. Questa fine settimana noi _____ in campagna. (andare)

Future Tense of Irregular Verbs

In the future tense, the verbs *dare*, *stare*, and *fare* simply drop the final *–e* of their infinitives and form the stems *dar–*, *star–* and *far–*, respectively; the stem of *essere* is *sar–*. These stems are then combined with the regular future-tense endings.

The verbs listed in **TABLE 18-3** also have an irregularly shortened stem in the future tense (usually, because the vowel *a* or *e* is dropped from the infinitive).

TABLE 18-3

IRREGULAR FUTURE-TENSE STEMS			
INFINITIVE	FUTURE STEM	INFINITIVE	FUTURE STEM
andare	andr–	potere	potr–
avere	avr–	sapere	sapr–
cadere	cadr–	vedere	vedr–
dovere	dovr–	vivere	vivr–

Also be aware of the spelling of verbs with infinitives ending in *–ciare* and *–giare*. These verbs drop the *i* before adding the future endings to the root: *tu comincerai, noi viaggeremo*. Also, verbs with infinitives ending in *–care* and *–gare* add an *h* to the root for the future to preserve the hard sound of the *c* or *g* of the infinitive: *io cercherò, loro pagheranno*.

The Future Perfect Tense

How to express the idea of "I will have" or "they will have"? Use the *futuro anteriore* or future perfect tense. Here is what it looks like:

Alle sette avremo già mangiato. (By seven we'll already have eaten.)
Noi avremo parlato al padre di Anna. (We will already have spoken to Anna's father.)

The *futuro anteriore* is a compound tense formed with the regular future-tense form of the auxiliary verb *avere* or *essere* and the past participle of the acting verb. **TABLE 18-4** contains the full conjugation forms of verbs *in futuro anteriore.*

	FUTURO ANTERIORE CONJUGATIONS OF AVERE AND ESSERE	
PERSON	**SINGULAR**	**PLURAL**
I	*(io) avrò avuto, sarò andato(a)*	*(noi) avremo avuto, saremo andati(e)*
II	*(tu) avrai avuto, sarai andato(a)*	*(voi) avrete avuto, sarete andati(e)*
III	*(lui, lei, Lei) avrà avuto, sarà andato(a)*	*(loro, Loro) avranno avuto, saranno andati(e)*

A Long, Long Time Ago

The remote past tense (*passato remoto*) is a simple tense and is formed by one word. In general, it refers to the historical past or to events that have happened in the distant past relative to the speaker.

Follow this format to form the *passato remoto* of regular verbs. For –*are* verbs, drop the infinitive ending and add one of these personal endings to the root: –*ai, –asti, –ò, –ammo, –aste, –arono* (see **TABLE 18-5**).

	CONJUGATING PARLARE IN THE REMOTE PAST	
PERSON	**SINGULAR**	**PLURAL**
I	*(io) parlai*	*(noi) parlammo*
II	*(tu) parlasti*	*(voi) parlaste*
III	*(lui, lei, Lei) parlò*	*(loro, Loro) parlarono*

For –*ere* verbs, drop the infinitive ending and add these personal endings to the root: –*ei, –esti, –é, –emmo, –este, –erono* (see **TABLE 18-6**). Note that many regular –*ere* verbs have an alternative form in the first person singular, third person singular, and third person plural forms.

TABLE 18-6	CONJUGATING *RICEVERE* IN THE REMOTE PAST		
PERSON	SINGULAR	PLURAL	
I	(io) ricevei (ricevetti)	(noi) ricevemmo	
II	(tu) ricevesti	(voi) riceveste	
III	(lui, lei, Lei) ricevé (ricevette)	(loro, Loro) riceverono (ricevettero)	

For *–ire* verbs, drop the infinitive ending and add these personal endings to the root: *–ii, –isti, –í, –immo, –iste, –iron*o (see **TABLE 18-7**).

TABLE 18-7	CONJUGATING *CAPIRE* IN THE REMOTE PAST		
PERSON	SINGULAR	PLURAL	
I	(io) capii	(noi) capimmo	
II	(tu) capisti	(voi) capiste	
III	(lui, lei, Lei) capí	(loro, Loro) capirono	

Here are a few examples of how the remote past is used in Italian:

Dante si rifugiò a Ravenna. (Dante took refuge in Ravenna.)
Petrarca morì nel 1374. (Petrarca died in 1374.)
Michelangelo nacque nel 1475. (Michelangelo was born in 1475.)

The Literary Past

Used primarily in literary contexts, the *trapassato remoto* (known in English as the preterite perfect) is a compound tense formed with the *passato remoto* of the auxiliary verb *avere* or *essere* and the past participle of the acting verb. To see how *avere* and *essere* conjugate in the remote past tense, see **TABLES 18-8** and **18-9**.

TABLE 18-8	CONJUGATING *AVERE* IN THE REMOTE PAST		
PERSON	SINGULAR	PLURAL	
I	(io) ebbi	(noi) avemmo	
II	(tu) avesti	(voi) aveste	
III	(lui, lei, Lei) ebbe	(loro, Loro) ebbero	

TABLE 18-9	CONJUGATING *ESSERE* IN THE REMOTE PAST		
PERSON	**SINGULAR**		**PLURAL**
I	(io) fui		(noi) fummo
II	(tu) fosti		(voi) foste
III	(lui, lei, Lei) fu		(loro, Loro) furono

In each sentence set in the *trapassato remoto*, you will encounter an expression of time, such as the following: *appena* (scarcely), *dopo che* (as soon as), *finché non* (up until), or *quando* (when). For example:

Partirono, quando ebbero ricevuto la notizia. (They were leaving when they received the notice.)

Renata entrò, appena Giorgio fu uscito. (Renata entered just after Giorgio had left.)

Andò a casa, quando ebbe finito di lavorare. (He went home when he had finished working.)

I Owe, I Owe, So Off to Work I Go

By now you probably have had enough of verb tenses and verb endings, so let's turn our attention back to nouns. You probably know that for every *professore* there is a *professoressa*, and for every *studente* there is a *studentessa*. But how about other nouns of profession, status, or relation that have a male and a female version?

Most masculine nouns ending in *–tore* become feminine by changing *–tore* to *–trice* (see **TABLE 18-10**).

TABLE 18-10	GENDERED NOUNS: FROM *–TORE* TO *–TRICE*		
MASCULINE	**FEMININE**		**ENGLISH**
attore	*attrice*		actor
autore	*autrice*		author
direttore	*direttrice*		director
imperatore	*imperatrice*		emperor/empress

GENDERED NOUNS: FROM –*TORE* TO –*TRICE* (CONTINUED)		
lavoratore	*lavoratrice*	worker
pittore	*pittrice*	painter
scrittore	*scrittrice*	writer
stiratore	*stiratrice*	presser
traditore	*traditrice*	traitor
traduttore	*traduttrice*	translator

Some masculine nouns become feminine by changing their final vowel to –*a* (see **TABLE 18-11**).

TABLE 18-11

GENDERED NOUNS THAT GAIN –*A* IN THE FEMININE		
MASCULINE	FEMININE	ENGLISH
cameriere	*cameriera*	waiter/waitress
cassiere	*cassiera*	bank teller
figlio	*figlia*	son/daughter
giardiniere	*giardiniera*	gardener
infermiere	*infermiera*	nurse
marchese	*marchesa*	marquis/marchioness
padrone	*padrona*	boss, owner
portiere	*portiera*	doorman/doorwoman
sarto	*sarta*	tailor/dressmaker
signore	*signora*	Mr./Mrs.

Take note that there are certain names of professions that end in –*a* regardless of whether the term refers to a male or a female. In such case, the gender distinction is made by the definite article: *il giornalista/la giornalista, il dentista/la dentista*. The plurals of these professions follow the same general rule as with any other noun: Plural masculine nouns end in –*i* (*i giornalisti, i dentisti*), plural feminine nouns end in –*e* (*le giornaliste, le dentiste*).

Finally, certain masculine nouns become feminine by replacing their final vowel with –*essa* (see **TABLE 18-12**).

TABLE 18-12

GENDERED NOUNS THAT GAIN AN *-ESSA* IN THE FEMININE		
MASCULINE	FEMININE	ENGLISH
avvocato	avvocatessa	lawyer
campione	campionessa	champion
conte	contessa	count/countess
dottore	dottoressa	doctor
oste	ostessa	host/hostess
poeta	poetessa	poet
principe	principessa	prince/princess
profeta	profetessa	prophet
sacerdote	sacerdotessa	high priest/priestess
studente	studentessa	student

Seasons in the Sun

The weather in Italy varies greatly by region and season. During *l'inverno* (winter), there can be ice storms and below-freezing weather even in the south of Italy. Many Italians head to the Alps for *una settimana in bianca* (winter vacation). *La primavera* (spring) is so beautiful, there's even a pasta dish named after it—*pasta primavera*—which is tossed with seasonal fresh vegetables.

ESSENTIALS

Visiting museums and churches when it's hot and humid can dampen your enthusiasm even for Michelangelo's statue of David. Something else to consider if you're planning to visit Italy in the summer: Many restaurants in the larger tourist cities are closed during August, since their proprietors are on vacation.

L'estate (summer) in Italy can be brutally hot, even in the northern regions, and many Italians take the month of August off. There's usually a mass exodus to the beaches and mountains, anywhere for cool breezes and a place to sit in the shade. *L'autunno* (autumn) is a splendid time, when the grapes and olives are harvested (the harvest is known as *la vendemmia*) and the leaves change in the hills. Although November tends to be rainy, it can be an ideal time to visit Italy, since fewer tourists are present.

Mark Your Calendar

Here are some points worth mentioning about the Italian calendar: The Italian week begins on Monday. The days of the week, the names of the seasons, and the names of months are not capitalized in Italian. And, finally, there is an explanation for why *settembre* (September) is the "seventh" month, *ottobre* (October) is the "eighth," *novembre* (November) is the "ninth," and *dicembre* (December) is the "tenth": A very long time ago, the Roman calendar began in March, so September, October, November, and December were the seventh, eighth, ninth, and tenth months of the year. For a complete list of months (*i mesi*), refer to **TABLE 18-13**.

TABLE 18-13

MONTHS OF THE YEAR			
gennaio	January	*luglio*	July
febbraio	February	*agosto*	August
marzo	March	*settembre*	September
aprile	April	*ottobre*	October
maggio	May	*novembre*	November
giugno	June	*dicembre*	December

Another bit of trivia: When a religious festival or holiday falls on a Tuesday or Thursday, Italians oftentimes *fare il ponte*, or make a four-day holiday, by taking off the intervening Monday or Friday. To learn Italian days of the week (*giorni della settimana*), take a look at **TABLE 18-14**.

TABLE 18-14

DAYS OF THE WEEK			
lunedì	Monday	*venerdì*	Friday
martedì	Tuesday	*sabato*	Saturday
mercoledì	Wednesday	*domenica*	Sunday
giovedì	Thursday		

Here are a few other phrases you might find useful:

Che giorno è oggi? (What day is it today?)
Oggi è martedì. (Today is Tuesday.)
Domani è mercoledì. (Tomorrow is Wednesday.)
Ieri è stato lunedì. (Yesterday was Monday.)

It's no joke! April Fool's Day is referred to as *Pesce d'Aprile* in Italy. As in many other countries, it's traditionally a day of practical jokes, pranks, and silliness. The origin of this custom is ancient and ambiguous, but one thing is certain: Much buffoonery and hilarity is always bound to take place.

Closed for the Holidays

One thing to remember if you visit Italy: Check the calendar. Not only are there holidays that are part of the government calendar, but many towns and cities celebrate saints' days and local festivals. The tourist board should have this information available, but here are the country's official national holidays, when everything shuts down—including museums, public buildings, and many retail shops (see **TABLE 18-15**).

TABLE 18-15

NATIONAL HOLIDAYS IN ITALY		
January 1	*Capodanno*	New Year's Day
January 6	*Epifania*	Feast of the Epiphany
Easter Monday	*Pasquetta*	Little Easter
April 25	*Festa della Resistenza*	Liberation Day
May 1	*Festa dei Lavoratori*	Labor Day
August 15	*Ferragosto*	Feast of the Assumption
November 1	*Ognissanti*	All Saints' Day
December 8	*Immacolata Concezione*	Immaculate Conception of the Blessed Virgin Mary
December 25	*Natale*	Christmas
December 26	*Festa di Santo Stefano*	St. Stephen's Day

È NATALE! (IT'S CHRISTMAS DAY!)

CHIARA: *Svegliati, presto! È venuto Babbo Natale!*
(Wake up, hurry up! Santa Claus came!)

FABIO: Ma sei pazza? È troppo presto. È l'alba!
(Are you crazy? It's too early. It's just dawn!)

CHIARA: Non dirmi che non sei curioso?
(Don't tell me that you aren't curious?)

FABIO: *Va bene, ma poi torno a dormire!*
(All right, but then I'm going back to sleep!)

CHIARA: *Guarda, questo è per te!*
(Look, this is for you!)

FABIO: *E qua c'è il tuo nome!*
(And here is your name!)

CHIARA: *Un pallone da calcio?!*
(A soccer ball?!)

FABIO: *Una Barbie!*
(A Barbie?!)

CHIARA: *Credo che questa volta Babbo Natale si sia confuso,*
poverino . . .
(I believe this time Santa Claus got mixed up, poor man . . .)

FABIO: *Sarà stato troppo stanco probabilmente . . . non è uno*
scherzo portare i regali a tutti i bambini in una sola sera.
(He probably was too tired. Bringing gifts to all the kids in
just one night is not a joke.)

CHIARA: *Guarda altri pacchi! e ci sono anche per mamma e papà!*
(Look more gifts! And there are even some for Mom and Dad!)

FABIO: *Aspetta! Corro a svegliarli!*
(Wait! I'll run and wake them up!)

CHAPTER 19
Home Sweet Home

What are Italian homes like, and what's a *portacenere*? Why do Italians prefer to live in the same hometown they grew up in? Find out how to refer to various family members, and review the many ways to say "you" in Italian—you won't need a tuxedo to formally address the prime minister, as long as you know the right pronoun and verb form.

Home Is Where the Hearth Is

Houses in Italy run the gamut from the modest to the extravagant. There are many surviving *villas* and Renaissance *palazzi* (palaces) that were originally built by popes, dukes, and wealthy traders. There are *case coloniche* (farmhouses) in Tuscany, chalet-type homes in the Alps, and modern apartment buildings in the large cities such as Rome, Milan, and Naples.

In the south of Italy, in the town of Alberobello, you will find *i trulli*, white-washed conical buildings that were built centuries ago and are being restored today. On the Amalfi coast, in the five towns of *Le Cinque Terre*, and in other coastal towns, houses cling to the hillside overlooking the Mediterranean Sea. Whatever the type of building, one thing is clear: There is always that certain warmth and hospitality that Italians are famous for.

To feel at home with the vocabulary of *la casa* (the home), review **TABLE 19-1**.

TABLE 19-1

VOCABULARY: THE HOME			
apartment	*l'appartamento*	garden	*l'orto*
attic	*la soffitta*	hallway	*l'ingresso*
bathroom	*il bagno*	house	*la casa*
ceiling	*il soffitto*	kitchen	*la cucina*
cellar	*la cantina*	living room	*il soggiorno*
closet	*l'armadio*	roof	*il tetto*
dining room	*la sala da pranzo*	staircase	*la scala*
door	*la porta*	study	*lo studio*
elevator	*l'ascensore*	wall	*la parete*
floor	*il pavimento*	window	*la finestra*

Campanilismo, taken from the word for bell tower (*campanile*), is a concept that refers to the regional focus of Italian society. For centuries, the Italian peninsula was composed of independent regions with very distinct dialects, cultures, and interests. Even nowadays, most Italians identify first with their hometown, then their region, third with the north or south of Italy, and finally, with the nation itself.

La casa bianca

A man's house is his castle. Home is where the heart is. There are many expressions to describe the relationship between houses, homes, and life in general. Here are a few common ones:

A casa del ladro non si ruba. (There's no honor among thieves.)
Antonio è di casa. (Antonio is one of the family.)
Tutto casa e famiglia (a stay-at-home type)
Non sapere neanche dove stia di casa (not to know the slightest thing about something)
Metter su casa (to set up house, to settle down)

ESSENTIALS   A *casalinga* is a housewife. It's also the term used for simple, unpretentious cooking. Restaurants in Italy often advertise their food as *la cucina casalinga*, the Italian equivalent of home cooking.

Domestic Bliss

Similar to the fashion industry, the style and functionality of Italian furnishings are renowned the world over. Italian craftsmen have an eye for detail, and Italians fill their homes with tasteful, useful furniture. When it's time for home decorating in Italian, refer to **TABLE 19-2** for some useful vocabulary.

TABLE 19-2

VOCABULARY: FURNISHINGS			
ashtray	*il portacenere*	mattress	*il materasso*
bed	*il letto*	picture	*il quadro*
carpet	*il tappeto*	pillow	*il cuscino*
chair	*la sedia*	sheets	*le lenzuola*
couch	*il divano*	table	*il tavolo*
desk	*la scrivania*	television	*la televisione*
drapery	*le tende*	umbrella stand	*il portaombrelli*
dresser	*il cassettone*	upholstery	*la tappezzeria*
furniture	*i mobili*	wallpaper	*la carta da parati*
lamp	*la lampada*	wine rack	*il portabottiglie*

Are Italian men really inseparable from their mothers?
So many unmarried men still live with their parents, even past the age of thirty, that there's a name for it, *mammismo*, and sons who are afflicted with extreme cases of it are called *mammoni!*

The Italian Family

The Italian family is one of the most enduring strengths of Italian culture. Even today, with increased mobility due to cars, airplanes, and other modes of transportation, many Italians prefer to live in the same town that they grew up in, raise their own family in familiar surroundings, and cheer on the same hometown soccer team that they've rooted for since childhood.

This cultural trait makes for very strong community bonds and traditions, and for strong family bonds as well. For vocabulary of *la famiglia* (the family), see **TABLE 19-3**.

TABLE 19-3

VOCABULARY: THE FAMILY			
brother	*il fratello*	mother	*la madre*
brother-in-law	*il cognato*	mother-in-law	*la suocera*
daughter	*la figlia*	nephew/niece	*il/la nipote (di zii)*
family	*la famiglia*	parents	*i genitori*
father	*il padre*	relative	*il parente*
father-in-law	*il suocero*	sister	*la sorella*
grandchild	*il/la nipote (di nonni)*	son	*il figlio*
grandfather	*il nonno*	uncle	*lo zio*
grandmother	*la nonna*	wife	*la moglie*
husband	*il marito*		

IL FICCANASO (THE BUSYBODY)

GIORGIO: *Come stai oggi?*
(How are you today?)

VIRGILIO: *Sto bene, grazie.*
(I'm fine, thanks.)

GIORGIO:	*Sei francese?*
	(Are you French?)
VIRGILIO:	*Certo che no, sono italiano.*
	(Of course not, I'm Italian.)
GIORGIO:	*Dove vivi?*
	(Where do you live?)
VIRGILIO:	*In Italia, e tu?*
	(In Italy, and you?)
GIORGIO:	*Io vivo in Svezia. Hai una casa?*
	(I live in Sweden. Do you have a house?)
VIRGILIO:	*Sì, con un giardino.*
	(Yes, with a garden.)
GIORGIO:	*Quanti anni hai?*
	(How old are you?)
VIRGILIO:	*Ho solo ventuno anni.*
	(I'm only twenty-one.)
GIORGIO:	*Sei sposato?*
	(Are you married?)
VIRGILIO:	*Sì, da due anni.*
	(Yes, for two years.)
GIORGIO:	*Hai dei bambini.*
	(Do you have any children?)
VIRGILIO:	*Sì, ho due gemelli!*
	(Yes, I have twins!)
GIORGIO:	*Dov'è tua moglie?*
	(Where's your wife?)
VIRGILIO:	*È uscita con i bambini.*
	(She's gone out with the children.)
GIORGIO:	*Hai una famiglia numerosa?*
	(Do you have a big family?)
VIRGILIO:	*Sì, ho molti zii e zie.*
	(Yes, I have many aunts and uncles.)

Forms of Address

As you already know, there are four ways of saying "you" in Italian: *tu, voi, Lei,* and *Loro. Tu* (for one person) and *voi* (for two or more people) are the familiar forms, used only with family members, children, and close friends.

Lei (for one person, male or female) and its plural *Loro* are used in more formal situations to address strangers, acquaintances, older people, or people in authority. *Lei* and *Loro* are written with a capital *L* to distinguish them from *lei* (she) and *loro* (they). For example:

Lei, professore, e anche Lei, signorina. (You, professor, and also you, miss.)
Non Loro, signore e signori. (Not you, ladies and gentlemen.)

In contemporary Italian speech, it is extremely rare to make adjectives, past participles, and so on agree in gender with *Lei* if the subject is masculine, so the correct way of saying "You are wrong, general" is *Lei è cattivo* [not *cattiva*], *generale.* But the object pronouns are the same as they would be with a feminine subject:

ArriverderLa, dottore! (Goodbye, doctor!)
Devo darLe una notizia importante. (I must give you important news.)

Therefore, the object pronouns generally impose agreement when they precede the participle:

Colonello, l'ho sempre amata. (Colonel, I always loved her.)

ALERT

The capitalization of *Lei,* when used as a courtesy address, is becoming less and less common, even in formal correspondence.

Possiamo darci del tu?

An Italian will often ask: "*Possiamo darci del tu?*" which figuratively means "May we switch to the *tu* form?" This question is addressed when two people get to know each other better, and can switch to a more informal way of conversing. Such a request is hardly ever refused; the difficulty is to keep track of whom one has passed on to *tu* terms with.

There are, of course, cases in which you can dare *del tu* immediately. Children are always addressed as *tu*, and young people would almost invariably use the *tu* form with each other right from the start: A university student who employs *Lei* with a fellow student would be considered a real stuffed shirt. Colleagues in certain professions, for example, in journalism, are expected to address each other as *tu*, or *compagni* (colleagues).

No Need to Be Formal

In the early years of the twentieth century, *lei* had become the preferred courtesy form, especially in northern and central Italy. Mussolini considered it both unmanly and foreign (presumably modeled on the Spanish *usted*, though there is little evidence for this), and tried to ban it in favor of *voi*. The result, however, was that *tu*, an extremely intimate form, became more popular as a form of address between friends.

Today, *voi* is still in common use only in southern Italy, apart from certain formulaic phrases in business correspondence, where it is generally capitalized:

Riscontriamo la Vostra pregiata del 6 u.s. [ultimo scorso] per comunicarVi . . . (Having received your esteemed letter of the sixth of last month, we wish to inform you . . .)

Tu is used to address God ("*Padre nostro, che sei nei cieli . . .*") and the common man ("*Vota socialista!*"); it is also used as the unique form of address in a number of central Italian dialects.

WORD SEARCH: HOME SWEET HOME

You won't find a Tuscany villa in this word search puzzle, but there is a casa with a few visiting family members hidden among the furniture. Check your answers in Appendix A.

```
Q  U  A  D  R  D  A  P  O  R  T  A  O  T  M
B  A  C  I  N  O  M  O  R  D  A  P  A  O  P
O  È  I  P  O  T  N  R  I  I  A  P  G  O  A
N  T  N  A  F  V  A  I  L  L  P  L  R  L  D
I  R  O  T  I  N  E  G  P  E  I  T  B  I  R
C  O  M  L  N  R  I  D  Z  O  A  B  D  B  T
S  E  D  O  E  F  R  Z  S  O  T  G  O  O  S
U  A  N  T  S  P  E  E  M  O  E  E  T  M  E
C  I  I  E  T  R  D  B  Z  N  R  R  I  A  N
U  L  P  T  R  I  R  E  I  Z  F  D  R  R  I
C  G  O  I  A  E  P  T  O  G  E  A  A  I  F
I  I  E  I  L  G  O  M  N  M  S  P  M  U  Q
N  M  R  L  S  C  R  I  V  A  N  I  P  U  Q
A  A  I  N  A  V  I  R  C  S  E  D  O  A  H
M  F  A  M  I  G  L  E  T  T  O  T  T  E  T
```

CASA	FINESTRA	MOGLIE	QUADRO
CUCINA	GENITORI	NIPOTE	SCRIVANIA
CUSCINO	LETTO	NONNA	SEDIA
FAMIGLIA	MARITO	PADRE	TETTO
FIGLIA	MOBILI	PORTAOMBRELLI	

Chapter 20

A Subjective Point of View

When you shop in Italy, it's all about style and fashion. It's also subjective—what you like, what you prefer, what the salesperson suggests. That's what the subjunctive tense is all about too—it will allow you to discuss your feelings, needs, and desires.

I Doubt It

Language is fluid, and usage changes. A case in point is the subjunctive (*il congiuntivo*), which in English is rapidly becoming extinct. Phrases like "I suggest you go home immediately" and "Robert wishes that you open the window" are not in frequent use anymore.

In Italian, though, the subjunctive tense is alive and flourishing, both in speaking and writing. Rather than stating facts, it expresses doubt, possibility, uncertainty, or personal feelings. It can also express emotion, desire, or suggestions. **TABLE 20-1** provides examples of three regular verbs conjugated in the present subjunctive tense.

TABLE 20-1

PRESENT SUBJUNCTIVE				
PRONOUN	*—ARE* VERB	*—ERE* VERB	*—IRE* VERBS	
	parlare	scrivere	sentire	capire
che io	parli	scriva	senta	capisca
che tu	parli	scriva	senta	capisca
che lui/lei/Lei	parli	scriva	senta	capisca
che noi	parliamo	scriviamo	sentiamo	capiamo
che voi	parliate	scriviate	sentiate	capiate
che loro/Loro	parlino	scrivano	sentano	capiscano

Typical phrases that call for the subjunctive tense include:

Credo che . . . (I believe that . . .)
Suppongo che . . . (I suppose that . . .)
Immagino che . . . (I imagine that . . .)
È necessario che . . . (It is necessary that . . .)
Mi piace che . . . (I'd like that . . .)
Non vale la pena che . . . (It's not worth it that . . .)
Non suggerisco che . . . (I'm not suggesting that . . .)
Può darsi che . . . (It's possible that . . .)
Penso che . . . (I think that . . .)
Non sono certo che . . . (I'm not sure that . . .)
È probabile che . . . (It is probable that . . .)
Ho l'impressione che . . . (I have the impression that . . .)

Certain verbs such as *suggerire* (to suggest), *sperare* (to hope), *desiderare* (to wish), and *insistere* (to insist) require use of the subjunctive.

A Subjunctive Statement

Complete the following with the correct subjunctive forms of the verb in parentheses. Then check your answers in Appendix A.

1. Voglio che voi _____. (dormire)
2. Hai paura che io _____. (avere ragione)
3. Perché ordini che loro _____? (salire)
4. Ordiniamo che tu _____ in biblioteca. (andare)
5. Mi dispiace che voi _____ triste. (essere)
6. Tu insiste che io _____ domani. (partire)
7. Speriamo che voi _____ qui. (restare)
8. È possibile che lui lo _____. (leggere)
9. È difficile che voi lo _____. (incontrare)
10. Credo che loro _____. (arrivare presto)

I Believed So

Of course, as you've probably figured out by now, if there's a *congiuntivo presente*, there's a *congiuntivo passato* (present perfect subjunctive—and I don't ever remember my grade-school teacher using that term). And like other verb tense formations, the *congiuntivo passato* is a compound tense formed with the *congiuntivo presente* of the auxiliary verb *avere* or *essere* and the past participle of the acting verb (see **TABLE 20-2**).

TABLE 20-2

CONGIUNTIVO PASSATO OF THE VERBS AVERE AND ESSERE		
PRONOUN	AVERE	ESSERE
che io	*abbia avuto*	*sia stato(–a)*
che tu	*abbia avuto*	*sia stato(–a)*
che lui/lei/Lei	*abbia avuto*	*sia stato(–a)*
che noi	*abbiamo avuto*	*siamo stati(–e)*
che voi	*abbiate avuto*	*siate stati(–e)*
che loro/Loro	*abbiano avuto*	*siano stati(–e)*

Here are a few examples of the *congiuntivo passato*:

Mi dispiace che abbia parlato così. (I'm sorry that he spoke that way.)
Siamo contenti che siano venuti. (We're glad they came.)
Non credo che siano andati in Italia. (I don't believe they went to Italy.)

It Would Be Possible

The imperfect subjunctive (*congiuntivo imperfetto*) is required when the verb in the dependent clause is in a past tense or the conditional. For conjugations of three regular verbs, see **TABLE 20-3**.

TABLE 20-3

CONJUGATING VERBS IN THE IMPERFECT TENSE			
PRONOUN	CANTARE	SAPERE	FINIRE
che io	cantassi	sapessi	finissi
che tu	cantassi	sapessi	finissi
che lui/lei/Lei	cantasse	sapesse	finisse
che noi	cantassimo	sapessimo	finissimo
che voi	cantaste	sapeste	finiste
che loro/Loro	cantassero	sapessero	finissero

Here are a few examples of the *congiuntivo imperfetto*:

Credevo che avessero ragione. (I thought they were right.)
Non era probabile che prendessimo una decisione. (It wasn't likely we would make a decision.)
Non c'era nessuno che ci capisse. (There was no one who understood us.)
Il razzismo era il peggior problema che ci fosse. (Racism was the worst problem there was.)

The Subjunctive in Time

Complete the following with the correct subjunctive forms of the verbs in parentheses. Check your answers in Appendix A.

1. I genitori volevano che i figli _____. (fare i compiti)
2. Lui ordinò che loro _____ immediatamente. (finire)
3. Era necessario che Carlo lo _____. (dire)
4. Hanno insistito che tu lo _____. (scrivere)
5. Vorrei che voi _____ i buoni. (fare)
6. Io preferirei che voi lo _____. (spiegare)
7. Desideravano che noi _____ a casa. (essere)
8. Volevo che Giancarlo _____ la verità. (dire)
9. Suggerirei che tu _____. (partire)
10. Tu vorresti che io ti _____ il mio orologio. (dare)

Did You Think So?

To complete the fourth of the subjunctive-tense verb forms, there's the *congiuntivo trapassato*, which is a compound tense. Again, form this tense with the *congiuntivo imperfetto* of the auxiliary verb *avere* or *essere* and the past participle of the acting verb (see **TABLE 20-4**).

TABLE 20-4

TRAPASSATO CONGIUNTIVO OF THE VERBS AVERE AND ESSERE		
PRONOUN	AVERE	ESSERE
che io	avessi avuto	fossi stato(–a)
che tu	avessi avuto	fossi stato(–a)
che lui/lei/Lei	avesse avuto	fosse stato(–a)
che noi	avessimo avuto	fossimo stati(–e)
che voi	aveste avuto	foste stati(–e)
che loro/Loro	avessero avuto	fossero stati(–e)

Here are a few examples of the *trapassato congiuntivo*:

Speravo che avessero capito. (I was hoping they had understood.)
Avevo paura che non avessero risolto quel problema. (I was afraid they hadn't resolved that problem.)
Non volevo che tu lo facessi così presto. (I didn't want you to do it as soon.)

When I Grow Up

For every occupation there's a name, and for every task there's an apt description. Remember that dreaded phrase, "What do you want to be when you grow up?" For a review of occupations, see **TABLE 20-5**.

TABLE 20-5

VOCABULARY: OCCUPATIONS			
baker	*il fornaio*	lawyer	*l'avvocato*
bank teller	*il cassiere*	librarian	*il bibliotecario*
bricklayer	*il muratore*	mailman	*il postino*
butcher	*il macellaio*	mechanic	*il meccanico*
carpenter	*il carpentiere*	painter	*l'imbianchino*
cobbler	*il calzolaio*	plumber	*l'idraulico*
dressmaker	*la sarta*	secretary	*la segretaria*
fisherman	*il pescatore*	tailor	*il sarto*
gardener	*il giardiniere*	truck driver	*il camionista*
journalist	*il giornalista*	writer	*lo scrittore*

On Strike

Bus strike, taxi strike, pilot strike—it seems there's always a strike in Italy. One reason is that the unions have a strong presence in all the trades; *fare lo sciopero* is almost a regular negotiating tactic. But have patience—in Italy, unlike other European countries, most strikes are over quicker than they happen. The transportation unions even plan the strikes so as not to interfere with other means of transportation—for instance, if the taxi drivers go on strike for the afternoon, it's highly unlikely that the bus drivers or train engineers would strike at the same time. A lot of time it's for show—and they don't want to inconvenience too many people.

Fashion and Style

Italians have a flair for fashion and enjoy showing off their style. When they take their *passeggiata* (evening stroll) in the town square, they like to dress up and *fare una bella figura* (cut a fine figure), talk to their friends, and catch up on news. There are a number of specialty shops too, and shopkeepers take special pride in their window displays. **TABLE 20-6** presents a list of various shops and stores you might encounter.

TABLE 20-6

VOCABULARY: SHOPS AND STORES	
antique shop	*l'antiquario*
bakery	*il panificio*
barber shop	*il barbiere*
bookshop	*la libreria*
butcher shop	*la macelleria*
dairy	*la latteria*
department store	*il grande magazzino*
drug store	*la drogheria*
fish market	*la pescheria*
flower shop	*il fioraio*
fruit/vegetable market	*il mercato frutta/verdura*
jewelry store	*la gioelleria*
laundry	*la lavanderia*
perfume shop	*la profumeria*
real estate agency	*l'agenzia immobiliare*
stationery store	*la cartoleria*
supermarket	*il supermercato*
tailor shop	*il sarto*

Looking for the drugstore? Maybe you want to study at the library? This word search will start you in the right direction if you're looking for the *gioelleria* or the *supermercato*. Check your answers in Appendix A.

```
M E C C A N I C O I A N R O F
A V V O C A O I A L L E C A M
C A R T A V V O C A T O B I B
E T C C A S S I E R E G O R D
L S A R A O E R O T A C S E P
L C L E S I D A E I A O D H A
E A Z R B A R C R F I B C C N
R R O T A C R E M R E P U S I
I T L A T R H T L O B C S E F
A O A B S G B O O L N I E P I
R L I P O S T I N O E I B M C
A E O R P E S L L I B O C A I
B R D C B A R B I E R E I A O
G I A R D I N I E R E G A G A
D A A I R E R B I L L E C A M
```

BARBIERE	**DROGHERIA**	**MACELLAIO**	**PESCHERIA**
BIBLIOTECARIO	**FORNAIO**	**MACELLERIA**	**POSTINO**
CALZOLAIO	**GIARDINIERE**	**MECCANICO**	**SARTO**
CARTOLERIA	**GIOELLERIA**	**PANIFICIO**	**SUPERMERCATO**
CASSIERE	**LIBRERIA**	**PESCATORE**	

CHAPTER 21

Italy by Plane, Train, and Automobile

I would have gone to Italy, but . . . I should have bought that ticket, but . . . Whether by train, plane, boat, or car, get yourself to Italy. There won't be any excuses after you learn these vocabulary words and the conditional tenses (which were used in the first two sentences of this paragraph).

Fly Away

You can practice your Italian even before arriving in Italy if you fly on Alitalia, the Italian national airline. Its planes have a red, white, and green color scheme and the crew wears uniforms designed by—who else?—Italian designers. Many other airlines have several daily scheduled flights into the country from worldwide destinations. Ready to get on the airplane? **TABLE 21-1** has some useful vocabulary for your airplane trip.

TABLE 21-1

VOCABULARY: ON THE PLANE			
aircraft	*l'aereo*	land	*atterrare*
airline	*la compagnia aerea*	landing	*l'atterraggio*
approach	*avvicinarsi*	pilot	*il pilota*
arrival	*l'arrivo*	reservation	*la prenotazione*
crew	*l'equipaggio*	return flight	*il volo di ritorno*
destination	*la destinazione*	seat belt	*la cintura di sicurezza*
emergency exit	*l'uscita d'emergenza*	stopover	*lo scalo*
flight	*il volo*	takeoff	*il decollo*
flight attendant	*l'assistente di volo*	ticket	*il biglietto*
helicopter	*l'elicottero*	wing	*l'ala*

Or Take the Train

Rail travel in Italy is relatively easy, and most cities and towns have rail service. There are several different levels of trains on the *Ferrovie dello Stato* or *FS* (Italian State Railway). Avoid the *locale*, which stops at every station along a line—it's only slightly more expensive to ride the *diretto* or *espresso*, which stops only at major stations. Then there's the *rapido*, or InterCity (IC) train, which travels only to the largest cities. The Eurostar trains are the fast trains, which can be pricey but cut down on travel time considerably.

If you travel by train in Italy, you'll see small, waist-high machines throughout the train station with the admonition *convalidare il biglietto*. You must punch your ticket prior to boarding; otherwise you'll be subject to a *multa* (fine).

To find out what *il biglietteria* is and how to inquire about the departure, as well as for other useful vocabulary, see **TABLE 21-2**.

TABLE 21-2

VOCABULARY: BY TRAIN	
arrival/departure	*arrivi/partenze*
change trains	*cambiar treno*
connection	*la coincidenza*
couchette sleeper	*la carrozza cuccette*
dining car	*il vagone ristorante*
express train	*il direttissimo*
fast train	*il diretto*
first-aid station	*il pronto soccorso*
information office	*le informazioni*
long distance express	*il rapido*
money exchange	*il cambio*
motorail service	*la littorina*
platform	*il binario*
rail car	*l'automotrice*
restaurant	*il ristorante*
restroom	*il gabinetto*
sleeper/sleeping car	*il vagone letto*
suburban train	*il treno suburbano*
ticket window	*la biglietteria*
timetable	*l'orario*
waiting room	*la sala d'aspetto*

What, No Air Conditioning?

Not all Italian hotels have air conditioning, so you'll have to get used to it. And in the economy *pensioni* and *alberghi*, you'll probably have to walk down the hall to use the bathroom. But then, you're here to see the ancient ruins, the Donatello sculptures, and the *affreschi* (frescoes) by Ghirlandio, not to watch TV in your hotel room. For some help in how to check in and other related vocabulary, see **TABLE 21-3**.

TABLE 21-3

VOCABULARY: CHECKING IN			
bath	*il bagno*	mattress	*il materasso*
bill	*il conto*	mirror	*lo specchio*
blanket	*la coperta*	pillow	*il cuscino*
concierge	*il portinaio*	plug	*la spina*
corridor	*il corridoio*	refrigerator	*il frigorifero*
drapery	*la tenda*	room	*la camera*
elevator	*l'ascensore*	shower	*la doccia*
heating	*il riscaldamento*	sink	*il lavandino*
lamp	*la lampada*	terrace	*il terrazzo*
lobby	*l'atrio*	towel	*l'asciugamano*

In big tourist towns and at expensive hotels the staff almost always speaks at least enough English to help those who haven't yet mastered Italian. Still, trying to speak Italian will definitely ingratiate you in the eyes of the staff—and it might even get you a better room.

On One Condition Only

The present-conditional tense (*condizionale presente*) is equivalent to the English constructions of "would" + verb (for example: I would never forget). Forming conditionals is easy: Just take any verb, drop the final –*e* in its infinitive form, and add an appropriate ending—endings are the same for all three conjugation groups of verbs. The only spelling change occurs with *–are* verbs, which change the *a* of the infinitive ending to *e*. For details, see **TABLE 21-4**.

TABLE 21-4

CONJUGATING VERBS IN THE PRESENT CONDITIONAL			
PRONOUN	*–ARE*	*–ERE*	*–IRE*
	parlare	credere	sentire
io	parlerei	crederei	sentirei
tu	parleresti	crederesti	sentiresti
lui, lei, Lei	parlerebbe	crederebbe	sentirebbe
noi	parleremmo	crederemmo	sentiremmo
voi	parlereste	credereste	sentireste
loro, Loro	parlerebbero	crederebbero	sentirebbero

Reflexive verbs follow the same scheme, with the addition of the reflexive pronouns *mi, ti, si, ci, vi,* or *si* when conjugating them: *mi laverei, ti laveresti, si laverebbe, ci laveremmo, vi lavereste, si laverebbero.* Here are some examples of conditional-tense sentences:

Vorrei un caffè. (I would like a coffee.)
Scriverei a mia madre, ma non ho tempo. (I would write to my mother, but I don't have time.)
Mi daresti il biglietto per la partita? (Would you give me a ticket for the game?)

Please note that the verbs in the conditional tense have the same root as in the future tense. If you review the irregular future-tense verbs in Chapter 18, you will have the stems you might need for the conditional tense.

In Good Condition

Complete the following sentences using the *condizionale presente* of the verbs in parentheses. Check your answers in Appendix A.

1. Io _____ mangiare la pizza. (preferire)
2. Che cosa Le _____ fare? (piacere)
3. Noi _____ cercare subito un parcheggio. (dovere)
4. Lui _____ noleggiare una macchina. (volere)
5. _____ darmi l'orario dei treni? (potere)
6. Le ragazze _____, ma non ricordano le parole. (cantare)
7. Teresa _____ tedesco, ma non ricorda i verbi. (parlare)
8. Tu _____ di non capire, ma sei impulsivo. (fingere)
9. Gli studenti _____ i corsi, ma non è obbligatorio. (frequentare)
10. Voi _____ il segreto, ma non sapete come. (scoprire)

We Could Have Danced All Night . . .

But at the stroke of midnight my coach turns into a *zucca!* The conditional perfect (*condizionale passato*), like all compound tenses in Italian, is formed with the *condizionale presente* of the auxiliary verb *avere* or *essere* and the past participle of the acting verb. Conjugated forms of *avere* and *essere* appear in **TABLE 21-5**.

TABLE 21-5

CONDIZIONALE PRESENTE OF THE VERBS AVERE AND ESSERE		
PERSON	SINGULAR	PLURAL
I	*(io) avrei, sarei*	*(noi) avremmo, saremmo*
II	*(tu) avresti, saresti*	*(voi) avreste, sareste*
III	*(lui, lei, Lei) avrebbe, sarebbe*	*(loro, Loro) avrebbero, sarebbero*

Here are a few examples of the *condizionale passato* in action. Remember that verbs conjugated with *essere* must change their endings to agree in number and gender with the subject:

Avremme potuto ballare tutta la notte. (I could have danced all night.)
Avreste dovuto invitarlo. (You ought to have invited him.)
Saremmo andati volentieri alla Scala, ma non abbiamo potuto.
    (We would gladly have gone to La Scala, but we weren't able to.)
Mirella sarebbe andata volentieri al cinema. (Mirella would have been
    happy to go to the cinema.)

You Could Have Been Right

Complete the following sentences using the *condizionale passato* of the verbs in parentheses. Then check your answers in Appendix A.

1. Ieri sera io _____ volentieri alla festa, ma ho dovuto studiare. (tornare)
2. Hanno scritto che _____ a teatro prima delle otto. (arrivare)
3. Io non gli _____ quelle informazioni ma mi hanno forzato. (chiedere)
4. Noi _____ vedere un film senza sottotitoli. (preferire)
5. Ha detto che _____ i biglietti per tutti. (comprare)
6. Loro _____ ma cominciò a piovere. (uscire)
7. Io _____ ma non avevo la macchina. (venire)
8. Mario _____ a casa presto, ma è partito. (stare)
9. Voi _____ telefonare prima di partire. (potere)
10. Loro _____ prima di partire. (cenare)

Botticelli Till You Drop

On your mark, get set, sightsee! It's tempting to try to see everything that's in the guidebooks, checking off churches and museums and historical monuments like a grocery list. Here's a tip: Do as the Italians do and slow down. Enjoy a walk down the street, chat up a store clerk, listen to schoolchildren singing.

Stendhal's syndrome is a malady first pointed out by the writer himself in the 1800s. Marked by shortness of breath, dizziness, and heart palpitations, it's usually suffered by tourists when they are overwhelmed by the magnificence of all the art in churches and museums in Italy.

The real Italy isn't in a tour or a book or a museum—it's experienced during a delicious lunch in a small, out-of-the-way *trattoria*, in a park with the smell of cyprus trees everywhere, or in the sound of the church bells every hour. After all, this is the country of *la dolce vita*. For your own *giro turistico* (sightseeing tour), check out the vocabulary in **TABLE 21-6.**

TABLE 21-6	VOCABULARY: SIGHTSEEING
district	*il quartier*
embassy	*l'ambasciata*
excavations	*gli scavi*
farmhouse	*la cascina*
fountain	*la fontana*
gallery	*la galleria*
gate	*il portone*
landscape	*il paesaggio*
memorial	*il monumento commemorativo*
mountain	*la montagna*
museum	*il museo*
old town	*il centro storico*
palace	*il palazzo*
park	*il parco*
port	*il porto*
river	*il fiume*
subway	*la metropolitana*
taxi	*il tassì*
valley	*la valle*
waterfall	*la cascata*

A ROMA (IN ROME)

Massimo è arrivato a Roma, ma non riesce ad orientarsi. Una donna si chiede se ha bisogno di aiuto. (Massimo has arrived in Rome, but he can't find his way about. A woman asks him if he needs help.)

MASSIMO:	*Mi sono perso. Dove sono? Non riesco a trovare il mio albergo.*
	(I'm lost. Where am I? I can't find my hotel.)
SIGNORA:	*Lei è a Roma!*
	(You're in Rome!)
MASSIMO:	*Sì, lo so! Ma a Roma, dove? Questa è Piazza di Spagna?*
	(Yes, I know that! But where in Rome? Is this the Spanish Square?)
SIGNORA:	*Quale via sta cercando?*
	(Which street are you looking for?)
MASSIMO:	*Questa. È scritta qui. Una strada dalle parte di via Vittorio Veneto.*
	(This one. It's written here. A street not far from Vittorio Veneto Street.)
SIGNORA:	*Qual è l'indirizzo?*
	(What's the address?)
MASSIMO:	*Com'era . . . mmm . . . l'ho dimenticato! L'indirizzo è nella borsa . . . che ho lasciato in albergo. Via Nazionale.*
	(How did it go . . . mmm . . . I forgot! The address is in my bag . . . that I left at the hotel. Via Nazionale.)
SIGNORA:	*Come si chiama l'albergo?*
	(What's the name of the hotel?)
MASSIMO:	*Albergo Fiorino. È qui vicino. Aspetti un attimo. L'ho scritto sulla mia agenda.*
	(It's the Hotel Fiorino. It's nearby. Wait a minute, I wrote it in my journal.)
SIGNORA:	*Mi lasci pensare.*
	(Let me think.)
MASSIMO:	*Lei sa dove si trova? Scusi? Io spero che lei sappia dov'è!*
	(Do you know where it is? Sorry? I hope you know where it is!)

SIGNORA: *È questo?*
(Is this it?)

MASSIMO: *Sì, è su questo pezzo di carta. No, questo è il mio indirizzo. Mi faccia vedere. Sì.*
(Yes, it's on this piece of paper. No, that's my address. Let me see. Yes.)

SIGNORA: *Non si preoccupi!*
(Don't worry!)

MASSIMO: *È lontano? Come ci posso arrivare? Non mi piace girare per la città di notte.*
(Is it far? How can I get there? I don't like wandering around town at night!)

SIGNORA: *Non riesco a leggere.*
(I can't read it.)

MASSIMO: *C'è scritto "via Nazionale." Comincia per "N." Un attimo, forse ce l'ho anche qui.*
(It's written "via Nazionale." It begins with an "N." One moment, I might also have it here.)

SIGNORA: *So dove si trova!*
(I know where it is!)

MASSIMO: *Sono nella direzione giusta? Devo andare a sinistra? È a destra?*
(Am I going the right way? Do I have to turn left? Is it right?)

SIGNORA: *Forse sarebbe meglio prenders l'autobus.*
(It might be better to take the bus.)

MASSIMO: *È così lontano? Non posso andare a piedi? Dov'è l'autobus?*
(Is it that far? Can't I walk? Where is the bus?)

SIGNORA: *Deve tornare indietro.*
(You have to turn back.)

MASSIMO: *Davvero? È sicuro? Ma, io vengo da lì!*
(Really? Are you sure? But I've just come from there!)

SIGNORA: *Deve andare sempre dritto.*
(Just go straight ahead.)

MASSIMO: *E poi? Fino a dove? Non devo girare a destra?*
(And then? Until where? Don't I have to turn right?)

SIGNORA: *Giri a destra dopo i giardini.*
(You turn right after the gardens.)

MASSIMO:	*I giardini? Benissimo. È lontano?*
	(The gardens? All right. Is it far?)
SIGNORA:	*Vedi il primo semaforo?*
	(Do you see the first traffic light?)
MASSIMO:	*Sì. Laggiù in fondo? La luce rossa? No, non lo vedo.*
	(Yes. Right over there? The red light? No, I can't see it.)
SIGNORA:	*Ha una piantina?*
	(Do you have a map?)
MASSIMO:	*Sì, ce l'ho. Ecco qua, è un po' vecchia . . . da qualche parte dovrei averla!*
	(Yes I do. Here it is. It's a bit old . . . it's around here somewhere.)
SIGNORA:	*Quando uno si perde, dovrebbe consultare una piantina!*
	(When you're lost, you should use a map!)
MASSIMO:	*Lei ha ragione. Io non ho proprio il senso dell'orientamento, comunque, a che serve, se poi perdo la piantina?*
	(You're right. In any case, I don't really have a sense of direction. What use would it be then, if I lose the map?)
SIGNORA:	*Vede? Noi siamo qui.*
	(See? We're here.)
MASSIMO:	*Vedo. Dov'è il nord? Sono indicati anche i mezzi pubblici?*
	(I see. Where is north? Does it show public transportation?)
SIGNORA:	*C'è un ufficio di informazioni turistiche duecento metri di qua.*
	(There's a tourist information office two hundred meters from here.)
MASSIMO:	*Prima della rotonda? Dopo la farmacia? Di fronte all'ufficio postale?*
	(Before the traffic circle? After the pharmacy? Opposite the post office?)
SIGNORA:	*Non può sbagliare.*
	(You can't go wrong.)
MASSIMO:	*Lei non mi conosce. Lo vedremo! Lei che è così gentile, non sa indicarmi una banca?*
	(You don't know me! We'll see! As you're so kind, could you tell me where to find a bank?)
SIGNORA:	*Sì, dop quel palazzo.*
	(Yes, after that building.)

MASSIMO:	*Quel palazzo in stile barocco? Mille grazie.*	
	(That baroque style building? Thank you very much.)	
SIGNORA:	*Pensa di riuscire ad orientarsi, adesso?*	
	(Do you think you can find your way now?)	
MASSIMO:	*Sì, credo proprio di sì.*	
	(Yes, I really think so.)	

Grab Your Life Preservers

Italy is a peninsula with beaches that encircle most of the country and has a rich maritime history. There are the islands of Capri and Ischia off of Naples, and the Aeolian Islands where volcanoes still spew lava. There are the islands of Sicilia and Sardegna (or Sardinia), homes to two very different cultures, yet still part of Italy. Then there's *La Serenissima* (the Most Serene One), otherwise known as Venezia, the city on the sea, with lagoons instead of streets and narrow, twisting walkways.

Venezia is accessible primarily by *vaporetto*, water taxi, or *gondola*. The city itself is comprised of 118 bodies of land in a lagoon, connected to the mainland by a thin causeway.

For some maritime vocabulary, navigate to **TABLE 21-7**.

TABLE 21-7

VOCABULARY: ON BOARD			
anchor	*l'ancora*	gangway	*la passerella*
barge	*la scialuppa*	lifeboat	*la scialuppa di salvataggio*
bay	*la baia*	lighthouse	*il faro*
boat	*la barca*	mast	*l'albero*
bow	*la prua*	motorboat	*il motoscafo*
captain	*il capitano*	pier	*il pontile*
deck	*la coperta*	rudder	*il timone*
ferry	*il traghetto*	sailboat	*la barca a vela*
fishing trawler	*la barca da pesca*	steamer	*il vaporetto*

CHAPTER 22

A Language Renaissance

Mention the Renaissance, and most people immediately think of *la Cappella Sistina*, the town of Florence, or the Medici family. It was a time of tremendous achievement not only in the arts, architecture, and politics, though, but also in the study of literature. The formation of a linguistic academy pushed forward the idea of a national language and exerted a powerful influence on the evolution of Italian.

A Prince of Politicians

The gradual development of the Italian language during the fourteenth and fifteenth centuries culminated in the Renaissance works of such writers as Ludovico Ariosto, Torquato Tasso, and Nicolò Machiavelli.

Machiavelli was a writer and statesman, Florentine patriot, and original political theorist, and his works included *The History of Florence*, *Life of Castruccio Castracani*, *Murder of Vitellozzo Vitelli*, *The Art of War*, and *Madragale*. However, Machiavelli is best known for *Il principe* (*The Prince*), the definitive manual of modern politics. The main theme of this work is that all means may be used in order to maintain authority, and that the worst acts of the ruler are justified by the treachery of the government. Nicolò Machiavelli's ideal prince was an amoral and calculating tyrant capable of unifying Italy. Over the centuries, without benefit of the historical context in which it was written, *Il principe* brought Machiavelli a reputation of amoral cynicism and immoral manipulation.

However, *Il principe* did make some interesting points. It focused on a suggested code of conduct for rulers and a description of a leader's character and personality. Machiavelli's underlying theme was that freedom is at risk when corruption is prevalent and that there is need for good laws and leaders in a free society. He also suggested a remedy for corruption, the urgent need to punish corrupt leaders, the role of the people in maintaining a good state, and how corrupt leaders discredit their governments.

FACTS

Machiavelli died in Florence in 1527, and his political writings became more widely known in the second half of the sixteenth century. Ultimately considered dangerous, they were placed on the Church Index of officially banned books in 1564.

To Coin a Phrase

Many of Machiavelli's thoughts, such as "it is much more secure to be feared, than to be loved" have survived the centuries as slogans.

Machiavelli drew upon examples from both ancient and more recent history, and also used his own experiences. What distinguished Machiavelli's *Il principe* from other such works is the originality and practicality of his thinking. Neither the attempts to interpret Machiavelli's ideas as first steps to democratic thoughts or examples of evil reflect a balanced view of his writing. Here are a few examples of his thoughts from *Il principe*:

- It is necessary to take such measures that, when they believe no longer, it may be possible to make them believe by force. (Chapter VI)
- A man who wishes to act entirely up to his professions of virtue soon meets with what destroys him among so much that is evil. (Chapter XV)
- Hence it is necessary for a prince wishing to hold his own to know how to do wrong, and to make use of it or not according to necessity. (Chapter XV)
- We have not seen great things done in our time except by those who have been considered mean; the rest have failed. (Chapter XVI)

Fresh-Baked Pronouns and Adjectives

In a land well-renowned for its culinary traditions, perhaps it was inevitable that the national language academy of Italy would be named for a by-product of the bread-making process. *L'Accademia della Crusca*, or the Academy of the Chaff, was founded in Florence in 1582 to maintain the purity of the language. Still in existence today, the academy was the first such institution in Europe and the first to produce a modern national language.

ESSENTIALS

The major work of *l'Accademia della Crusca* was the compilation of A. F. Grazzini's *Vocabulario*, a dictionary of "pure" words first published in 1612 and later taken as a model by other European states.

Corn Flakes and Crusty Florentines

The academy developed out of the informal meetings of a group of Florentine intellectuals, including A. F. Grazzini, Giambatista Deti, Bernardo Zanchini, Bernardo Canigiani, and Bastiano de' Rossi, between 1570 and 1580. They ironically called themselves *Crusconi* (the bran flakes) with the intention of giving a jocular tone to their conversations, impatient as they were with the solemnity surrounding the erudite but futile discussions of the *Sacra Accademia Fiorentina*. In 1582, the *Crusconi* gave formal status to their assembly, christening it with the name of *Accademia*.

Leonardo Salviati (*L'Infarinato*, "the floured one") joined the group at this time and gave it renewed impetus. Salviati interpreted in a new sense the name of *crusca* (bran): "As if to say that the academy should undertake a separation of the good from the bad." Together with Grazzini, Salviati gave the academy a new linguistic direction, setting as its goal the promotion of a Florentine language according to the model of vernacular classicism established by Pietro Bembo, who idealized the fourteenth-century Italian authors, especially Boccaccio and Petrarca. The Florentines differed from the purist Bembo to the extent that they included their national poet Dante among this privileged group.

FACTS

The academy's headquarters are still located at the historical *Villa Medicea di Castello* just outside Florence, and is open for touring groups. The sixteenth-century garden is adorned with statues, fountains, and an artificial grotto by Giambologna, a sculptor to the Medici court.

When the number of members reached several dozen, and the offices and responsibilities of the members were established, it was decided that each member should adopt a nickname, motto, and device having to do with bran and the oven.

The "Question of the Language"

La questione della lingua, an attempt to establish linguistic norms and codify the language, engrossed writers of all persuasions. Grammarians during the fifteenth and the sixteenth centuries attempted to confer upon the pronunciation, syntax, and vocabulary of fourteenth-century Tuscan the status of a central and classical Italian speech. Eventually this classicism, which might have made Italian another dead language, was widened to include the organic changes inevitable in a living tongue.

In the dictionaries and publications of the *Accademia della Crusca*, which was accepted by Italians as the authority in Italian linguistic matters, compromises between classical purism and living Tuscan usage were successfully effected. The most important literary event of the fifteenth century did not actually take place in Florence. In 1525, the Venetian Pietro Bembo (1470–1547) set out his proposals (*Prose della volgar lingua*, 1525) for a standardized language and style. His models were Petrarca and Boccaccio, whose writings were thus elevated to the status of modern classics. It follows, then, that the language of Italian literature is modeled on the dialect spoken in Florence in the fifteenth century.

The Academy Today—Still Fresh

L'Accademia della Crusca is still active and vigorous today, and their affinity for symbology has not waned a bit. The academy's symbol is a flour bolter, a machine used to separate the flour from the bran in milling operations. The traditional furnishings of the academy consist of *pale* (baker's shovels), which are individual coats of arms of the members of the academy from the sixteenth to the eighteenth century. The iconography of these shovels draws on the symbolism of the cultivation of grain, the baking of bread, and other products of the flour and of the *crusca*.

There are also *gerle* (baker's baskets), which are ceremonial academic chairs in the shape of baskets. The earliest examples date from

1642. Then there are *sacchi* (sacks), cabinets where the academic secretary kept the flour—the status, regulations, and other writings read and approved by the censorship academics.

Not Just Bread and Water

The academy has other, more serious resources too. For those interested in Italian linguistics, the history of the Italian language, and philological studies, there is the historical archive that consists of early diaries, literary manuscript texts, and correspondences from early academy members. The library at the academy consists of language texts, dictionaries, lexicons, and works devoted to the study of Italian and to linguistics in general.

Washing His Words in the Arno

Although not a Renaissance author, Alessandro Manzoni, who wrote during the nineteenth century, was instrumental in the development of the Italian language. His novel *I promessi sposi* (The Betrothed), a historical reconstruction of a seventeenth-century Milan ravaged by plague and under Spanish domination, tells the story of Renzo and Lucia, two lovers who overcome all obstacles to be together.

Manzoni proposed that contemporary spoken Florentine should form the basis of Italian. From the first published version (1825–1827) to its final form (1840–1842), he reworked *I promessi sposi* in a long series of painstaking revisions. The work is also significant because it served as the benchmark for literary Italian, which, after the unification of Italy in the late 1800s, became standard Italian. The *unificazione linguistica* was as important to the newly formed nation as its political structure.

CHAPTER 23
Grab Some Culture

L earn more about the culture of Italy, and you'll learn more about its language. Today, Italians have a broad range of interests, including playing sports, watching movies, and reading books and magazines. They have a lot of time to do it too, since most Italians have four weeks of vacation annually.

Lights, Camera, Action!

Italian movies are a great way to practice your language listening skills. Many times, too, the dialogue is spoken in dialect or with an accent—it's not always easy for the actor to change his diction. Italian cinema has had several genres. During the 1940s *neorealismo* emphasized location shooting and authentic drama. In the 1950s, the lighthearted *la commedia all'italiana*, with stars such as Totò, left audiences howling. Progressive directors in the 1960s, such as Federico Fellini and Michelangelo Antonioni, created films of great individual expression.

Here is a list of recommended films related to the Italian language. Pass the popcorn and watch *lo schermo* light up with Roberto Benigni, Sophia Loren, Marcello Mastroianni, and many others.

- *Ladri di biciclette (Bicycle Thief)*, 1948. Many critics consider this Oscar-winning classic to be one of the greatest films ever made. Vittorio De Sica used nonprofessional actors to tell the simple, human tragedy of a working man whose bike, which he needs for his job, is stolen, sending him and his son on a harrowing search through the streets of Rome.
- *Riso amaro (Bitter Rice)*, 1948. Silvana Mangano became an international sensation with her performance as a shapely city woman working in the rice fields of Italy's Po Valley after World War II. The sexy Mangano is caught in a love triangle with the respectable Raf Vallone and the unscrupulous Vittorio Gassman.
- *Ciao professore!*, 1993. A tender and often hilarious comedy from Lina Wertmuller that centers on a teacher who is mistakenly assigned to a third-grade class in an impoverished town in Southern Italy. The teacher soon faces the Mafia, truancy, and pupils with family problems as he tries to steer his students in the right direction.
- *Nuovo Cinema Paradiso*, 1988. A charming, bittersweet tribute to the power of movies which won 1989's Best Foreign Film Academy Award. A film director looks back on his childhood in Sicily, where he served as an apprentice to the projectionist at his small town's only movie theater. (Directed by Giuseppe Tornatore.)
- *Morte a Venezia (Death in Venice)*, 1971. This is Luchino Visconti's brilliant version of Thomas Mann's classic story. Dirk Bogarde stars as

a jaded, middle-aged composer on holiday on Venice who spots a handsome young boy on the beach. His doomed obsession with the youth renews his interest in living.

- *Divorzio all'Italiana (Divorce, Italian Style)*, 1961. Marvelous Oscar-winning farce starring Marcello Mastroianni as a man facing midlife crisis who discovers it's easier to kill his annoying wife than divorce her. Eventually he falls for a gorgeous younger woman, played by Stefania Sandrelli.

- *Il Giardino dei Finzi-Contini (The Garden of the Finzi-Continis)*, 1962. Director Vittorio De Sica's Oscar-winning drama centers on an upper-class Jewish family living in Fascist Italy, oblivious at first to the growing tide of anti-Semitism that soon threatens their existence.

- *Il postino*, 1994. A lovely romance set in a small Italian town during the 1950s where exiled Chilean poet Pablo Neruda has taken refuge. A shy mailman befriends the poet and uses his words—and, ultimately, the writer himself—to help him woo a woman with whom he has fallen in love. (With Massimo Troisi, who died a day after filming ended, and Philippe Noiret.)

- *La strada (The Road)*, 1954. Federico Fellini's Oscar-winning study of members of a traveling circus troupe. The film relates how a brutal strongman uses a simpleminded woman who loves him, forcing her to find solace with a good-hearted clown.

- *Le sette bellezze (Seven Beauties)*, 1976. Giancarlo Giannini stars in Lina Wertmuller's dark seriocomic movie as a small-time hood in World War II Italy trying to support his sisters. His desperate attempts to stay alive take him from jail to a mental hospital, and eventually put him in the hands of an obese concentration camp commandant.

SSENTIALS

The movie *Ladri di Saponette* (1989), also known as *The Icicle Thief* in English, is a shameless parody of Vittoria De Sica's neorealist classic *Ladri di Biciclette* (*The Bicycle Thief*). It's a black-and-white film that satirizes TV commercials and lampoons advertising. The video has no relation to De Sica's film—but is worth mentioning for its own warped version of the small screen.

The Art of Dubbing

Italy is a nation that shies away from subtitles, and dubbing in Italian movies is acknowledged to be first-rate. In fact, Italy has an internationally renowned dubbing school and tradition. Dubbing and voice-over for film, video, and documentary scripts requires training in a formal setting. For years, the same actors and actresses have dubbed the voices of well-known actors. Ferruccio Amendola, for instance, was an outstanding dubber who gave the Italian voices to actors such as Al Pacino, Dustin Hoffman, and Robert De Niro.

What's on TV?

Another way to exercise that aural muscle is Italian television. In general, news reporters tend to speak with the least inflected voices, modulated in a standard Italian meant to appeal to a wide audience.

RAI channels (RAI1, RAI2, and RAI3, pronounced "*raiuno*," "*raidue*," and "*raitre*") are vaguely educational, state-owned channels. *Italia 1*, *Rete 4*, and *Canale 5* are networks owned by two-time prime minister Silvio Berlusconi. TMC and TMC2 are stations put out by Telemontecarlo, an independent media company. Production values on Italian TV shows can be a surprise to those accustomed to the slick programs common in the United States.

A Reading List

There are a number of Italian texts, both classic and contemporary, that are must-reads for anyone interested in the history, culture, and language of Italy. Whether it's a trip to hell and back, a year's worth of love poems, or ribald, coarse humor during the plague, there's a tale for everyone.

As you might remember, Dante, Petrarca, and Boccaccio were the trio that first popularized literary Italian. During the Renaissance, writers such as Ludovico Ariosto, Nicolò Machiavelli, and Torquato Tasso blazed new trails with epic poetry, dramas, and political works. Dramatists such as

Vittorio Alfieri and Carlo Goldoni and the poet Ugo Foscolo led a literary revival in the eighteenth century.

In the twentieth century, the poet Gabriele D'Annunzio, the dramatist Luigi Pirandello, and writers Alberto Moravia, Cesare Pavese, and Italo Calvino all made their mark in Italian literature.

What follows are just a few of the many classics in Italian literature. Instead of getting yourself English translations, seek out bilingual texts that are printed side by side in Italian and English. It's a terrific way to read the original work and practice your Italian skills.

- *Non si paga, non si paga (Can't Pay? Won't Pay!)*. Nobel Prize–winning playwright Dario Fo tells the story of a Milan housewife Antonia, who steals a large number of groceries from her local supermarket during a mass protest against rising prices. Knowing that her husband, Giovanni, will disapprove, she persuades her dimwitted friend, Margherita, to help her hide the booty in her father-in-law's allotment shed. Giovanni's unexpected return home prompts a mad rush to conceal the shopping during which Margherita stashes some bags under her coat and assumes the guise of a pregnant woman. There follows an increasingly frantic series of confusions, police searches, and misunderstandings that spiral into high farce.
- *Canzoniere (Collection of Poems)*. Francesco Petrarca, one of the great early Renaissance humanists, wrote love poetry in the "vulgar" tongue. His *Canzoniere* had enormous influence on the poets of the fifteenth and sixteenth centuries. Head over heels in love with Laura, Petrarca wrote 365 poems, one passionate poem a day, dedicated to his true love.
- *Commedia (The Divine Comedy)*. The epic poem by Dante, begun in exile in 1306, allegorically describes the poet's (and, by implication, mankind's) journey through life to salvation. The *Commedia* is the central and culminating literary work of medieval Europe. It is systematically structured in *terza rima*, with three *cantiche* (*Inferno, Purgatorio,* and *Paradiso*).
- *Il decamerone (The Decameron)*. Written by the Italian humanist writer Giovanni Boccaccio almost 650 years ago, *Il decamerone*

contains a hundred tales supposedly told in ten days by a party of ten young people who had fled from the Black Death in Florence. Regarded as his masterpiece and a model for Italian classical prose, its influence on Renaissance literature was enormous.

- *Il fu Mattia Pascal (The Late Mattia Pascal)*. Luigi Pirandello's remarkable work about Pascal, a landowner fallen on hard times and trapped in a miserable marriage, who runs away from home and wins a lot of money at the gaming tables in Monte Carlo. Meanwhile, a dead body has been found in his village, and his neighbors assume it is Pascal—that he has killed himself. Seizing the chance to create a new life, Pascal travels to Rome under an assumed name, struggles to invent a different identity, fails, and returns home. There, he finds his wife has remarried. Now he must act out the role of a living ghost.

FACTS

Italic script was a style of handwriting adopted in fifteenth-century Italy by papal scribes and later (c. 1500) adapted for printing. Italic cursive letters eliminate unnecessary lifts of the pen, permitting rapid legible handwriting.

- *Il principe (The Prince)*. The definitive manual of modern politics written by the Italian Renaissance political philosopher Nicolò Machiavelli almost 500 years ago.
- *I promessi sposi (The Betrothed)*. Alessandro Manzoni's powerfully characterized historical reconstruction of plague-ravaged seventeenth-century Lombardy. The simple attempts of two poor silk weavers to marry are used to explore the corrupt and oppressive rule of the Spaniards and, by implication, of the later Austrians. The novel also forged the literary Italian, which, after the unification of Italy, became standard Italian (see Chapter 22).
- *Orlando Furioso*. A romance epic by the Italian poet Ludovico Ariosto. Orlando goes mad because his lady, Angelica, marries a Moorish youth, but he is cured in time to defeat Agramante, king of Africa, who has been besieging Paris. Ariosto invents fantastic episodes and complicated romantic intrigues and adventures.

- *I rusteghi (The Tyrants).* Carlo Goldoni, a dramatist who wrote 250 plays, based this three-act comedy on the society of his native Venice.

Extra, Extra, Read All about It!

After you've learned how to ask for directions in Italian, can count to *dieci miliardi*, and have read about Mario and Maria's classmates for the *ennesimo* (umpteenth) time, you'll want to find out more about current events in Italy. After all, how else can you expect to *fare pettegolezzi* (gossip) without being up-to-date on the latest news?

Italian publications can be found on the newsstands of many large cities, at airports, and online. *Panorama* and *L'Espresso* are weekly newsmagazines similar to *Time* or *Newsweek*. Both include news, science, politics, medicine, sports, lifestyle, and personalities. Some familiar magazines are also published in Italy, such as *Le Scienze*, which is the Italian version of *Scientific American*.

In Italy, you are what you read, and newspapers are a sign of how important politics are to Italians. Many people swear allegiance to certain publications, depending on their party affiliations. One benefit of reading newspapers or magazines is the exposure to current usage, jargon, and idioms. Like any other language, Italian is dynamic, and that is reflected in contemporary style and usage.

The most popular national daily papers are *Il Corriere della Sera*, a conservative publication from Milan, and *La Repubblica*, a liberal paper from Rome. Other popular papers include *La Stampa* (conservative, published in Torino and owned by Fiat) and *Il Messaggero* (liberal, published in Rome). *Il Sole 24 Ore* is the *Wall Street Journal* of Italian newspapers, while the pink-colored *La Gazzetta dello Sport* is a favorite among *i tifosi* (fans, enthusiasts) to keep track of their favorite soccer team.

Surf the Italian Web

Many people have access to the Web nowadays, so why not use the new technology for improving your Italian skills? Whether it's browsing a news site, requesting travel information, or even taking an interactive Italian lesson on a Web site designed specifically for English speakers, there are many ways to use the Web to advance your language abilities. To get yourself started, review the vocabulary listed in **TABLE 23-1**.

TABLE 23-1

VOCABULARY: THE INTERNET	
address	*l'indirizzo*
browser	*il navigatore*
to click	*cliccare*
computer	*il computer*
control panel	*il pannello di controllo*
dialogue box	*la finestra di dialogo*
to download	*scaricare*
e-mail box	*la casella di posta elettronica*
folder	*la cartella*
icon	*l'icona*
Internet	*la rete*
keyboard	*la tastiera*
online	*in linea*
page	*la pagina*
password	*la parola d'accesso*
printer	*la stampante*
to reboot	*rifare il booting*
search engine	*il motore di ricerca*
site	*il sito*

Here are a few online Italian dictionaries that you might find helpful as you browse Italian Web sites:

✐ *www.yourdictionary.com*
✐ *www.lai.com/lai/glossaries.html*
✐ *www.garzanti.it*
✐ *www.virgilio.it/servizi/dizionario/*

CHATTARE AD INTERNET (INTERNET CHAT)

ROBERTO: *A che cosa assomigli? Sei alta?*
(What do you look like? Are you tall?)

RENATA: *No, sono bassa!*
(No, I'm short!)

ROBERTO: *Hai i capelli biondi?*
(Are you fair-haired?)

RENATA: *Sì, sono bionda.*
(Yes, I'm fair-haired.)

ROBERTO: *Di che colore sono i tuoi occhi?*
(What color are your eyes?)

RENATA: *Grigio blu.*
(Blue-gray.)

ROBERTO: *Sei magra?*
(Are you slim?)

RENATA: *Non proprio, diciamo che non sono grassa.*
(Not exactly, but let's say I'm not fat.)

ROBERTO: *E che cosa indossi?*
(And what are you wearing?)

RENATA: *Il mio maglione preferito e un paio di jeans.*
(My favorite sweater and a pair of jeans.)

ROBERTO: *Che cosa stai facendo in questo momento?*
(What are you doing now?)

RENATA: *Sto parlando con te!*
(I'm talking to you!)

Il rock and roll

You might know The Beatles, the Rolling Stones, Britney Spears, Michael Jackson, and Creed. But how about Claudio Baglioni, Laura Pausini, Vasco Rossi, Eros Ramazzotti, and Jovanotti? Or Claudio Villa, Mina, Domenico Modugno, Gianni Morandi, and Adriano Celentano? Modern Italian pop stars have been filling the airwaves for decades with their version of rock, soul, funk, and dance music.

It was Guglielmo Marconi, an Italian physicist, who invented the radio in 1895. He achieved the first successful wireless trans-Atlantic transmission.

Soccer, What a Kick

Imagine no professional football, hockey, or basketball leagues. Now imagine the weather was mild enough so that everyone played baseball, and only baseball, practically every day of the year. In Italy, that's the situation with soccer, a truly national pastime. Every town has a *squadra* that, theoretically, could play in the top league depending on the caliber of play. Fans are incredibly loyal to their teams, even to the point of hysteria. The national soccer team, called *gli Azzurri* for the blue color of their jerseys, is ranked world-class. If you're serious about learning Italian, it's a good idea to at least familiarize yourself with the sport so you can talk to your Italian friends about their favorite team.

Besides soccer, other popular sports in Italy include skiing, swimming, hiking, mountain climbing, and bicycling. Each May, Italy hosts the *Giro d'Italia*, a grueling month-long cross-country race. For some sports-related vocabulary, see **TABLE 23-2**.

TABLE 23-2

VOCABULARY: SPORTS			
auto racing	*la corsa automobilistica*	fishing	*la pesca*
ball	*il pallone*	game	*il gioco*
bicycling	*il ciclismo*	handball	*la pallamano*
boat racing	*la corsa nautica*	hunting	*la caccia*
bowling	*il gioco dei birilli*	mountain climbing	*l'alpinismo*
boxing	*il pugilato*	race	*la gara*
championship	*il campionato*	rowing	*il canottaggio*
competition	*la gara*	skiing	*sciare*
defeat	*la sconfitta*	soccer	*il calcio*
fencing	*la scherma*	victory	*la vittoria*

CHAPTER 24

Art in High Places

Quick, think of a famous Italian artist. Or name a period of art history that drew inspiration from Italy. What about a theatrical presentation that's associated with Italian singers? It's practically impossible not to come up with several artists immediately, to recall the Renaissance, or to think of the opera. The many cultural riches of Italy can entertain you and at the same time help you learn Italian.

Ya Gotta Have Art

Whether you travel to Italy, page through a coffee-table book featuring Italian artists, or listen to opera on the radio, the plethora of Italian art is unavoidable.

A wide variety of amazing artwork has been created in Italy from before the Roman Empire up to the present day, and it provides a unique way to study the language while learning more about the artistic patrimony of Italy.

ESSENTIALS

When referring to a particular artistic period in a century between 1100 and 1900, Italians drop the *mille* (thousand). For example, the 1300s are called *il Trecento*, the 1400s are called *il Quattrocento*, and so on.

On a First-Name Basis

Michelangelo, Raffaello, Leonardo, and Donatello have at least one thing in common: Most people nowadays know these artists by their first names. Obviously, they had *cognomi* (last names) too:

- Michelangelo Buonarroti
- Raffaello Sanzio
- Donato di Betto Bardi (Donatello)
- Leonardo da Vinci

Other well-known names are Giotto di Bondone, Tommaso Giovanni di Simone Guidi (Masaccio) and Alessandro di Mariano Filipepi (Sandro Botticelli).

FACTS

There's a price to pay for everything—even church. Some churches in Italy now request an entrance fee to offset the cost of maintenance, claiming that the artwork found on their walls, by such artists as Filippo Brunelleschi, Masaccio, and Giotto, are equal to any found in museums. Town residents are exempt from paying.

Have You Lost Your Marbles?

Marble, wood, bronze. If it was solid and durable, chances are an artist would grab a chisel and begin to sculpt. Donatello, for example, was an extremely influential Florentine sculptor of the *Quattrocento*. He did freestanding sculptures in marble, bronze, and wood, and was also known for a new way of doing shallow relief that gave a sense of depth through using perspective rather than through the use of high relief. Michelangelo believed it was his duty to liberate the figure that was straining to be released from the marble. His slave series, several of which can be viewed in Florence's *Galleria dell'Accademia*, are perhaps the best examples of how he chipped away just enough marble to liberate the figures.

At the Museum

So do you want to see these great works of art for yourself? If so, check out these top-ten not-to-be-missed Italian museums:

1. *Galleria dell'Accademia, Firenze*
2. *Galleria Borghese, Roma*
3. *Galleria degli Uffizi, Firenze*
4. *Museo della Scuola Grande di San Rocco, Venezia*
5. *Museo di Capodimonte, Napoli*
6. *Musei Vaticani* (a group of several museums housing world-class treasures)
7. *Palazzo Farnese, Roma*
8. *Museo del Risorgimento, Milano*

9. *Museo Egizio and Galleria Sabauda, Torino*
10. *Galleria Regionale della Sicilia, Palermo*

You're standing on line at the *Uffizi* in Florence or the *Capodimonte Museum* in Naples and can't wait to see all that amazing artwork. Or you're a student in an art history class studying Michelangelo, Ghirlandaio, and Caravaggio. Put your free time to good use and review some vocabulary words that relate to art and museums (**TABLE 24-1**).

TABLE 24-1

VOCABULARY: AT THE MUSEUM			
apprentice	*l'apprendista*	paint, to	*dipingere*
art	*l'arte*	paint	*la vernice*
artist	*l'artista*	paintbrush	*il pennello*
canvas	*la tela*	painter	*il pittore*
caption	*la didascalia*	relief	*il rilievo*
corridor	*il corridoio*	Renaissance	*il Rinascimento*
frame	*la cornice*	sculpt	*scolpire*
gallery	*la galleria*	sculptor	*scultore*
marble	*il marmo*	sculpture	*la scultura*
masterpiece	*capolavoro*	studio	*la bottega*

Hitting the High C

There might not be another pastime in Italy that is more closely associated with the Italian language than opera. The theatrical form, combining acting, singing, and classical music, originated in Italy more than 400 years ago. Most operas were originally sung in Italian, and today there are historic opera houses throughout Italy where the divas still sing.

The common operatic term *bel canto* (beautiful singing) points out why so many people refer to Italian as a language that's "sung" by native speakers. Since Italian speakers place the vowels in a forward position (in front of the mouth) just as singers do when singing, it's easy for Italians to switch from speaking to singing. That's probably why so many Italians seem to be blessed with "natural" singing voices. The formation of vowels is integral not only in singing opera but in speaking Italian as well.

QUESTIONS?

Just who is the *prima donna*?
Well, she's the principal female singer in an opera or concert organization! The term literally means "first lady," and has mutated in current usage to mean an extremely sensitive, vain, or undisciplined person.

If you want to get a head start on understanding a performance, be sure to read the *libretto* (literally, "little book") first. The *libretto* is a play-by-play of all the action onstage, and reading it will enhance your time at the theater. Although you might not be able to follow the songs word for word, what's more important is to get a feel for the action, the excitement, and the drama.

Here are just a few operas that are recognized as masterpieces and are sure to give you a thrill:

- *Aida*, by Giuseppi Verdi, was first produced in Cairo in 1871. The opera is set in ancient Egypt and is named after the Ethiopian princess who is its heroine.
- *Il Barbiere di Siviglia (The Barber of Seville)* is a comic opera composed by Gioacchino Rossini and first produced in Rome in 1816. The barber of the title is Figaro, a character who also appears in Mozart's *Le Nozze di Figaro*, a sequel.
- *La Bohème* is an opera in four acts by Giacomo Puccini, first produced in Turin in 1896.
- *Rigoletto* is an opera by Verdi produced in Venice in 1851. The title is taken from its baritone hero, a tragic court jester. "*La donna è mobile*" (the woman is fickle) is its most famous aria.
- *La Traviata* is another opera written by Verdi. The title is variously interpreted to mean "the fallen woman" or "the woman gone astray." The work, in three acts, was first performed in Venice in 1853.

If you ever have the opportunity, hearing a performance at Milano's *La Scala* will leave you speechless. *Bravissimi!* To help you find your way out there, you might need to know a few vocabulary words (see **TABLE 24-2**).

TABLE 24-2

VOCABULARY: AT THE THEATER			
act	*l'atto*	musical	*il musicale*
backstage	*il retroscena*	overture	*il preludio*
ballet	*il balletto*	performance	*la rappresentazione*
ballet dancer	*il ballerino*	play	*l'opera drammatica*
cadence	*la cadenza*	producer	*il produttore*
check room	*il guardaroba*	production	*la messa in scena*
comedy	*la commedia*	program	*il programma*
comic opera	*l'opera buffa*	scene	*la scena*
concert	*il concerto*	scenery	*lo scenario*
conductor	*il direttore d'orchestra*	show	*lo spettacolo*
costumes	*i costumi*	singer	*il cantante*
curtain	*il sipario*	song	*il canzone*
dance	*la danza*	stage	*il palcoscenico*
duet	*il duetto*	symphony	*la sinfonia*
intermission	*l'intervallo*	tenor	*il tenore*
lyric	*il lirico*	ticket	*il biglietto*
music	*la musica*	voice	*la voce*

AL CONCERTO (AT THE THEATER)

MONICA: *Siamo stati proprio fortunate ad avere questi posti.*
(We were really lucky to get these seats.)

FRANCESCA: *In quale fila siamo?*
(Which row are we in?)

MONICA: *Siamo nell'ultima fila.*
(We're in the last row.)

FRANCESCA: *Spero che si riesca a sentire qualcosa.*
(I hope we'll be able to hear something!)

ADRIANA: *Ma tu sai quale concerto danno?*
(But do you know what concert they're showing?)

FRANCESCA:	*No, nessuno me l'ha mai detto.*
	(No, no one ever told me.)
ADRIANA:	*È un concerto di musica classica di una solista bravissima!*
	(It's a classical music concert with an incredible soloist!)
FRANCESCA:	*Io pensavo che fosse un concerto di musica jazz!*
	(I thought it was a jazz concert!)
ADRIANA:	*Stanno eseguendo brani ai Bach e di Mozart.*
	(They are playing works by Bach and Mozart.)
FRANCESCA:	*Che musica stupenda!*
	(What superb music!)
ADRIANA:	*Tu sai suonare qualche strumento?*
	(Can you play any musical instruments?)
FRANCESCA:	*Io so suonare il pianoforte, e tu?*
	(I can play the piano, and yourself?)
ADRIANA:	*Io sono.*
	(I play.)
FRANCESCA:	*Che cosa suoni? Il pianoforte? Il tamburo?*
	(What do you play? The piano? Drums?)
ADRIANA:	*No, no!*
	(No, no!)
FRANCESCA:	*La chitarra? Il clarinetto? L'armonica?*
	(The guitar? The clarinet? The harmonica?)
ADRIANA:	*Nessuno di questi!*
	(None of these!)
FRANCESCA:	*Che cosa, allora? Uno strumento a percussione? Il violino?*
	(What then? A percussion instrument? The violin?)
LUIGI:	*Stai zitto! Non sento la musica!*
	(Be quiet! I can't hear the music!)
FRANCESCA:	*Scusami tanto!*
	(So sorry!)

Home of the Golden Arches

McDonald's might have served billions of hamburgers beneath its neon arches, but it was the Romans who put the *arco* in *architettura*, using this design element to build aqueducts, stadiums, villas, and palaces. Learning about architecture is another way to increase your Italian vocabulary, whether you'd like to learn about the three primary orders of columns—*corinto, dorico,* or *ionico*—or the many different types of architectural styles—*bizantino, gotico, romanico, rinascimento, manierismo, barocco.* Another example? The palladium window derives from an Italian architect, Andrea Palladio, who led a revival of classical architecture in sixteenth-century Italy and designed many major buildings, including the church of *San Giorgio Maggiore* in Venice, built in 1566.

ESSENTIALS

If you're interested in learning more about architecture and have some time on your hands, try the ten-volume treatise *De Architectura* written in the first century B.C. by Vitruvius, a Roman architect and military engineer. The work is considered the bible of classical architectural theory and also served to inspire the Italian Renaissance's architects and educated men.

Holier Than Thou

If a priest wanted to teach his congregation about the Bible, and virtually all the common folk were illiterate, how else could he convey his message? With pictures! That's one reason why so many churches in Italy have paintings, frescoes, and mosaics everywhere. Commissioned artists created pictorial representations of Biblical stories, from the flood to the martyrdom of saints, from heaven to hell, from Christ's birth to His crucifixion and resurrection. Since very few people could read, this was one way for them to visualize the sermons offered from the pulpit. Images of sinners burning in Hell probably convinced a number of churchgoers to mind their actions.

It's not surprising to see so many impressive-looking churches in a country where the seat of Roman Catholicism is located. Throughout Italy, there are cathedrals and basilicas in styles such as Byzantine, Gothic, Romanesque, and Renaissance. If you're looking for some of the best examples of celestial art and architecture, you can't go wrong visiting these churches:

- *Basilica di San Francesco, Assisi:* Built in memorial of St. Francis, this unique church, with two separate levels, has a number of important frescoes by artists such as Giotto, Cimabue, Simone Martini, and Pietro Lorenzetti.
- *Cattedrale, Battistero, e Campanile, Pisa:* It's not just the Leaning Tower of Pisa! The green-and-white marble stonework of the adjacent buildings is every bit as stunning.
- *Duomo e Battistero, Firenze:* The octagonal *duomo* by Filippo Brunelleschi can be seen for miles around, while the ceiling of the Baptistery is covered in amazing mosaics.
- *Basilica di San Marco, Venezia:* The curving domes of the church are encrusted with golden mosaics that are the epitome of Byzantine art.
- *San Miniato al Monte, Firenze:* This church overlooking a hillside has many important frescoes.
- *Sant'Ambrogio, Milano:* This is an amazing Gothic church in the center of the city. Visitors can even walk on the roof for a closeup look at the spires.
- *Santa Maria Novella, Firenze:* Wealthy businessmen commissioned several of the city's most important Renaissance artists to create frescoes in the chapels that line this church.

For some architectural jargon in Italian, see **TABLE 24-3**.

TABLE 24-3

VOCABULARY: ARCHITECTURE			
abbey	*l'abbazia*	cloister	*il chiostro*
altar	*l'altare*	crypt	*la cripta*
arch	*l'arco*	crucifix	*il crocifisso*
balcony	*la loggia*	Last Supper	*il cenacola*
baptistery	*il battistero*	nave	*la navata*
bell tower	*il campanile*	palace	*il palazzo*
canopy	*il baldacchino*	pilaster	*il pilastro*
chapel	*la cappella*	refectory	*il refettorio*
church	*la chiesa*	rose window	*il rosone*

A City in Ruins

There's something almost otherworldly about historical ruins—maybe it's the thought of connecting with an ancient people, admiring their craftsmanship, or wondering about the lives of those who lived long before us. At the *Foro Romano* (Roman Forum), for example, Roman senators would meet to conduct the business of governing the empire. Today, you can wander the *Via Antica* and see many of the buildings and monuments that date back over 2000 years.

There are many other incredible ancient ruins in Italy, and you might consider taking a tour from an Italian speaker to learn twice—first the language, and second the history of the location. Take a guidebook along to translate the terms you don't understand, and then describe what you've seen in Italian. Here are a few places worth visiting:

- **Pompeii.** One of the most popular ghost towns, it was leveled in A.D. 79 when Mount Vesuvius erupted and covered the entire city in ash. Thousands of years later, it is still Italy's most-visited tourist attraction. Today, it's still possible to see many houses and public buildings that were part of the city.
- **The Colosseum.** This structure was the scene of gladiator fights, naval battles, chariot races, and fights with hungry lions. What remains of this huge *anfiteatro* is remarkable, considering that emperors and popes mined the ruins for centuries to use its marble for other buildings in Rome.
- **Etruscan ruins.** These ruins are older than the Roman Empire, and there are a number of sites you can visit throughout Tuscany.
- **Roman Forum.** Imagine Caesar walking the stones of the *Foro Romano*, planning and scheming for domination of the Western world.
- **Sicily**. This is the motherlode of Greek archeological finds. The best-preserved Greek temples in the world today are found not in Greece but in Sicily. Remarkable examples can be found at Syracuse, Agrigento, Selinunte, and Segesta. The theater at Taormina is among the best preserved in the world.

CHAPTER 25

Passports Please!

You've conjugated verbs, learned to roll your *r*s, can pronounce double consonants, and know the difference between *passato prossimo* and *passato remoto*. Now you want to practice your Italian in Italy! Before you go, here is practical information about traveling, including survival phrases, embassy and consulate information, and tour suggestions. *Buon viaggio!*

Get Your Papers In Order

Before your first taste of authentic *crostini misti* and a glass of *Chianti*, you'll have some paperwork to do. Check to see if you need a passport to enter Italy and return home (returning to the United States with an expired passport is illegal).

Visas are generally required for citizens of the United States only if they stay in Italy for longer than three months. If that's the case, you'll need an application form, a detailed itinerary, proof of adequate medical insurance, a valid return airline ticket, and proof of accommodations. Also carry two or more forms of identification on your person, including at least one photo ID. Many banks require several IDs in order to cash traveler's checks.

I've Got Nothing to Hide

Going through *la dogana* (customs) shouldn't be much of a bother as long as you have all the right identification. In addition, if you've purchased goods and gifts at a duty-free shop, you'll have to pay a duty on the value of those articles that exceeds the allowance established by the Italian customs service.

FACTS

Freedom of movement isn't just for those wearing stretch pants. If you're an EU citizen you can take the EZ-Pass lanes at the airport and breeze right through customs. It's all part of the efforts to ease border-patrol regulations and ease travel between participating countries.

"Duty-free" simply means that you don't have to pay a tax in the country of purchase. Be sure to keep receipts for major purchases while in Italy—non-EU (European Union) citizens can claim a refund for the value added tax (VAT or IVA).

L'ARRIVO IN ITALIA (ARRIVING IN ITALY)

LUIGI: *Buongiorno!*
(Good morning!)

FILIPPO: *Salve!*
(Hello!)

LUIGI: *Lei è inglese?*
(Are you English?)

FILIPPO: *Esatto, sono inglese.*
(That's right, I'm English.)

LUIGI: *Come va?*
(How are you?)

FILIPPO: *Molto bene, e Lei?*
(Very well, and you?)

LUIGI: *Bene grazie. Lasci che l'aiuti. Mi dia una delle sue valigie.*
(Fine, thanks. Let me help you. Give me one of your suitcases.)

FILIPPO: *Non si preoccupi, sono molto leggere.*
(Don't worry, they're very light.)

LUIGI: *Ne è sicuro?*
(Are you sure?)

FILIPPO: *Se proprio insiste . . .*
(If you really insist . . .)

LUIGI: *Eccoci qui. Questa è la macchina. Aspetti, le apro la portiera.*
(Here we are. There's the car. Wait, I'll open the door for you.)

FILIPPO: *Posso mettere questi nel cofano?*
(Can I put this in the trunk?)

LUIGI: *Ora, mi racconti un po' di Lei.*
(Now, tell me a bit about yourself.)

FILIPPO: *Che cosa vuole sapere? Sono inglese. Non parlo molto bene l'italiano.*
(What would you like to know? I'm English. I don't speak Italian very well.)

LUIGI: *Lei ha fratelli o sorelle? Non ne parlava nella sua lettera.*
(Do you have any brothers or sisters? You didn't say in your letter.)

FILIPPO: *Sì, ho tre sorelle.*
(Yes, I have three sisters.)

LUIGI: *Ha dei bambini?*
(Do you have any children?)

FILIPPO: *No, non sono sposato.*
(No, I'm not married.)

LUIGI: *Lei ha vissuto in Francia?*
(Have you lived in France?)

FILIPPO: *No, ho vissuto in Germania per cinque anni.*
(No, I've lived in Germany for five years.)

LUIGI: *Incontrerà un sacco di gente simpatico durante il suo soggiorno in Italia.*
(You'll meet a lot of nice people during your stay in Italy.)

FILIPPO: *Non vedo l'ora!*
(I can't wait!)

LUIGI: *Ecco, siamo arrivati a casa. Benvenuto tra noi!*
(Here we are, back home. Welcome!)

FILIPPO: *Molto carina!*
(Very nice!)

LUIGI: *Ormai, siamo amici. Possiamo darci del tu?*
(Now that we're friends, we can drop the formalities, can't we?)

FILIPPO: *Con piacere, anzi, grazie di avermel chiesto.*
(With pleasure, in fact, thanks for asking.)

Where's My Wallet?

Sometimes it happens no matter what you do to prevent it. You thought your wallet was safe in your pocket but you misplaced it. Or, your passport fell out of your pocket on that rough ride from Naples to the island of Capri. If you lose your passport, immediately notify the local police and the nearest embassy or consulate. There are consulates in most major Italian cities including Florence, Milan, Naples, Palermo, and Venice. They answer the phone around the clock and also have lists of English-speaking doctors and lawyers.

ESSENTIALS

The U.S. Embassy and Consulate is at Via V. Veneto, 119a, 00187 Rome. They issue new passports the same day but are closed on U.S. and Italian holidays.

Making a Telephone Call

At some point you'll want to speak on the telephone, either to make hotel reservations, purchase tickets to a show, or arrange for a taxi to pick you up. The *alfabeti telefonici* (phonetic alphabet) is useful when spelling out words over the telephone, for example, or when speaking to officials.

Italians tend to use the names of Italian cities (when there is a corresponding town) rather than proper nouns to spell out words. For example, while you might say "M as in Michael," an Italian is more likely to say *M come Milano* (M as in Milan). **TABLE 25-1** will give you examples for all other letters, including those five foreign letters that sometimes appear in Italian.

TABLE 25-1

THE TELEPHONE ALPHABET: *A COME ANCONA*			
A	*Ancona*	N	*Napoli*
B	*Bologna*	O	*Otranto*
C	*Como*	P	*Padova*
D	*Domodossola*	Q	*quarto*
E	*Empoli*	R	*Roma*
F	*Firenze*	S	*Savona*
G	*Genova*	T	*Torino*
H	*hotel*	U	*Udine*
I	*Imola*	V	*Venezia*
J	*Jérusalem*	W	*Washington*
K	*kilogramma*	X	*Xeres*
L	*Livorno*	Y	*York*
M	*Milano*	Z	*Zara*

Telephones aren't the only way to communicate in Italy. New Internet cafés, Internet bars, and even Internet laundromats are popping up everywhere, so you can access Web-based e-mail providers and even surf the Web while in Italy. (Also see Chapter 23 for ideas on browsing the Italian Web, as well as related vocabulary.)

The Government Merry-Go-Round

Sometimes it seems as though the Italian government strives to reach new levels of dysfunctionality. After all, there have been close to sixty governments since the country formed a democratic republic in 1946 following World War II, and political scandals seem to be the norm rather than the exception. On the other hand, it may be that term limits are simply a theoretical concept, and politicians and their parties mutate as the economy, geopolitics, and social programs demand.

FACTS

Wondering where all the Machiavellian intrigue takes place? In Rome there's the *Palazzo Montecitorio*, where the Chamber of Deputies is located. *Palazzo Madama* is the Senate seat, and the president of Italy lives in the *Palazzo del Quirinale*, a splendid former papal palace. *Palazzo Chigi* is the center of the Italian government.

Much like many democratic governments today, the Italian government is divided into three branches. The executive branch has two members: the *presidente*, who is elected by an electoral college, and the *primo ministero*, who is generally the leader of the party that has the largest representation in the Chamber of Deputies (the prime minister is also sometimes called *il Presidente del Consiglio dei Ministri*). The legislative branch consists of a bicameral *Parlamento*, which includes the *Senato della Repubblica* and the *Camera dei Deputati* (Chamber of Deputies). The *Corte Costituzionale* (Constitutional Court) rounds out the government. For a more in-depth look at Italian government, visit the official Italian government Web site at *www.governo.it*.

Survival Phrases: Don't Leave Home Without Them

As you get to the end of this book, you may not remember the difference between transitive and intransitive verbs, or the indirect object pronouns. However, make sure you commit to memory the following Italian phrases, essential for visitors who would like to ingratiate themselves with native Italians. If you try to communicate in Italian, it's likely they'll return the thoughtfulness with goodwill and graciousness.

A domani! (See you tomorrow.)
A presto! (See you soon.)
Arrivederci! (Good-bye!)
Buon giorno! (Good morning!)
Buon pomeriggio! (Good afternoon!)
Buona sera! (Good evening!)
Buonanotte! (Good night!)
Come sta? (How are you?)
Come va? (How're you doing?)
Ci sentiamo bene. (We're feeling fine.)
Ciao! (Hi!/Bye!)
Come si chiama? (What is your name?)
Di dov'è? (Where are you from?)
Piacere di conoscerla. (Pleased to meet you.)
Siamo qui da una settimana. (We've been here for a week.)

Italy in Overdrive

Roma non è stata fatta in un giorno. Rome wasn't built in a day. And obviously there's no way to explore all the wonderful history of the town, to soak up the atmosphere of its beautiful parks and gardens, to visit the churches and museums overstuffed with magnificent art in just one day either.

But suppose you were limited to just twenty-four hours apiece in what are arguably Italy's three most-visited cities. Here's a suggested high-velocity walking tour (no stopping inside museums!) that would take in many of the most famous monuments and attractions—with the caveat that you will return at a much more leisurely pace to give each city its proper time. So grab a map, lace up your most comfortable walking shoes, and get ready for a tour that would make a Ferrari proud.

Touring Rome

Begin in *Piazza Navona* and take in the incredible Fountain of the Four Rivers sculpture by Bernini. Next is the Pantheon, one of the largest domes of its kind in the world. No dawdling, though! Close by is the *Galleria Doria Paphilj*, a collection of classical and Renaissance art. Make sure you've got three coins in your pocket, since the next stop is the Trevi Fountain. Further on (a lot further on!) is *Piazza Trinità dei Monti*. Walk to the top of the Spanish Steps for a panoramic view of St. Peter's.

ALERT

One way to cover the large distances quickly in Rome is with the *metropolitana* (the subway). The subway entrances are marked with a white "M" on a red square.

Back down at the base of the steps walk to *Piazza del Popolo*, where you can see artwork by Caravaggio and Raffaello in the *Chiesa di Santa Maria del Popolo*. Next stop is the huge *Ara Pacis* and Mausoleum of Augustus near the river. Last stop is *Chiesa San Luigi dei Francesi*, home to three of Caravaggio's most famous paintings. This is the most strenuous of all tours since the city is so big, and you haven't even made it across the Tiber to see Vatican City.

A Quick Tour of Florence

Start at the *centro storico* at the Baptistery and take in Ghiberti's Gates of Paradise, the ten world-famous gilded panels on the eastern doors. Right across the piazza there's the *Duomo*, where you can snap a few photos of Brunelleschi's dome and Giotto's campanile. Next, head toward the *Basilica di San Lorenzo*, which was commissioned by the Medici family. If you had time, you'd visit the *Cappelle dei Medici* as well as the Laurentian Library, both located within the church's complex.

FACTS

The Medici were a powerful and influential Italian family of bankers and merchants whose members effectively ruled Florence for much of the fifteenth century and from 1569 were grand dukes of Tuscany. Cosimo and Lorenzo de' Medici were notable rulers and patrons of the arts in Florence; the family also included four popes (including Leo X) and two queens of France (Catherine de' Médicis and Marie de Médicis).

The next stop is the *Bargello*, which once functioned as a prison, and now houses Renaissance sculpture from most of the masters. Next, your feet will carry you to an outdoor sculpture garden, the *Loggia dei Lanzi* off *Piazza Signoria*. From there you can see the long line of people waiting to enter the overwhelming *Uffizi* museum (a must-see if you have more time). Then, make your way to the *Chiesa Santa Croce*, a church that houses the tombs of many of Florence's most famous citizens, including Galileo, Michelangelo, and Machiavelli. Finally, head toward the *Arno*, where you can capture a wonderful view of the *Ponte Vecchio* in the distance.

A Race Around Venice

Your tour begins in *Piazza San Marco*. Step inside the *Basilica di San Marco* and marvel at the mosaics. Adjacent to it is the *Palazzo Ducale*, a wonderful museum that you don't have time for. If you look up, you'll see that the long shadow being cast is from the *Campanile*, the bell tower made famous by all those Canaletto paintings of Venice.

Next, take a long, meandering walk to the *Rialto* bridge and visit the nearby markets. From there, hop a *vaporetto* to the *Accademia* stop. Take note that the *Gallerie dell'Accademia* has some of the finest art in the world, including works by Bellini, Carpaccio, and Titian. Walk to the *Collezione Peggy Guggenheim*, a collection of modern art. Your tour ends at the *Chiesa Santa Maria della Salute*, one of the best vistas of the city.

Take a Picture

As you tour these amazing sites, chances are you'll want to take some pictures. Here's a list of words related to taking photos (**TABLE 25-2**).

TABLE 25-2

VOCABULARY: THE PHOTO SHOP	
black and white	*la pellicola in bianco e nero*
camera	*la macchina fotografica*
color film	*la pellicola a colori*
develop, to	*sviluppare*
enlargement	*l'ingrandimento*
exposure	*la posa*
film, to	*filmare*
film	*la pellicola*
flash bulb	*il flash*
lens	*l'obiettivo*
movie camera	*la cinepresa*
negative	*il negativo*
photo	*la foto*
photograph, to	*fotografare*
print	*la copia*
roll (of film)	*il rullino*
self timer	*l'autoscatto*
shutter	*l'otturatore*
viewfinder	*il mirino*
yellow filter	*il filtro giallo*

APPENDIX A
Answer Key

CHAPTER 2: WHAT YOU SEE IS WHAT YOU HEAR

1. True: The Italian alphabet contains 26 letters.
2. The punctuation mark (!) is called *il punto esclamativo* in Italian.
3. False: Italian word pairs like *sera/serra* and *dona/donna* are not pronounced the same.
4. Usually, Italian words are stressed on the next-to-last syllable.
5. Italian is a phonetic language, which means most words are pronounced as written.

CHAPTER 4: NOUNS AND ARTICLES

1. *aranciata*   *aranciate*
2. *vitello*   *vitelli*
3. *albicoca*   *albicoche*
4. *torta*   *torte*
5. *pesce*   *pesci*
6. *polpetta*   *polpette*
7. *gelato*   *gelati*
8. *bruschetta*   *bruschette*
9. *risotto*   *risotti*
10. *arancino*   *arancini*

---

1. *un agnello* (a lamb)
2. *un cavallo* (a horse)
3. *un elefante* (an elephant)
4. *un'aquila* (an eagle)
5. *un orso* (a bear)
6. *una vipera* (a snake)
7. *una volpe* (a fox)
8. *uno sciacallo* (a jackal)
9. *una giraffa* (a giraffe)
10. *una tartaruga* (a turtle)

---

1. *Quella foto è vecchia.* (That photograph is old.)
2. *Quell'automobile è una Fiat.* (That car is a Fiat.)
3. *Come sono bravi quegli avvocati!* (How clever are those lawyers!)
4. *È irlandese quello studente?* (Are those students Irish?)
5. *Sono facili quelle ricette?* (Are those recipes easy?)
6. *Quei bambini hanno i capelli biondi.* (Those kids have blond hair.)
7. *Quell'ospedale è grande.* (That hospital is large.)
8. *Com'è bello quello negozio!* (How good is that business!)

CHAPTER 5: *ESSERE* AND *AVERE*: DON'T LEAVE HOME WITHOUT THEM

1. *Massimo non è qui, è da sua zia.* (Massimo is not here, he is at his aunt's house.)
2. *Ragazze, siete a scuola alle tre?* (Children, are you at school at three o'clock?)
3. *La sabato io sono sempre a casa.* (Saturdays I always stay at home.)
4. *Voi siete di Torino?* (Are you from Torino?)
5. *Dove sono i tuoi genitori?* (Where are your parents?)
6. *Noi siamo pronti a studiare.* (We're ready to study.)
7. *Monica, sei italiana?* (Monica, are you Italian?)
8. *Luisa non è americana: è canadese.* (Luisa isn't American, she's Canadian.)

---

1. *Anna Maria ha la penna in mano.* (Anna Maria has a pen in her hand.)
2. *Tu hai una bella voce.* (You have a beautiful voice.)
3. *Voi avete dieci dollari.* (You have ten dollars.)
4. *Io ho tre sorelle.* (I have three sisters.)
5. *Alessandra ha una macchina italiana.* (Alessandra has an Italian car.)
6. *Gli studenti hanno molti compiti da fare.* (The students have a lot of homework to do.)
7. *Oggi noi abbiamo ospiti in casa.* (Today we have guests at home.)
8. *Stefano e Antonio hanno un cane.* (Stefano and Antonio have a dog.)

---

1. *Che ora è? Che ore sono?* (What time is it?)
2. *Non hanno amici in Italia. Non ha amici in Italia.* (They don't have friends in Italy. He doesn't have friends in Italy.)
3. *Di dove sono i tuoi zii? Di dov'è il tuo zio?* (Where are your uncles from? Where is your uncle from?)
4. *Voi avete molto fame? Tu hai molto fame?* (Are you hungry?)
5. *Loro sono americane. Lei è americana.* (They are American. She is American.)
6. *Hai due pizze. Avete due pizze.* (You have two pizzas.)
7. *Abbiamo sete? Ho sete?* (Are we thirsty? Am I thirsty?)
8. *Lui è molto occupato. Loro sono molto occupati.* (He is very busy. They are very busy.)
9. *Sono italiane le tue cugine? È italiana la tua cugina?* (Are your cousins Italian? Is your cousin Italian?)
10. *Ho un gatto. Abbiamo un gatto.* (I have a cat. We have a cat.)

CHAPTER 6: BIG, RED, ROUND, AND DELICIOUS

1. *La pizza è calda.* (The pizza is hot.)
2. *La madre di Lorenza è generosa.* (Lorenza's mother is generous.)
3. *I fiori sono rossi.* (The flowers are red.)
4. *La torta è buona.* (The cake is delicious.)
5. *Il gatto è nero.* (The cat is black.)
6. *Carla è magra.* (Carla is thin.)
7. *I bambini sono cattivi.* (The infants are bad.)
8. *Voi siete timidi.* (You are timid.)
9. *L'appartamento è moderno.* (The apartment is modern.)
10. *Le case non sono nuove.* (The houses are new.)

1. *I nostri libri sono grossi.* (Our books are big.)
2. *La sua rivista è interessante.* (Her/his magazine is interesting.)
3. *La mia giacca è nera.* (My jacket is black.)
4. *Le loro motociclette sono rosse.* (Their motorcycles are red.)
5. *La tua cravatta è bella.* (Your tie is pretty.)
6. *Le loro amiche sono brave.* (Their friends are good.)
7. *I vostri vicini sono italiani.* (Your neighbors are Italian.)
8. *Il tuo giardino è bello.* (Your garden is pretty.)
9. *Il mio cappotto è leggero.* (My coat is light.)
10. *Le nostre maglie sono pesante.* (Our vests are heavy.)

CHAPTER 7: BY THE NUMBERS

1. 34: *trentaquattro*
2. 86: *ottantasei*
3. 2.514: *duemilacinquecentoquattordici*
4. 19: *diciannove*
5. 3: *tre*
6. 108: *centotto*
7. 6: *sei*
8. 16: *seidici*
9. 35.015: *trentacinquemilaquindici*
10. 7: *sette*

1. *cinquecentosessantotto:* 568
2. *trecento:* 300
3. *nove:* 9
4. *milleundici:* 1.011
5. *trentatré:* 33
6. *novantanove:* 99

7. *milleottocentododici:* 1.812
8. *un milione:* 1.000.000
9. *ventisette:* 27
10. *quattro:* 4

1. *dodici + tredici = venticinque*
2. *sei + sessantanove = settantacinque*
3. *trenta + quarantotto = settantotto*
4. *sessantasei + trentaquattro = cento*
5. *cento + duecentoventiquattro = trecentotrentaquattro*
6. *mille – novecentonovantasette = tre*
7. *millequattrocentonovantadue – millequattrocentoquattro = ottantotto*
8. *ventuno – diciassette = quattro*
9. *novantaquattro – sessantadue = trentadue*
10. *cinque – due = tre*

1. 1,15: *È l'una e un quarto.*
2. 20,20: *Sono le venti e venti.*
3. 23,00: *Sono le ventitre.*
4. 3,30: *Sono le tre e mezzo.*
5. 7,25: *Sono le sette e ventiquattro.*
6. 16,45: *Sono le diciassette meno un quarto.*
7. 4,10: *Sono le quattro e dieci.*
8. 9,00: *Sono le nove.*
9. 18,40: *Sono le diciotto meno venti.*
10. 19,55: *Sono le venti meno cinque.*

CHAPTER 8: FIRST-CONJUGATION VERBS

1. *Loro camminano lentamente.* (They walk slowly.)
2. *Tu guidi la macchina.* (You drive the car.)
3. *Adriana non trova il quaderno.* (Adriana cannot find the notebook.)
4. *Marco guarda l'orologio.* (Marco looks at the clock.)
5. *Io compro i biglietti.* (I buy the tickets.)
6. *Voi cantate ad alta voce.* (You sing in a high voice.)
7. *Lavorate fino a tardi voi?* (Are you working late?)
8. *Io alzo il ricevitore.* (I raise the receiver.)
9. *Noi impariamo la lezione.* (We learn the lessons.)
10. *Loro arrivano in ritardo.* (They arrive late.)

1. *La regina regna.* (The queen reigns.)
2. *Io e Marco marciamo per molte ore.* (Marco and I march for many hours.)
3. *Io assaggio la zuppa.* (I taste the soup.)
4. *Tu avvinghi forte.* (You squeeze strongly.)
5. *Lei invecchia molto.* (She ages a lot.)
6. *Voi noleggiate la macchina.* (You rent a car.)
7. *Marco parcheggia la motocicletta.* (Marco parks the car.)
8. *Loro racconciano i pantaloni.* (They mend the pants.)

---

1. *Voi quando andate a trovare vostro padre all'ospedale?* (When are you going to see your father at the hospital?)
2. *Ciao, Silvio, come vai?* (Hi Silvio, how are you?)
3. *Bambini, perché non state ziti?* (Children, why don't you be quiet?)
4. *Noi andiamo in treno a Pisa.* (We go by to train to Pisa.)
5. *Danno un film di Fellini.* (They're showing a film by Fellini.)
6. *Io sto per uscire.* (I am leaving.)
7. *Chi va a Bologna?* (Who is going to Bologna?)
8. *Lei va in aeroplano a Roma.* (She goes by plane to Rome.)
9. *Monica da una festa.* (Monica gives a party.)
10. *Noi stiamo per mangiare.* (We are eating.)

CHAPTER 9: SECOND- AND THIRD-CONJUGATION VERBS

1. *Il professore non risponde.* (The professor does not answer.)
2. *Noi beviamo un caffè.* (We drink a coffee.)
3. *Loro vedono un film.* (They see a film.)
4. *Io vendo la macchina.* (I sell the car.)
5. *Tu leggi i giornali.* (You read the papers.)
6. *Io prendo due aspirine.* (I take two aspirin.)
7. *Noi non crediamo la storia.* (We don't believe the story.)
8. *Voi correte ogni sera.* (You run every night.)
9. *Anna Maria perde sempre le chiavi!* (Anna Maria always loses the keys!)
10. *Roberta e Fabrizio scrivono volentieri delle lettere.* (Roberta and Fabrizio willingly write the letters.)

---

1. *Loro sentono il campanello.* (They hear the bell.)
2. *Il cuoco bolle le patate.* (The cook boils the potatoes.)
3. *Franco apre la scatola.* (Franco opens the box.)
4. *Io offro il caffè alle amiche.* (I offer coffee to the friends.)
5. *Voi scoprite la verità.* (You discover the truth.)
6. *Noi apriamo la finestra.* (We open the window.)
7. *Marcantonio veste bene.* (Marcantonio dresses well.)
8. *Tu sfuggi il pericolo.* (You escape the danger.)

9. *Voi partite oggi.* (You are leaving tomorrow.)
10. *Io servo le bevande.* (I serve the beverages.)

---

1. *I fratelli ubbidiscono ai genitori.* (The brothers obey their parents.)
2. *Loro puliscono la case.* (They clean the house.)
3. *Io preferisco rimanere qui.* (I prefer to remain here.)
4. *Noi capiamo la professoressa.* (We understand the professor.)
5. *Gianfranco riferisce il suo messaggio.* (Gianfranco is referring to his message.)
6. *Beatrice dimagrisce durante l'estate.* (Beatrice slims down during the summer.)
7. *I pronomi sostituiscono i nome.* (Pronouns substitute for nouns.)
8. *Noi capiamo tutto.* (We understand everything.)
9. *Tu finisci gli esami.* (You finish the exams.)
10. *Le studentesse capiscono la lezione.* (The students understand the lesson.)

---

1. *vero: veramente*
2. *certo: certamente*
3. *felice: felicemente*
4. *veloce: velocemente*
5. *triste: tristemente*
6. *leggero: leggermente*
7. *speciale: specialmente*
8. *preciso: precisamente*
9. *forte: fortemente*
10. *largo: largamente*

CHAPTER 10: NEGATIVE WORDS AND CONSTRUCTIONS

1. *Loro non mangiano troppo.* (They don't eat too much.)
2. *Non hanno visto Roberta ieri sera.* (They didn't see Roberta last night.)
3. *Non mi sono svegliato alle sette.* (I didn't wake up at seven o'clock.)
4. *Patrizia non vuole venire adesso.* (Patrizia doesn't want to come now.)
5. *Non voglio andare al cinema.* (I don't want to go to the cinema.)
6. *Non lo avete dimenticato.* (You didn't forget it.)
7. *I suoi amici non mi visitano.* (Their friends don't visit me.)
8. *Il facchino non porta i bagagli.* (The porter doesn't carry the baggage.)

9. *Non conosciamo quelle ragazze.* (We don't know those girls.)
10. *Non vado alle Alpi ogni inverno.* (I don't go to the Alps during the winter.)

1. *Non abbiamo chiamato affatto.* (We didn't call them at all.)
2. *Non è ancora arrivato.* (It hasn't arrived yet.)
3. *Voi non siete entrati neppure.* (You did not even enter.)
4. *Non avete mai visto quel film.* (You never saw that film.)
5. *Loro non hanno punto sciato.* (They haven't skied at all.)
6. *Non siete mai andati a nuotare.* (You never went swimming.)
7. *Non hai visto nessuno spettacolo.* (You didn't see any performance.)
8. *Non ho visto nessuno.* (I saw no one.)
9. *Non mi sono ancora svegliato.* (I had not woken up yet.)

1. *Neanche/nemmeno/neppure le mie cugine hanno molto denaro.* (None of my cousins have a lot of money.)
2. *Neanche/nemmeno/neppure Viviana lo sa e neanch'io/nemmeno io/neppure io lo so.* (Not even Viviana nor I know it.)
3. *Neanche/nemmeno/neppure Luisa viene.* (Not even Luisa will come.)
4. *Neanche/nemmeno/neppure noi lo abbiamo fatto.* (Neither would we have done it.)
5. *Neanche/nemmeno/neppure loro sono ricco.* (Neither of them are rich.)

CHAPTER 11: TENSE ABOUT TENSES? DON'T BE!

1. *Nino ha lavorato tutto il giorno.* (Nino worked all day.)
2. *Ieri mia madre ha cucinato un piatto tipico toscano.* (Yesterday my mother cooked a typical Tuscan dish.)
3. *Loro hanno demolito tutte le vecchie case.* (They demolished all the old houses.)
4. *Il professore ha spiegato molto chiaramente l'uso degli ausiliari.* (The professor explained very clearly the use of the auxiliaries.)
5. *Conosco bene Firenze perché ci ho abitato per dieci anni.* (I know Florence well because I lived there for ten years.)
6. *Qualcuno ha bussato alla porta.* (Someone knocked on the door.)
7. *Noi abbiamo comprato molte cose.* (We bought many things.)
8. *Loro hanno ballato tutta la notte.* (They danced all night.)
9. *Io ho avuto un terribile raffreddore.* (I had a terrible cold.)
10. *Noi abbiamo mangiato tutta la pizza!* (We ate all the pizza.)

1. *Le ragazze sono state a Modena.* (The girls were in Modena.)
2. *Luca è arrivato in ritardo.* (Luca arrived late.)
3. *L'opera è durata due ore.* (The opera lasted two hours.)
4. *Noi siamo andati in montagna.* (We went to the mountains.)
5. *Quei vini si sono piaciuti a tutti.* (Everyone liked these vines.)
6. *Le ragazze sono uscite alle undici.* (The girls left at eleven o'clock.)
7. *Paola è ritornata tarde.* (Paola returned late.)
8. *Loro sono restati a casa di Vincenzo.* (They remained at Vincenzo's house.)

CHAPTER 12: ASKING QUESTIONS IN ITALIAN

1. *Noi abbiamo paura?* (Are we frightened?)
2. *Francesca viene a casa, no?* (Francesca is coming home, right?)
3. *La squadra ha perso la partite, non è vero?* (The team lost the match, isn't it true?)
4. *Noi ci siamo alzati presto, no?* (We woke up early, no?)
5. *Gli studenti sono tornati?* (The students returned?)
6. *I ragazzi vanno a casa, no?* (The children are going home, right?)
7. *Voi vi sedete qui, non è vero?* (You are sitting here, isn't it true?)
8. *La mamma prepara la cena, è vero?* (Mama prepares dinner, right?)
9. *Il vino costa molto?* (The wine costs much?)
10. *Luigi ha tradotto quel libro?* (Luigi translated that book?)

1. *Che cosa preferisci: la birra o il vino?* (What do you prefer: beer or wine?)
2. *Quanti caffè bevi al giorno?* (How much coffee do you drink a day?)
3. *Come ti chiami?* (What is your name?)
4. *Quando è il tuo compleanno?* (When is your birthday?)
5. *Quanti anni hai?* (How old are you)
6. *Chi è l'autore dell'Orlando Furioso?* (Who is the author of *Orlando Furioso*?)
7. *Quanti temi hai scritto quest'anno?* (How many compositions did you write this year?)
8. *Quale è la capitale d'Italia?* (Which is the capital of Italy?)
9. *Perché non mi aiuti?* (Why don't you help me?)
10. *Quando è stato abbattuto il muro di Berlino?* (When was the Berlin Wall knocked down?)

1. *Ho due sorelle. Quante sorelle hai?* (I have two sisters. How many sisters do you have?)
2. *Perché non mi piacciono! Perché non mangi i pomodori?* (Because I don't like them. How come you aren't eating the tomatoes?)
3. *Sono alle tre. Che ore sono?* (It's three. What time is it?)
4. *Abbiamo una Fiat. Quale tipo di macchina avete?* (I have a Fiat. Which kind of car do you have?)
5. *È in Sicilia. Dov'è Palermo?* (It's in Sicily. Where is Palermo?)
6. *Non avete mangiato niente. Che cosa abbiamo mangiato?* (You didn't eat anything. What did we eat?)
7. *Parto domani. Quando parti?* (They leave tomorrow. When are you leaving?)
8. *Ne avete tre. Quanti fratelli abbiamo?* (You have three. How many brothers do we have?)
9. *Sono di Trieste. Di dov'è sei?* (They are from Trieste. Where are you from?)
10. *Vogliamo quelle! Quale scarpe volete?* (We would like those! Which shoes would you like?)

CHAPTER 13: MAKING SENSE OF THE LA-DI-DAS

1. *La lezione comincia alle dieci.* (The lesson starts at ten o'clock.)
2. *Scriviamo spesso agli zii.* (We often write to our uncles.)
3. *Vive a Bologna, ma lavora a Milano.* (He lives in Bologna, but he works in Milano.)
4. *Finalmente comincio a capire la grammatica italiana!* (Finally I am beginning to understand Italian grammar!)
5. *A che ora torni a casa? Alle sei?* (At what time are you returning home? At six o'clock?)
6. *Andiamo a Napoli ogni anno.* (We go to Naples every year.)
7. *Giovanna studia a Bologna ogni estate.* (Giovanna studies at Bologna every summer.)
8. *È nata a Palermo.* (She was born in Palermo.)

---

1. *Mi servono dieci dollari. Puoi prestarmeli?* (I need ten dollars. Can you lend it to me?)
2. *Ti piace quel ragazzo?* (Do you like that boy?)
3. *Mi occorrono le forbice.* (I need scissors.)
4. *Bastano dopo dieci pagine per un saggio.* (Ten pages is sufficient for an essay.)
5. *Quanti fogli vuoi? Me ne occorrono due.* (How many sheets do you want? I need two of them.)
6. *Ci serve il tuo aiuto.* (We need your help.)
7. *Ci dispiace molto che tu non sia potuto venire.* (We're very sorry that you cannot come.)

8. *Ai Rossi manca molto la figlia.* (The Rossis miss their daughter very much.)
9. *Non mi piace il pesce.* (I don't like fish.)
10. *Mi mancana molto i miei genitori.* (I miss my parents very much.)

CHAPTER 14: I COMMAND YOU!

1. *Mangiate la minestra!* (Eat the soup!)
2. *Telefona a Gino!* (Telephone Gino!)
3. *Dì questo a tuo padre!* (Give this to your father!)
4. *Fate questo favore!* (Do this favor!)
5. *Guarda allo specchio!* (Look into the mirror!)
6. *Esci subito!* (Leave immediately!)
7. *Girate a destra!* (Turn right!)
8. *Bevete il latte!* (Drink the milk!)
9. *Sbrigati, è tardi!* (Hurry, it's late!)
10. *Spegnete la radio!* (Turn off the radio!)

---

1. *Fabio, non mangiare addesso; ceneremo presto!* (Fabio, don't eat now, we're going to eat soon!)
2. *Pierino, non dire parolacce!* (Pierino, don't say curse words!)
3. *Mamma, non preparare la cena per me: sono invitata a cena fuori.* (Mama, don't prepare supper for me: I was invited to eat out.)
4. *Aspettate ragazzi; non siate sempre così impazienti!* (Wait, children; don't always be so impatient!)
5. *Bambini, non scrivete sulle pareti!* (Kids, don't write on the walls!)
6. *Roberta, non essere così cattiva con la sorellina!* (Roberta, don't be so bad with your little sister!)
7. *Monica, non toccare la pentola; è piena di acqua calda!* (Monica, don't touch the pot, it's filled with hot water.)
8. *Davide, non parlare con la bocca piena!* (David, don't speak with a full mouth!)
9. *Ragazzi, non giocate a pallone in questa strada; è pericoloso!* (Children, don't play ball in this street; it's dangerous!)
10. *Gianna, non essere così pessimista! La vita è troppo bella!* (Gianna, don't be such a pessimist! Life is too beautiful!)

CHAPTER 15: PASTA, PRONOUNS, AND PORCINI

1. *Io e tu: noi*
2. *Marco: lui*
3. *Giorgio e Maria: loro*
4. *Tu e lei: voi*

5. *Gli studenti: loro*
6. *Cinzia: lei*

---

1. *Professore, per favore, vorrei parlarLe.* (Professor, please, I would like to speak to you.)
2. *Tuo figlio ti assomiglia molto: è il tuo ritratto.* (Your son resembles you a lot: he's a portrait of you.)
3. *Io sono affezionatissima a mia nonna: le voglio molto bene.* (I am very fond of my grandmother: I love her very much.)
4. *Massimo guardava la ragazza e le sorrideva.* (Massimo watched the girl and smiled at her.)
5. *È maleducato: quando gli parlo, lui non mi risponde mai.* (He's rude: when I speak to him, he never answers me.)
6. *Devi imparare a non toccare le cose che non ti appartengono.* (You must learn not to touch the things that don't belong to you.)

---

1. *Riportiamo il libro a lei. Glielo riportiamo.* (We bring the books back to her. We bring them back to her.)
2. *Restituisci il quaderno a lui. Glielo restituisci.* (You return the notebook to him. You return it to him.)
3. *Presto la macchina a Paolo. Gliela presto.* (I lend the car to Paolo. I lend it to him.)
4. *Mandate i regali ai bambini. Li mandate loro.* (You give the gifts to the children. You give them to them.)
5. *Mi zio porta i documenti ai signori. Mi zio li porta loro.* (My uncle carries the documents to the men. My uncle brings them to them.)
6. *Date la palla alle ragazze. La date loro.* (You give the ball to the girls. You give it to them.)
7. *Do il libro agli studenti. Lo do loro.* (I give the book to the students. I give it to them.)
8. *Inviano i pacchi a lui. Glieli inviano.* (They send the packages to him. They send them to him.)
9. *Prestiamo le fotografie a Luisa. Gliele prestiamo.* (We lend the photos to Luisa. We lend them to her.)
10. *Do la penna a Martina. Gliela do.* (I give the pen to Martina. I give it to her.)

CHAPTER 16: YOUR BODY AND YOUR SELF

1. *Il signor Rossi si laurea in medicina.* (Mr. Rossi is graduating in medicine.)
2. *Massimo si siede vicino alla porta.* (Massimo sits near the door.)
3. *Io mi chiamo Anna Grazia.* (My name is Anna Grazia.)

4. *Mia madre non lavora: si dedica interamente alla famiglia.* (My mother doesn't work: she devotes herself entirely to the family.)
5. *Perché tu non ti prendi una vacanza?* (Why don't you take a vacation?)
6. *Giorgio si guadagna la vita lavorando in un bar.* (Giorgio earns his living working in a bar.)
7. *Cinzia si compra una gonna per la festa.* (Cinzia buys a skirt for the party.)
8. *Il ghiaccio, col calore, si scioglie.* (Ice, with heat, melts.)
9. *Il cristallo è fragile: si rompe facilmente.* (Crystal is fragile: it breaks easily.)
10. *Io e mio fratello ci scriviamo una lettera alla settimana.* (My brother and I write a letter to each other every week.)

---

1. *I miei parenti si visitano spesso.* (My relatives visit often.)
2. *Ci conosciamo molto bene, noi due!* (We know each other well, us two.)
3. *Purtroppo Giuseppe e Lidia non si capiscono più.* (Unfortunately Giuseppe and Lidia no longer understand each other.)
4. *Voi vi vedete tutti i giorni?* (Would you like to see each other every day?)
5. *Gli spagnoli e i portoghese, quando parlano si capiscono fra loro.* (The Spanish and the Portuguese, when they speak, understand each other.)
6. *A questo incrocio si scontrano sempre tante macchini.* (At this intersection there are always many cars crashing into each other.)
7. *Alberto e Caterina si amano sul serio: vogliono sposarsi.* (Alberto and Caterina love each other seriously: they want to marry each other.)
8. *Anna e Angela si incontrano al museo.* (Anna and Angela meet each other at the museum.)
9. *Voi vi salutate ogni giorno.* (You greet each other every day.)
10. *I signori si rispettano molto.* (The men respect each other a lot.)

CHAPTER 17: MORE FUN WITH VERBS

1. *Come, tu non puoi nemmeno assaggiarlo?* (Why, you don't even want to taste it?)
2. *Ragazzi, questa sera volete andare a mangiare una pizza?* (Children, this evening would you like to go eat a pizza?)
3. *Tu pui accompagnarmi dal parrucchiere oggi alle due?* (Can you accompany me to the hairdresser today at two o'clock?)
4. *In casa nostra, noi figli sia maschi che femmine,*

dobbiamo aiutare nostra madre. (In our house, we males as well as females, we must help our mother.)

5. *Hanno bisogno di una seconda macchina, ma non possono permettersela.* (They need a second car, but they cannot afford it.)

6. *Vi accompagno io. A che ora dovete essere all'aeroporto?* (I'll accompany you. What time do you need to be at the airport?)

7. *L'aereo parte alle sette, ma i passeggeri devono presentarsi un'ora prima.* (The plane leaves at seven o'clock, but the passengers must show up one hour before.)

8. *Perché tu non vuoi venire alla festa?* (How come you don't want to come to the party?)

1. *Oggi vado a fare una gita in campagna.* (Today I'm taking a trip in the countryside.)

2. *La tua casa è molto lontana, prima ho preso l'autobus e poi ho fatto un pezzo di strada a piedi.* (Your house is very far from here, first I took the bus and then I walked.)

3. *Per mantenersi in forma e in buona salute è bene fare dello sport.* (To stay in shape and in good health it's good to practice sports.)

4. *C'è molta gente allo sportello dei biglietti, devi fare la coda per una mezz'oretta.* (There are many people at the ticket window; you must wait in line for a half hour.)

5. *Ogni mattina, prima di uscire, io faccio colazione con la mia famiglia.* (Every morning, before leaving, I have breakfast with my family.)

6. *Prendo il treno dell 12,40 per Milano e devo ancora fare la valigia.* (I am taking the 12:40 train for Milano and I still have to pack my suitcase.)

7. *Oggi vado in centro a fare le spese, devo comprare diverse cose.* (Today I am going into the center of town to go shopping, I must buy many things.)

8. *Maria va al mercato ogni mattina e fa la spesa, dopo torna a casa e fa da mangiare per tutta la famiglia.* (Maria goes to the market every day and does the food shopping, then she returns home and prepares a meal for the whole family.)

9. *Il serbatoio della macchina è vuoto, se voglio partire devo fare il pieno al distributore.* (The gas tank of the car is empty, if I want to leave I must fill it up at the service station.)

10. *Ho comprato un dolce, posso fare a metà con te se lo vuoi.* (I bought a pastry, I can split it with you if you want it.)

11. *Oggi tu fai una visita al tuo amico che è ammalato.* (Today you are paying a visit to your friend who is sick.)

CHAPTER 18: BACK TO THE FUTURE

1. *Quanto tempo tu resterai in Italia?* (How long are you going to stay in Italy?)

2. *Noi parteciperemo al nuovo concorso.* (We will participate in the new contest.)

3. *I genitori arriveranno il mese prossimo.* (The parents will arrive next month.)

4. *Io mi alzerò tardi domani.* (I will wake up late tomorrow.)

5. *Daniele noleggerà una macchina.* (Daniele will rent a car.)

6. *Sabato voi arriverete.* (Saturday you will arrive.)

7. *Tu e Luca parlerete di calcio.* (Luca and you will talk about soccer.)

8. *Gli studenti impareranno la matematica.* (The students will learn math.)

9. *Noi prenoteremo la settimana prossima.* (We will reserve next week.)

10. *Loro viaggeranno in autobus.* (They will travel by bus.)

1. *Noi partiremo per l'Italia il mese prossimo.* (We will leave for Italy next month.)

2. *Gli studenti leggeranno molti libri.* (The students will read many books.)

3. *Tu e Carlo ripeterete la lezione.* (Carlo and you will repeat the lesson.)

4. *Il negoziante venderà tutta la merce.* (The shopkeeper will sell all the merchandise.)

5. *Noi capiremo le nuove regole.* (We will understand the new regulations.)

6. *Gli atleti correranno per un'ora.* (The athletes will run for one hour.)

7. *Il bambino sentirà la mancanza dei genitori.* (The child will miss his parents.)

8. *La professoressa correggerà i compiti domani.* (The professor will correct the homework tomorrow.)

9. *Tu finirai i compiti domani mattina.* (You will finish the homework tomorrow morning.)

10. *Questa fine settimana noi andremo in campagna.* (This weekend we are going to the country.)

CHAPTER 20: A SUBJECTIVE POINT OF VIEW

1. *Voglio che voi dormiate.* (I hope that you are sleeping.)
2. *Hai paura che io abbia ragione.* (You are worried that I am right.)
3. *Perché ordini che loro salgano?* (How come you asked that they leave?)
4. *Ordiniamo che tu vada in biblioteca.* (We're asking that you go to the library.)
5. *Mi dispiace che voi siate triste.* (I'm sorry that you are sad.)
6. *Tu insiste che io parta domani.* (You insist that I leave tomorrow.)
7. *Speriamo che voi restiate qui.* (We hope that you stay here.)
8. *È possibile che lui lo legga.* (It is possible that he is reading it.)
9. *È difficile che voi lo incontriate.* (It is difficult for you to meet him.)
10. *Credo che loro arrivino presto.* (I think that they are arriving immediately.)

---

1. *I genitori volevano che i figli facessero i compiti.* (The parents wanted their children to do their homework.)
2. *Lui ordinò che loro finissero immediatamente.* (He wanted them to finish immediately.)
3. *Era necessario che Carlo lo dicesse.* (It was necessary that Carlo say it.)
4. *Hanno insistito che tu lo scrivessi.* (They insisted that you write it.)
5. *Vorrei che voi faceste i buoni.* (I hope that you are good.)
6. *Io preferirei che voi lo spiegaste.* (I would prefer that you explain it.)
7. *Desideravano che noi fossimo a casa.* (They wished that we were at home.)
8. *Volevo che Giancarlo dicesse la verità.* (I wished that Giancarlo spoke the truth.)
9. *Suggerirei che tu partissi.* (I suggest that you leave.)
10. *Tu vorresti che io ti dessi il mio orologio.* (You would like me to give you my watch.)

CHAPTER 21: ITALY BY PLANE, TRAIN, AND AUTOMOBILE

1. *Io preferirei mangiare la pizza.* (I would prefer to eat pizza.)
2. *Che cosa Le piacerebbe fare?* (What would you like to do?)
3. *Noi dovremmo cercare subito un parcheggio.* (We would like to find a parking lot immediately.)
4. *Lui vorrebbe noleggiare una macchina.* (He would like to rent a car.)

5. *Potresti darmi l'orario dei treni?* (Can you tell me the timetable for the trains?)
6. *Le ragazze canterebbero, ma non ricordano le parole.* (The girls would sing, but they don't remember the words.)
7. *Teresa parlerebbe tedesco, ma non ricorda i verbi.* (Teresa would speak German, but she doesn't remember the verbs.)
8. *Tu fingeresti di non capire, ma sei impulsivo.* (You might pretend to not understand, but you are impulsive.)
9. *Gli studenti frequenterebbero i corsi, ma non è obbligatorio.* (The students would attend the courses, but it is not mandatory.)
10. *Voi scoprireste il segreto, ma non sapete come.* (You could have discovered the secret, but you don't know how.)

---

1. *Ieri sera io sarei tornato volentieri alla festa, ma ho dovuto studiare.* (Yesterday evening I would have gladly returned to the party, but I had to study.)
2. *Hanno scritto che sarebbero arrivati a teatro prima delle otto.* (They wrote that they would have arrived at the theater before eight o'clock.)
3. *Io non gli sarei chiesto quelle informazioni ma mi hanno forzato.* (I would not have asked them for that information, but they forced me.)
4. *Noi avremmo preferito vedere un film senza sottotitoli.* (We would have preferred to see a film without subtitles.)
5. *Ha detto che avrebbe comprato i biglietti per tutti.* (He said that he would have bought tickets for everyone.)
6. *Loro sarebbero usciti ma cominciò a piovere.* (They would have left but it started to rain.)
7. *Io sarei venuto ma non avevo la macchina.* (I would have come but I didn't have a car.)
8. *Mario sarebbe stato a casa presto, ma è partito.* (Mario would have been home soon, but he's gone.)
9. *Voi avreste potuto telefonare prima di partire.* (You could have telephoned before leaving.)
10. *Loro avranno cenato prima di partire.* (They should have eaten first before leaving.)

A GAME OF SURVIVAL; PAGE 26

NO, NEVER, NO WAY!; PAGE 104

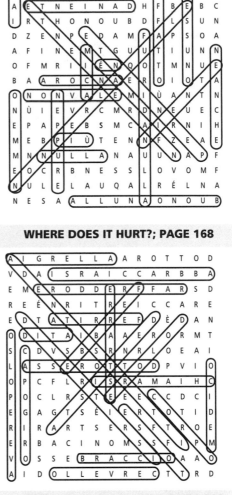

THE FIVE W'S; PAGE 124

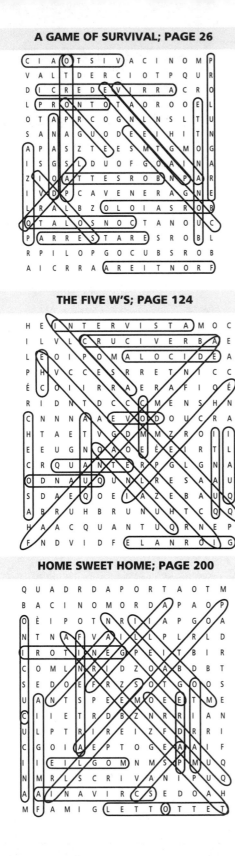

WHERE DOES IT HURT?; PAGE 168

HOME SWEET HOME; PAGE 200

SHOPPING, ITALIAN STYLE; PAGE 208

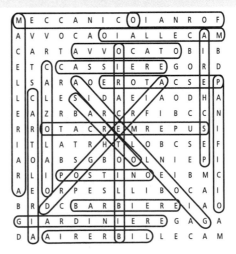

Italian Verb Reference Guide

Essere (to be)

PRESENTE		PASSATO PROSSIMO	
SINGULAR	PLURAL	SINGULAR	PLURAL
sono	siamo	sono stato(a)	siamo stati(e)
sei	siete	sei stato(a)	siete stati(e)
è	sono	è stato(a)	sono stati(e)

IMPERFETTO		TRAPASSATO PROSSIMO	
SINGULAR	PLURAL	SINGULAR	PLURAL
ero	eravamo	ero stato(a)	eravamo stati(e)
eri	eravate	eri stato(a)	eravate stati(e)
era	erano	era stato(a)	erano stati(e)

PASSATO REMOTO		TRAPASSATO REMOTO	
SINGULAR	PLURAL	SINGULAR	PLURAL
fui	fummo	fui stato(a)	fummo stati(e)
fosti	foste	fosti stato(a)	foste stati(e)
fu	furono	fu stato(a)	furono stati(e)

FUTURO SEMPLICE		FUTURO ANTERIORE	
SINGULAR	PLURAL	SINGULAR	PLURAL
sarò	saremo	sarò stato(a)	saremo stati(e)
sarai	sarete	sarai stato(a)	sarete stati(e)
sarà	saranno	sarà stato(a)	saranno stati(e)

CONDIZIONALE PRESENTE		CONDIZIONALE PASSATO	
SINGULAR	PLURAL	SINGULAR	PLURAL
sarei	saremmo	sarei stato(a)	saremmo stati(e)
saresti	sareste	saresti stato(a)	sareste stati(e)
sarebbe	sarebbero	sarebbe stato(a)	sarebbero stati(e)

CONGIUNTIVE PRESENTE		CONGIUNTIVE PASSATO	
SINGULAR	PLURAL	SINGULAR	PLURAL
sia	siamo	sia stato(a)	siamo stati(e)
sia	siate	sia stato(a)	siate stati(e)
sia	siano	sia stato(a)	siano stati(e)

CONGIUNTIVE INPERFETTO		CONGIUNTIVE TRAPASSATO	
SINGULAR	PLURAL	SINGULAR	PLURAL
fossi	fossimo	fossi stato(a)	fossimo stati(e)
fossi	foste	fossi stato(a)	foste stati(e)
fosse	fossero	fosse stato(a)	fossero stati(e)

IMPERATIVO	
SINGULAR	PLURAL
–	siamo
sii	siate
sia	siano

Avere (to have)

PRESENTE		PASSATO PROSSIMO	
SINGULAR	PLURAL	SINGULAR	PLURAL
ho	abbiamo	ho avuto	abbiamo avuto
hai	avete	hai avuto	avete avuto
ha	hanno	ha avuto	hanno avuto

IMPERFETTO		TRAPASSATO PROSSIMO	
SINGULAR	PLURAL	SINGULAR	PLURAL
avevo	avevamo	avevo avuto	avevamo avuto
avevi	avevate	avevi avuto	avevate avuto
aveva	avevano	aveva avuto	avevano avuto

PASSATO REMOTO

SINGULAR	PLURAL
ebbi	avemmo
avesti	aveste
ebbe	ebbero

TRAPASSATO REMOTO

SINGULAR	PLURAL
ebbi avuto	avemmo avuto
avesti avuto	aveste avuto
ebbe avuto	ebbero avuto

FUTURO SEMPLICE

SINGULAR	PLURAL
avrò	avremo
avrai	avrete
avrà	avranno

FUTURO ANTERIORE

SINGULAR	PLURAL
avrò avuto	avremo avuto
avrai avuto	avrete avuto
avrà avuto	avranno avuto

CONDIZIONALE PRESENTE

SINGULAR	PLURAL
avrei	avremmo
avresti	avreste
avrebbe	avrebbero

CONDIZIONALE PASSATO

SINGULAR	PLURAL
avrei avuto	avremmo avuto
avresti avuto	avreste avuto
avrebbe avuto	avrebbero avuto

CONGIUNTIVO PRESENTE

SINGULAR	PLURAL
abbia	abbiamo
abbia	abbiate
abbia	abbiano

CONGIUNTIVO PASSATO

SINGULAR	PLURAL
abbia avuto	abbiamo avuto
abbia avuto	abbiate avuto
abbia avuto	abbiano avuto

CONGIUNTIVO IMPERFETTO

SINGULAR	PLURAL
avessi	avessimo
avessi	aveste
avesse	avesser

CONGIUNTIVO TRAPASSATO

SINGULAR	PLURAL
avessi avuto	avessimo avuto
avessi avuto	aveste avuto
avesse avuto	avessero avuto

IMPERATIVO

SINGULAR	PLURAL
–	abbiamo

abbi	abbiate
abbia	abbiano

Regular Verb Endings

PRESENTE			
PERSON	**−ARE**	**−ERE**	**−IRE**
io	−o	−o	−o/−isco
tu	−i	−i	−i/−isci
lui, lei, Lei	−a	−e	−e/−isce
oi	−iamo	−iamo	−iamo
voi	−ate	−ete	−ite
loro, Loro	−ano	−ono	−ono/−iscono

IMPERFETTO			
PERSON	**−ARE**	**−ERE**	**−IRE**
io	−avo	−evo	−ivo
tu	−avi	−evi	−ivi
lui, lei, Lei	−ava	−eva	−iva
noi	−avamo	−evamo	−ivamo
voi	−avate	−evate	−ivate
loro, Loro	−avano	−evano	−ivono

PASSATO REMOTO			
PERSON	**−ARE**	**−ERE**	**−IRE**
io	−ai	−ei/−etti	−ii
tu	−asti	−esti	−isti
lui, lei, Lei	−ò	−é/−ette	−ì
noi	−ammo	−emmo	−immo
voi	−aste	−este	−iste
loro, Loro	−arono	−erono/−ettero	−irono

FUTURO SEMPLICE

PERSON	–ARE	–ERE	–IRE
io	–erò	–erò	–irò
tu	–erai	–erai	–irai
lui, lei, Lei	–erà	–erà	–irà
noi	–eremo	–eremo	–iremo
voi	–erete	–erete	–irete
loro, Loro	–eranno	–eranno	–irranno

CONGIUNTIVO PRESENTE

PERSON	–ARE	–ERE	–IRE
io	–i	–a	–a/–isca
tu	–i	–a	–a/–isca
lui, lei, Lei	–i	–a	–a/–isca
noi	–iamo	–iamo	–iamo
voi	–iate	–iate	–iate
loro, Loro	–ino	–ano	–ano/–iscano

CONGIUNTIVO IMPERFETTO

PERSON	–ARE	–ERE	–IRE
io	–assi	–essi	–issi
tu	–assi	–essi	–issi
lui, lei, Lei	–asse	–esse	–isse
noi	–assimo	–essimo	–issimo
voi	–aste	–este	–iste
loro, Loro	–assero	–essero	–issero

CONDIZIONALE PRESENTE

PERSON	–ARE	–ERE	–IRE
io	–erei	–erei	–irei
tu	–eresti	–eresti	–iresti
lui, lei, Lei	–erebbe	–erebbe	–irebbe

noi	–eremmo	–eremmo	–iremmo
voi	–ereste	–ereste	–ireste
loro, Loro	–erebbero	–erebbero	–irebbero

IMPERATIVO

PERSON	–ARE	–ERE	–IRE
io	–	–	–
tu	–a	–i	–i/–isci
lui, lei, Lei	–i	–a	–a/–isca
noi	–iamo	–iamo	–iamo
voi	–ate	–ete	–ite
loro, Loro	–ino	–ano	–ano/–iscono

VERBS THAT FUNCTION BOTH TRANSITIVELY AND INTRANSITIVELY

affogare	affondare	annegare
arricchire	aumentare	bruciare
cessare	cominiciare	congelare
continuare	cuocere	dimagrire
dimezzare	diminuire	finire
guarire	incominciare	ingrassare
iniziare	invecchiare	maturare
migliorare	mutare	peggiorare
raddopppiare	ricominciare	rimbecillire
ringiovanire	rinsavire	soffocare
terminare		

PARTICIPIO PASSATO

	–ARE	–ERE	–IRE
singular	-ato, –ata	-uto, –uta	-ito, ita
plural	-ati, –ate	-uti, –ute	-iti, –ite

VERBS WITH IRREGULAR PAST PARTICIPLES

INFINITIVE	PAST PARTICIPLE	INFINITIVE	PAST PARTICIPLE
accludere	accluso	aprire	aperto
assumere	assunto	cadere	caduto
chiedere	chiesto	chiudere	chiuso
convincere	convinto	correre	corso
cuocere	cotto	decidere	deciso
dipendere	dipeso	dipingere	dipinto
dire	detto	discutere	discusso
distinguere	distinto	dividere	diviso
esprimere	espresso	fare	fatto
leggere	letto	mettere	messo
morire	morto	muovere	mosso
nascere	nato	offendere	offeso
offendere	offeso	offrire	offerto
parere	parso	piacere	piaciuto
piangere	pianto	prendere	preso
rendere	reso	ridere	riso
rimanere	rimasto	rispondere	risposto
rompere	rotto	scegliere	scelto
scendere	sceso	scoprire	scoperto
succedere	successo	tradurre	tradotto
uccidere	ucciso	vedere	visto or veduto
venire	venuto	vincere	visto
vivere	vissuto		

APPENDIX C

Italian-to-English Glossary

abate: abbot
abbacchiato: downhearted
abbacchio: spring lamb
abbecedario: primer
abilmente: skillfully, cleverly
abruzzese: inhabitant of Abruzzi
accappatoio: bathrobe
accetta: hatchet
accompagnare: to accompany
acero: maple
aceto: vinegar
acqua: water
Acquario: Aquarius
adagio: slowly
addome: abdomen
adesso: now
aeroporto: airport
affardellare: to bundle together, to pack
affinché: so that; in order that
affittacamere: landlord
affittare: to rent
agganciare: to fasten, to attach
aglio: garlic
agnello: lamb
agosto: August
ahimè: alas
ala: wing
alba: dawn
albicocca: apricot
alice: anchovy
aliscafo: hydrofoil
alleanza: alliance
allegria: happiness
allegro: happy
allenare: to train
alluce: big toe
alluvione: flood
almeno: at least
altana: covered roof terrace
altura: hill
ambra: amber
ambulanza: ambulance
ametista: amethyst
ammattire: to go mad
ammiccare: to wink
ammobiliare: to furnish
amore: love
amuleto: amulet
anatra: duck
anche: also
ancora: still, again, yet
andare: to go
anello: ring
angolo: corner

anguilla: eel
anguria: watermelon
annacquare: to water down
anno: year
annullare: to annul
anta: shutter
antartico: Antarctic
antefatto: prior event
anteporre: to put before
anteprima: preview
anticipo: down payment
antilope: antelope
antipasti: appetizers
anziché: rather than
ape: bee
appartamento: apartment
appartenere: to belong
appendere: to hang
applaudire: to applaud
approvare: to approve, to accept
appunto: exactly
apribottiglia: bottle opener
aprile: April
aprire: to open
apriscatole: can opener
arachide: peanut
aragosta: lobster
arancia: orange
arazzo: tapestry
arbitro: referee
arcaico: archaic
arcangelo: archangel
arcobaleno: rainbow
argento: silver
aria: air
Ariete: Aries
aritmetica: arithmetic
armadio: closet
armonica: harmonica
arpa: harp
arrivare: to arrive
arrostire: to roast
arzillo: sprightly
ascella: armpit
ascensore: elevator
asciugarsi: to dry oneself
ascoltare: to listen to
asparago: asparagus
aspirapolvere: vacuum cleaner
assegno: check
assentarsi: to absent oneself
asso: ace
assoldare: to recruit
attendibile: reliable

attenersi: to attend to
atterrare: to land
attirare: to attract
atto: act
attore: actor
aula: classroom
autoritratto: self-portrait
autostrada: highway
autunno: autumn
avocado: avocado
avorio: ivory
avvelenare: to poison
azalea: azalea
azzurro: blue
babbeo: foolish, stupid
babbo: father, dad(dy)
baciare: to kiss
bacio: kiss
baco: worm
badia: abbey
baffi: mustache
bagno: bathroom, bath
bagordare: to carouse, to revel
baia: bay
baita: Alpine hut
balena: whale
balestra: crossbow
balocco: toy
bambino: child
bambola: doll
banale: banal, trite, commonplace
banca: bank
banchiere: banker
banco: counter
barba: beard
barbiere: barber
barca: boat
barrire: to trumpet
basette: sideburns
basilico: basil
basso: bass
battere: to beat, to hit, to strike
batteria: battery
Belgio: Belgium
bellicoso: belligerent
belva: wild beast
benché: although
beneducato: well-mannered
beneficenza: charity
berretto: cap
bestia: beast
betulla: birch
bevanda: drink
bianco: white

Bibbia: Bible
bibita: drink, beverage
biblioteca: library
bighellonare: to loaf
biglietto: ticket
Bilancia: Libra
bilancia: scale
binario: track, platform
biondo: blonde
birichino: naughty
birra: beer
bis: encore
biscia: grass snake
biscotto: cookie, biscuit
bistecca: steak
blandire: to soften
blatta: cockroach
bloccare: to block, to cut off
bocca: mouth
boccheggiare: to gasp
boiata: rubbish
boicottare: to boycott
bollettino: bulletin
bollire: to boil
bollo: stamp
bombetta: bowler hat
borotalco: talcum powder
borraccia: flask
borsa di studio: scholarship
bosco: woods, forest
botte: barrel
bottega: shop
bottiglia: bottle
bottone: button
bozzolo: cocoon
braccare: to hunt
braccio: arm
bramare: to desire, to yearn for
Brasile: Brazil
bricco: jug
briccola: catapult
brogliare: to intrigue
bruco: caterpillar
bruno: brown
brutto: ugly
bucaneve: snowdrop
budino: pudding
bufalo: buffalo
buio: dark; gloomy; somber
buongustaio: gourmet
buonumore: good temper
burattino: puppet
burro: butter
busta: envelope

bustarella: bribe
cabina di pilotaggio: cockpit
cabinovia: cableway
cacciavite: screwdriver
cacciucco: fish soup, chowder
cadere: to fall
cagionevole: delicate
caiaco: kayak
calabrese: inhabitant of Calabria
calamaro: squid
calca: throng, crowd
calcagno: heel
calciare: to kick
calcio: soccer
caldo: heat
caldura: summer heat
calendario: calendar
calmo: calm
calzini: socks
camera da letto: bedroom
cameriere: waiter
camicetta: blouse
caminetto: fireplace
cammeo: cameo
camminare: to walk
campagna: countryside
campana: bell
campano: inhabitant of Campania
canale: channel
cancello: gate
Cancro: Cancer
cane: dog
canella: cinnamon
canterano: chest of drawers
cantico: hymn
cantina: cellar
caotico: chaotic
capellini: angel hair pasta
capitare: to happen
capobanda: ringleader,
   bandmaster
Capodanno: New Year's Day
capolavoro: masterpiece
cappella: chapel, shrine
cappello: hat
cappotto: coat
capra: goat
Capricorno: Capricorn
carcere: jail, prison
caro: expensive
carota: carrot
carta: paper
carta di credito: credit card
cartolina: postcard

cascata: waterfall
cassetta postale: mailbox
cassetto: drawer
cassiere: cashier
castagna: chestnut
castigare: to punish
cavallo: horse
cavatappi: corkscrew
caverna: cave
cavolo: cabbage
celare: to hide, to conceal
celiare: to joke, to jest
cembalo: cymbal
cena: supper
centogrado: centigrade
centralino: switchboard
ceralacca: sealing-wax
cercare: to look for
cervo: deer
checchè: whatever
cherubino: cherub
chiacchiere: to chat
chiaro: clear
chiave: key
chiesa: church
chilogrammo: kilogram
chimica: chemistry
chioccio: harsh, hoarse
chirurgo: surgeon
chitarra: guitar
cigno: swan
Cina: China
cinghiale: wild boar
cinta: belt
cipolla: onion
circo: circus
cittadino: citizen
clarinetto: clarinet
classe: classroom
clima: climate
cognata: sister-in-law
cognato: brother-in-law
colapasta: colander
colare: to strain
colino: strainer
colla: glue
colle: hill
colma: high water
coltello: knife
compenetrare: to penetrate
compitare: to spell out
compleanno: birthday
conato: attempt, effort
concludere: to conclude

conferenza: lecture
confino: political exile
coniglio: rabbit
conte: count
conto: bill, account
contrarre: to contract
controllare: to check
corda: cord, rope
coriandolo: coriander
cornetto: cornet
corridoio: aisle
corsia: lane
corvo: raven
coscia: thigh
cosiddetto: so-called
costoso: costly
costume da bagno: bathing suit
cotone: cotton
covo: den
cozza: mussel
cranio: skull
cravatta: tie
creanza: politeness
crema: cream
crepitare: to crackle
crepuscolo: twilight
creta: clay
cricca: gang
cricco: carjack
crocicchio: crossroads
crocifiggere: to crucify
crogiolarsi: to bask
cronico: chronic
crostaceo: shellfish
cruciverba: crossword puzzle
cruscotto: dashboard
cucchiaino: teaspoon
cucchiaio: soup spoon
cucinare: to cook
cucire: to sew
cugina: cousin (female)
cugino: cousin (male)
cuoio: leather
curare: to cure
dabbasso: downstairs
dabbene: honest
daccapo: (once) again
dacché: since
damigella: bridesmaid
Danimarca: Denmark
danneggiare: to harm
danno: danger, harm
dappertutto: everywhere
dappoco: worthless

darno: dart
dattero: date
davanti: in front
davanzale: window sill
davanzo: more than enough
davvero: really, truly, indeed
dea: goddess
debellare: to defeat
debilitare: to weaken
debole: weak
debosciato: debauched
decano: dean
decantare: to praise
decapare: to pickle
decenne: decade
decifrare: to decipher
decollare: to take off
decollo: take off
decrepito: decrepit
decreto: decree, order, ruling
dedalo: maze
deflazione: deflation
deliberare: to deliberate, to discuss
demagnetizzare: to demagnetize
democratico: democratic
demordere: to give in
denaro: money
dentrificio: toothpaste
dentro: inside
depositare: to deposit
deprecare: to deprecate
depurare: to purify
derubare: to rob
deserto: desert
destino: destiny
destra: right
deviazione: detour
diabolica: diabolical
diario: diary, journal
dibattito: debate, discussion
dicembre: December
dieta: diet
dietro: in the back
difetto: defect
dilungare: to lengthen
dimettere: to dismiss
dimorare: to reside
dinosauro: dinosaur
dio: god
dipingere: to paint
direttiva: directive
dirittura: straight line
disalberare: to dismast
discordia: discord

disimballare: to unpack
dislessia: dyslexia
dispensa: pantry
distruggere: to destroy
ditale: thimble
ditto: finger
divano: sofa, couch
divincolarsi: to wiggle
dizionario: dictionary
dogana: customs
doganiere: customs agent
domani: tomorrow
domenica: Sunday
donna: woman
dono: gift
dopodomani: day after tomorrow
dormire: to sleep
dovunque: everywhere, anywhere
dozzina: dozen
drago: dragon
dritta: right hand
duca: duke
duchessa: duchess
duna: dune
dunque: therefore; well (then)
duomo: cathedral
durante: during, throughout
durone: hardened skin
e, ed (before vowels): and
ebano: ebony
ebbene: well (then)
ebreo: Hebrew, Jewish
eccellere: to excel
eccetto: except
eccezionale: exceptional
eclissi: eclipse
eco: echo
ecologia: ecology
economico: inexpensive
edicola: newsstand, bookstall
effigiare: to portray, to represent
Egitto: Egypt
elaborare: to elaborate, to draw up
elargire: to lavish
elefante: elephant
elementari: primary school
elenco: list, directory
elettrificare: to electrify
elezione: election
elica: propeller
elicottero: helicopter
eliminare: to eliminate
eliporto: heliport
elmetto: helmet

eludere: to elude, to escape
emaciato: emaciated
emergenza: emergency
emiliano-romagnolo: inhabitant of Emilia-Romagna
emisfero: hemisphere
emoteca: blood bank
emotivo: emotional
empire: to fill (up)
encomiare: to commend
endovenoso: intravenous
enorme: enormous, huge
enoteca: wine bar
entrambi: both
entrante: coming, next
entrare: to fit, to enter
epidemia: epidemic
Epifania: Epiphany (Jan. 6)
epoca: epoch, age, era, time
equatore: equator
equino: horse
erba: grass, herb
ergere: to raise, to lift up
erodere: to erode
eroe: hero
esatto: exact
esercito: army
esiguo: meager
esimio: outstanding, distinguished
esito: result
esodo: exodus
esotico: exotic
espatriare: to leave one's country
esplicare: to carry on
esplicito: explicit
est: east
estate: summer
estero: foreign
estraneo: outside, extraneous
estuario: estuary
etichetta: tag, label
etrusco: Etruscan
ettaro: hectare
eucalipto: eucalyptus
Europa: Europe
evadere: to escape, to run away
evanescente: vanishing
evasivo: evasive
evento: event
evitare: to avoid
evocare: to evoke
fa: ago
fabbrica: factory
fabbro: blacksmith

faccenda: thing, matter
facciata: façade
faceto: facetious, jesting
facinoroso: violent
facoltoso: wealthy, moneyed
fagiano: pheasant
fagiolo: bean
fagotto: bassoon
falce: scythe
falco: hawk
falcone: falcon
falegname: carpenter
falla: leak
fallace: deceptive
fallire: to fail, to be unsuccessful
falò: bonfire
fama: report, fame, rumor
fame: hunger
famiglia: family
famoso: famous; well-known
fanale: light, lamp
fango: mud, mire
fantascienza: science fiction
fantasma: ghost, phantom
fante: infantryman, foot soldier
fantino: jockey
fantoccio: puppet, marionette
fardello: bundle, package
farfugliare: to stumble, to mutter
farmacia: pharmacy
farmaco: drug
farneticare: to rave, to be delirious
fascismo: fascism
fase: phase
fauna: faun
fautore: supporter
fava: broad bean
favella: speech
favilla: spark
fazzoletto: handkerchief
febbraio: February
febbre: fever
fecola: potato flour
federa: pillowcase
felce: fern
felino: feline
felpato: plushy
feltro: felt hat
fermare: to stop
Ferragosto: Assumption Day (Aug. 15)
fervente: fervent, fervid, ardent
festa: holiday, festival

fetore: stench
fiammiferi: matches
fianco: hip
fiatone: heavy breathing, panting
fico: fig
fiducia: trust
figlia: daughter
figlio: son
fila: line, row
filza: string
fine settimana: weekend
finestra: window
finora: so far, up till now
fiocina: harpoon
firmare: to sign
fisarmonica: accordion
fischiare: to whistle
fisima: whim
fisso: set, fixed
fiume: river
flauto: flute
flettere: to bend
fluire: to flow
folla: crowd
forbici: scissors
forchetta: fork
formaggio: cheese
forte: strong
foschia: haze, mist
fosforo: phosphorus
fragola: strawberry
frana: landslide
Francia: France
francobollo: postage stamp
fratellastro: stepbrother, half brother
fratello: brother
freccia: arrow
frenare: to brake
friggere: to fry
friulano-giuliano: inhabitant of Friuli-Venezia Giulia
frustrare: to frustrate, to thwart
frutta: fruit
fulmine: lightning
fumetto: comic strip
fungo: mushroom
funivia: cableway
fuoco: fire
fuori: outside
fuorilegge: outlaw
futuro: future
gabbiano: seagull
gabbo: joke, hoax
gabinetto: toilet

gaffe: blunder
gagliardo: vigorous
galassia: galaxy
galera: prison
galleggiare: to float
galleria: tunnel, gallery
gallina: hen
galoppare: to gallop
gamba: leg
gancio: hook
garrire: to chirp
gasolio: diesel oil
gatto: cat
gattopardo: leopard
gazza: magpie
gelare: to freeze
gelato: ice cream
gelido: freezing
gelo: frost
gelosia: jealousy
gelsomino: jasmine
Gemelli: Gemini
genero: son-in-law
genitori: parents
gennaio: January
gente: people
genuflessione: genuflection
gergale: slang
Germania: Germany
gestore: manager, director
gettone: token
ghiacciaio: glacier
ghiaia: gravel
ghianda: acorn
ghignare: to sneer
ghindola: gland
ghirlanda: wreath, garland
ghisa: cast iron
già: already
giacca: jacket
giacere: to lie
giallo: yellow
Giappone: Japan
giara: jar
giardino: garden
giocare: to play
giorno feriale: weekday
giorno festivo: holiday
giovedì: Thursday
gioviale: jovial
girare: to turn
girasole: sunflower
girino: tadpole
gironzolare: to stroll about

giugno: June
giungla: jungle
giurare: to swear, to take an oath
giusto: just, right, correct
goffo: awkward
golfo: gulf
gomito: elbow
gomma: eraser
gonfiare: to inflate, to blow up
gonna: skirt
gorgo: whirlpool
gracile: delicate
gradasso: braggart
gradire: to appreciate, to enjoy
grana: grain
granaio: barn
granchio: crab
grande: big, large
grande schermo: movie screen
granduca: grand duke
granturco: maize
grappolo: bunch
grasso: fat
grattacapo: trouble
grattacielo: skyscraper
grattugia: grater
gravare: to burden
gravoso: onerous
Grecia: Greece
gregario: gregarious
gregge: flock, herd
greve: heavy
grigio: gray
griglia: grill
grilletto: trigger
grissino: breadstick
grotto: cave, grotto
grullo: silly
guadare: to ford
guanciale: pillow
guanti: gloves
guardare: to watch
gufo: owl
gustare: to taste
iato: hiatus
icona: icon
idillio: idyll
idraulico: plumber
iella: evil eye
ieri: yesterday
iettare: to jinx
igiene: hygiene, health
ignorare: to ignore
ignoto: unknown

illecito: illicit
illegale: illegal
illeggibile: illegible
illeso: unhurt, uninjured
illibato: chaste
illustre: distinguished
imballare: to pack, to wrap up
imbarcadero: jetty, wharf
imbottire: to stuff, to pad
imbrunire: to get dark
imbruttire: to make ugly
imbucare: to drop, to mail
imbuto: funnel
immaginare: to imagine
immenso: immense
immigrare: to immigrate
immissario: tributary
imparare: to learn
impasticciare: to make a mess (of)
impegno: engagement, commitment
imperizia: inexperience
impermeabile: raincoat
impietrito: petrified
impigrire: to make lazy
importare: to import
impostare: to mail
imprecare: to curse
imprestare: to lend
improprio: improper
in ritardo: later
inabitabile: uninhabitable
inatteso: unexpected
incartare: to wrap
incerata: oilcloth
incinta: pregnant
incitare: to incite
incivile: uncivilized, barbaric
incominciare: to start, to begin
incongruo: inadequate
incrocio: intersection, crossing
indenne: unharmed, unhurt
indire: to announce, to proclaim
indirizzo: address
indispettire: to irritate, to annoy
indole: nature, temperament
indovinare: to guess
indovinello: riddle
infatti: in fact
infermiere: nurse
infinito: infinitive
inflazione: inflation
influsso: influence
Inghilterra: England
ingresso: entrance

iniziare: to begin
insistere: to insist
insolito: unusual, strange, odd
intermezzo: intermission
internazionale: international
intero: entire, whole
intervallo: intermission
inutile: useless, hopeless
invece: instead
inverno: winter
inviare: to send
invito: invitation
ipoteca: mortgage
Irlanda: Ireland
ironia: irony
irrisorio: derisive, scornful
isola: island
istituto: institute
Italia: Italy
itinerario: itinerary
labbro: lip
labile: unstable, frail, weak
labirinto: labyrinth, maze
lacca: lacquer
lacrima: tear, drop
lacuna: gap
ladro: thief
laggiù: down there
lagnarsi: to moan, to groan
lago: lake
laido: filthy
lambire: to lap, to lick
lamiera: sheet metal
lampada: lamp
lampadario: chandelier
lampante: clear
lampo: lightning
lampone: raspberry
lancia: lance
lanciafiamme: flame-thrower
lancinante: piercing
landa: heath
lapidare: to stone
larghezza: width, breadth
largire: to lavish
largo: wide
lassù: up there
latente: latent, hidden
latte: milk
latteria: dairy store
lattina: can
lattuga: lettuce
lauro: laurel
lavadino: sink

lavagna: chalkboard
lavapiatti: dishwasher
lavarsi: to wash oneself
lavatrice: washing machine
laziale: inhabitant of Lazio
leale: loyal, sincere
lecito: right, allowed
legare: to tie up, to bind
leggere: to read
leggero: light
legno: wood
lembo: edge, hem, tip, end
lenticchia: lentil
lenzuolo: sheet
Leone: Leo
letizia: joy
lettera: letter
lettiga: stretcher
lettino: cot, crib
letto: bed
levante: east
levare: to raise, to lift up
levitare: to levitate
levriero: greyhound
lezione: lesson
libeccio: southwest wind
libellula: dragonfly
libero: free
libertà: freedom
libreria: bookstore
libro: book
liceo: high school
liguro: inhabitant of Liguria
limitare: to limit
limone: lemon
lingua: language, tongue
lino: flax, linen
liquefare: to melt
liso: worn, threadbare
litigare: to fight, argue
litro: liter
liuto: lute
locale: public place
lombardo: inhabitant of Lombardia
lontano: far
lotta: struggle
lotteria: lottery
lucano: inhabitant of Basilicata
lucchetto: padlock, lock
luce: light
lucidare: to shine, to polish
luglio: July
lumaca: snail
luna: moon

lunedì: Monday
lungomare: seafront
luogo: place
macabro: macabre
macchè: not at all
macchina: engine, machine
maciullare: to crush
madornale: gross
madre: mother
madrelingua: native language
madrina: godmother, sponsor, matron
maestro: teacher, expert
maga: sorceress
magazzino: store, warehouse, depot
maggio: May
maggiorana: marjoram
maggioranza: majority
maggiordomo: butler
magia: magic
maglio: mallet
maglione: sweater
mago: magician
magro: thin
maiale: pork, pig
malavita: underworld
maledetto: cursed, wicked, beastly
malfermo: shaky, unsteady
malgrado: in spite of
malo: bad, evil, wicked
mancanza: lack, want
mancia: tip
mandare: to send
mandolino: mandolin
mangiare: to eat
mangime: fodder
maniera: manner
manovello: winch, crank
mantello: cloak, mantle
mantenere: to keep
marchigiano: inhabitant of Le Marche
mare: sea
margine: margin, edge, border
marionetta: puppet
marito: husband
marmo: marble
martedì: Tuesday
martello: hammer
marzo: March
materasso: mattress
materia: subject
matita: pencil
matrigna: stepmother
mattina: morning

mattone: brick
meandro: meander
medaglia: medal, badge, token
medesimo: same
mediante: by
medico: doctor
Medioevo: Middle Ages
meglio: better
mela: apple
meno: less
menta: mint
mente: mind
mento: chin
menzogna: lie
mercato: market
mercoledì: Wednesday
merletto: lace
merluzzo: cod
mescolare: to mix
Messico: Mexico
mestiera: trade, job
mestola: ladle, dipper
metà: half
mettersi: to put on
mezzanotte: midnight
mezzogiorno: noon
miccia: fuse
miele: honey
minestra: soup
mischiare: to mix
misurare: to measure
mite: mild, gentle, meek
mito: myth
moglie: wife
molisano: inhabitant of Molise
monologo: monologue
monotono: monotonous
montagna: mountain
monumento: monument
morsicare: to nibble, to gnaw
mosaico: mosaic
mostra: exhibit, fair
mostro: monster
motivo: reason, cause, grounds
motocicletta: motorcycle
mucchio: heap, pile, mass
multa: fine, ticket
mummia: mummy
municipio: city hall
muraglia: wall
muratore: bricklayer
museo: museum
musicale: musical
nacchera: castanet

nano: dwarf
narrativa: fiction, narrative
nascente: dawning, rising
nascondere: to hide
naso: nose
nastro: ribbon, tape
Natale: Christmas
natura: nature
naufragare: to be shipwrecked
nazione: nation
neanche: not even
nebbia: fog, mist
nefando: wicked
nefasto: ill-omened, unlucky
negletto: neglected
negozio: store, shop, deal
nemmeno: not even
nenia: dirge
neolitico: Neolithic
nero: black
nespola: medlar
nesso: connection, link
nettare: nectar
neutro: neutral
neve: snow
nevicare: to snow
nibbio: kite
nido: nest
niente: nothing
ninnananna: lullaby
ninnolo: toy, plaything
nipote: nephew, niece, grandchild
nitido: neat, clear
nitore: brightness, lucidity
nitrire: to neigh, to whinny
niveo: snow-white
nocca: knuckle
nocciolina: peanut
noce: walnut
noce moscata: nutmeg
nocepesca: nectarine
nocivo: harmful
nodo: knot, bond, tie
noia: boredom, tedium
noioso: boring
noleggiare: to rent
nomade: nomadic
nomignolo: nickname
nomina: appointment
non: not
nonna: grandmother
nonno: grandfather
nonnulla: trifle
nonostante: in spite of

nord: north
noria: water wheel
norma: rule, regulation
Norvegia: Norway
nota: mark, note, list
notaio: notary
notizia: news
noto: well-known
notte: night
novella: short story
novello: new
novembre: November
novilunio: new moon
nozze: wedding, marriage
nube: clouds
nubile: unmarried, single woman
nuca: nape
nudo: naked, nude, bare
nullaosta: permit
nuora: daughter-in-law
nuotare: to swim
nutrire: to nourish
nuvola: cloud
nuziale: nuptial
oasi: oasis
obbligare: to oblige, to make, to compel
obbrobrio: infamy, disgrace
obelisco: obelisk
oberare: to overburden
obitorio: mortuary
oblio: oblivion
oboe: oboe
oca: goose
occhiaccio: scowl, ugly look
occhiali: glasses
occhieggiare: to ogle
occhiello: buttonhole
occidente: west
occorrere: to need
occultare: to hide
oceano: ocean
odiabile: hateful, loathsome, odious
offendere: to offend, to insult
officiare: to officiate
offrire: to offer
oggetto: object
oggi: today
oggigiorno: nowadays
ogiva: warhead
ogni: every, each
Ognissanti: All Saint's Day (Nov. 1)
ognuno: everyone, everybody
Olanda: Holland

olfatto: sense of smell
olio: olive
oliveto: olive grove
olona: sailcloth, canvas
oltranza: to the last, to the bitter end
ombelico: navel
ombra: shade, dark, shadows
omelia: homily
omettere: to omit
onda: wave
onerare: to burden, to weigh down
onestà: honesty, integrity
onomastico: name-day
onore: honor
onta: shame, dishonor
opale: opal
operaio: worker
opificio: factory
oppure: else, or
optare: to opt
ora di punta: rush hour
orafo: goldsmith
orario: schedule
orbita: orbit, limits
orco: ogre
orda: horde
ordinare: to order
ordire: plot
orecchio: ear
organo: organ
orgoglio: pride
Oriente: East, Orient
origano: oregano
origliare: to eavesdrop
orizzonte: horizon
orlare: to edge, to border
oroscopo: horoscope
orrore: horror, disgust
orso: bear
orsù: come on!
ortaggio: vegetable
orto: garden
ospitale: hospital
ossobuco: marrowbone
ostaggio: hostage
ostello: hostel
osteria: inn
ostrica: oyster
ostruire: to obstruct
ottimo: excellent, best
ottobre: October
ottone: brass
ovale: oval

ove: where
ovest: west
ovino: sheep
ovvio: obvious
pacchetto: package
pacchiano: garish
pace: peace
padella: frying pan
padiglione: pavilion
padre: father
padrino: godfather
padrone: master, owner, proprietor
pagamento: payment
pagare: to pay
pagina: page
pagliaccio: clown
pagnotta: loaf
paio: pair
palato: palate
palco: box seat
palcoscenico: stage, boards
paletta: spade
palla: ball
palpare: to feel
palude: marsh
pancetta: bacon
panchina: bread
pane: bread
paniera: basket, hamper
panificio: bakery
panino: roll
panno: cloth
pantaloni: pants, slacks, trousers
pantano: muddy land, swamp
pantofole: slippers
papà: dad, daddy, pop
papa: Pope
papiro: papyrus
paprica: paprika
parabrezza: windshield
paradiso: paradise, heaven
paralume: lampshade
parare: to adorn, to decorate
paraurti: bumper
parcheggiare: to park
parecchio: several, quite a few
parente: relative
parere: opinion
parete: wall
partenza: departure
pascere: to graze
Pasqua: Easter
passaporto: passport

passare: to pass
pasticceria: pastry shop
patata: potato
patrigno: stepfather
pavimento: floor
pavone: peacock
pece: pitch
pecora: sheep
pedaggio: toll
pedale: pedal
pedinare: to shadow
pelare: to pare, to peel
pelle: leather
penisola: peninsula
penna: feather, plumage
penuria: shortage, scarcity, lack
pera: pear
perdurare: to continue, to last, to go on
pericolo: danger, risk, hazard
pero: pear
perorare: to plead
perseguire: to pursue
pesce: fish
Pesci: Pisces
pezzo: piece
pianoforte: piano
pianterreno: ground floor
piattino: saucer
piede: foot
piemontese: inhabitant of Piemonte
pieno: full
piglio: to look
pillola: pill
pioggia: rain
piovere: to rain
piovigginare: to drizzle
piscine: swimming pool
pistola: pistol
più: more
piuttosto: rather
pizzicare: to pinch
pizzo: lace
pneumatico: tire
poco: not very much
poiché: since
pollo: chicken
polmone: lung
Polonia: Poland
polpo: octopus
polso: wrist
pomodoro: tomato
ponte: bridge

porta: door
portale: portal
portauovo: egg-cup
Portogallo: Portugal
positivo: positive
posteggiare: to park
pozzo: well
predone: robber
preferire: to prefer
prefisso: area code
pregare: to pray, to beg, to ask
pregno: pregnant
pregustare: to look forward to
preistorico: prehistoric(al)
prendere: to take
prenotare: to make a reservation
preporre: to place before
prestito: loan
prezzo: price
prima classe: first class
primavera: spring
primeggiare: to excel
primo ministro: prime minister
principale: main
principianti: beginners
profondo: deep
prolisso: verbose
promettere: to promise
promontorio: promontory
pronosticare: to predict
prontuario: handbook
prorompere: to burst out
prototipo: prototype
provenire: to derive
proverbio: proverb
pugliese: inhabitant of Puglia
pulire: to clean, to scrub
punteggio: score
qua: here
quaderno: notebook
quadrare: to make square, to tally
quadrato: square
quadretto: small picture
quadricipite: quadriceps
quadrifoglio: four-leaf clover
quadrivio: crossroad(s)
quadro: painting, picture
quadruplicare: to quadruplicate
quaggiù: down here
quaglia: quail
qualcuno: someone, somebody
qualifica: title, qualification
qualora: in case, if
qualsiasi: any

qualunque: any
quando: when
quantità: quantity
quanto: how much
quantunque: although
quarantina: quarantine
quaresima: Lent
quartabuono: bevel, triangle
quartiere: neighborhood
quarzo: quartz
quasi: almost, nearly
quassù: up here
quatto: crouching
quattrini: money
quattrocchi: face to face
quercia: oak
querela: action, suit
questione: issue
questura: police headquarters
qui: here
quietanza: receipt
quintetto: quintet
quotare: to assign a share to
quotidiano: daily paper
quoto: quotient
rabarbaro: rhubarb
rabbino: rabbi
rabbonire: to calm down, to pacify
rabbuiarsi: to become dark
racchio: ugly, ungainly
raccolta: collection
raccomodare: to repair
raccontare: to tell, narrate
racconto: narration, telling, story
raccordo: connection, link, joint
racimolare: to scrape together
radazzare: to swab
raddoppiare: to double
raddrizzare: to straighten
radersi: to shave oneself
radiare: to strike off
radice: root
rado: thin, sparse
radura: clearing, glade
ragazza: girl
ragazzo: boy
ragno: spider
rallegrare: to cheer up
ramanzina: reprimand
ramare: to cover with copper
rame: copper
rana: frog
rancore: resentment
randagio: stray

rango: rank
rapa: turnip
rapare: to crop
rapido: quick, fast
rapina: robbery, plunder, booty
rapporto: connection, report
rapsodia: rhapsody
rasare: to shave, to cut, to trim
rasoio: razor
rassicurare: to reassure
ratto: rat
ravanello: radish
razza: race, breed
re: king
realtà: reality
rebbio: fork, tine
recare: to carry, to bring, to bear
reddito: income, revenue
regalare: to give a gift
reggia: royal palace
regina: queen
regno: kingdom, realm
regola: rule
reintegrare: to restore
reliquia: relic
rena: sand
rene: kidney
reparto: unit, division, section
reputare: to consider
resa: surrender
respiro: breath
restaurare: to restore
ricchezza: wealth
ricco: rich
ricevuta: receipt, bill
ridacchiere: to giggle
rilassare: to relax
rima: rhyme
rimanere: to remain
Rinascimento: Renaissance
rio: stream
ripieno: stuffed, filled
riscaldare: to warm, to heat
riso: rice
ristorante: restaurant
ritmo: rhythm
rito: ritual
rivista: magazine
rivo: brook
robusto: stout, strong
rospo: toad
rosso: red
rubinetto: faucet
rugiada: dew

ruscello: stream
russo: Russian
sabato: Saturday
sabbia: sand
saccheggiare: to sack
sacerdote: priest
sacramento: sacrament
Sagittario: Sagittarius
sagra: festival
sagrestia: sacristy
sala d'aspetto: waiting room
sala da pranzo: dining room
salace: salacious
salario: salary
saldo: balance
salice: willow
salire: to get on, to board
salmone: salmon
salpare: to sail
salubre: healthy
salutare: to greet
sapone: soap
sardo: inhabitant of Sardegna
sassofono: saxophone
satira: satire
sbadiglio: yawn
sborsare: to pay
sbottare: to burst out
sbottonare: to unbutton
sbracarsi: to undo one's belt
sbucciare: to pare, to peel
scacchiera: chess board
scaffale: bookcase
scala: staircase
scaldarsi: to heat
scarpa: shoe
scatola: box
scegliere: to choose
scellerato: wicked
schiuma: foam
sciacallo: jackal
sciare: to ski
scimmia: monkey
scioglilingua: tongue-twister
sciopero: strike
scoiattolo: squirrel
scolapiatti: dish drainer
scolare: to drain
scombro: mackerel
scommettere: to bet
sconsigliare: to advise against
Scorpione: Scorpio
scorso: last, past
Scozia: Scotland

scrittoio: writing desk
scrostare: to scrape
scure: axe
sdraiarsi: to lie down
sebbene: although
secco: dry
secolo: century
sedativo: sedative
segreto: secret
semaforo: traffic light
senape: mustard
sentiero: path, footpath
sentito: sincere
senza: without
sera: evening
serbatoio: tank
serpente: snake
sesamo: sesame
sesso: sex
sete: thirst
settembre: September
settentrione: north
severo: severe, strict
sevizia: torture, mayhem
sfalsare: to stagger, to parry
sfarzo: pomp, splendor
sfidare: to challenge
sfogo: vent, outlet
sfornire: to deprive
sfortuna: misfortune, bad luck
sforzo: effort
sfuso: melted, loose, in bulk
sgabello: stool, footstool
siccome: as
siciliano: inhabitant of Sicily
sicurezza: safety
sicuro: safe, sure
signora: Mrs., Ms., woman
signore: Mr., Sir, man
sobbalzare: to bounce, to jolt
socio: associate, partner
soffio: breath, puff
soffitta: attic
soffitto: ceiling
soggetto: subject
soggiorno: living room
soglio: throne, seat
sogliola: sole
sogno: dream, wishful thinking
solamente: only
sole: sun
solito: usual, customary, habitual
solleone: summer heat
soltanto: only, all, just, alone

somigliare: to resemble
sopra: on top
sordo: deaf
sorella: sister
sorellastra: stepsister, half sister
sorridere: to smile
sorriso: smile
sotto: under
sottovoce: in a low voice
Spagna: Spain
spalla: shoulder
spazzacamino: chimney sweeper
spazzolino: toothbrush
specchio: mirror
spesso: often
spettacolo: show
spezia: spice
spiegare: to explain
spina: electric plug
spinaci: spinach
spingere: to push
spogliatoio: locker room
spolverare: to dust
sporco: dirty
sportello: ticket window
spugna: sponge
squadra: team
squalo: shark
stampella: hanger
stanza: room
Stati Uniti: United States
stazione: station
stirare: to iron
strada: street, road
strano: strange
strega: witch
stretto: tight
stupendo: stupendous
sudore: sweat
suggerire: to suggest
suocera: mother-in-law
suocero: father-in-law
suonare: to ring
supplemento: additional charge
surgelato: frozen food
sveglia: alarm clock
svendita: sale
Svezia: Sweden
Svizzera: Switzerland
tabacco: tobacco
tabù: taboo
tacchino: turkey
tacito: silent; tacit
taco: heel

tagliare: to cut
tale: such
talpa: mole
tamburello: tamborine
tamburo: drum
tappeto: rug, carpet
tappezzeria: tapestry
tappo: plug
tariffa: fare
tartaruga: tortoise
tasca: pocket
tasse: taxes
tavola: table
tazza: cup
teatro: theater
telefono: telephone
telepatia: telepathy
telescopio: telescope
tema: theme, subject, topic
temperino: pocketknife
tempesta: storm
tenaglia: pincers
tenda: curtain, hanging
tenore: tenor
tentare: to try, to attempt
tepore: warmth
terapia: therapy
tergicristallo: windshield wipers
terminare: to end, to finish, to
    terminate
terra: earth, land, country
testa: head
tetro: gloomy
tetto: roof
tifoidea: typhoid
tifone: typhoon
tigre: tiger
timballo: pie
timido: shy
timo: thyme
tintinnare: to tinkle
tintura: tint
tirata: pull, jerk, wrench
tirchio: stingy
tirocinio: apprenticeship
tizio: fellow
tomba: tomb, grave
tonaca: habit
tondo: round
tonno: tuna
topo: mouse
torace: chest
torba: peat
torcia: torch

Toro: Taurus
torre: tower
toscano: inhabitant of Tuscany
tovaglia: tablecloth
tovagliolo: napkin
tra: between
traffico: traffic
tragedia: tragedy
tragitto: journey, way, route
tralcio: shoot
tramare: to plot, to scheme
tramontana: north wind
tramonto: dusk
tramortire: to stun, to knock out
tranne: except for, but
trappola: trap
travalicare: to cross over, to pass
    over
treno: train
trentino-altoatesino: inhabitant of
    Trentino-Alto Adige
trepido: anxious
tresca: love affair, intrigue, plot
trinciare: to carve
triste: sad, sorrowful
tritare: to chop
trofeo: trophy
tromba: trumpet
trono: throne
troppo: too much, too many
trovare: to find
trovatore: troubador
tuba: tuba
tuffare: to dip, to plunge
tuffo: dive
Tunisia: Tunis
turbare: to disturb, to trouble
turbolento: unruly, turbulent
Turchia: Turkey
turista: tourist
turpiloquio: foul language
tuta: jumpsuit
tuttora: still
ubbidire: to obey
ubertà: fertility
ubriacarsi: to get drunk
ubriaco: drunk
uccelliera: aviary
uccello: bird
uccidere: to kill
udibile: audible
udienza: hearing, audience
udire: to hear, to listen to
uditorio: audience

ufficiale: official
ufficializzare: to make official
uggioso: boring
uguale: (exactly) the same
ultimare: to complete
ultimo: last, final
ululare: to howl
umanità: humanity
umbratile: shady, shadowy
umbro: inhabitant of Umbria
umile: humble, modest
umore: humor
un: a, an, one
una: a, an, one
uncinare: to bend, to hook, to crook
uncino: hook
ungere: to grease, to oil
unghiata: scratch, claw mark
unguento: ointment
unicorno: unicorn
unificare: to unify
unione: union, uniting
unire: to unite, to join, to combine
università: university
universo: universe
unno: Hun
uno: one, a, an
unto: greased, oiled
untore: plague spreader
uomo: man
uova: egg
uragano: hurricane, storm, tempest
uranio: uranium
urgente: urgent
urgente: urgent, pressing
urlare: to shout
urlo: roar, howl
urtone: violent knock, hard push
usato: used
usciere: usher, porter
uscire: to go out, to leave
uscita: exit
usignolo: nightingale
utile: useful
vacante: vacant
vacanza: vacation
vacca: cow
vagare: to wander
vaglia: money order
vago: vague
valanga: avalanche
valdostano: inhabitant of Val d'Aosta
valente: skillful

valevole: valid
valle: valley
valletto: valet
valoroso: valiant
vampiro: vampire
vandalo: vandal
vaneggiare: to rave
vaniglia: vanilla
vantaggio: advantage
vaporizzare: to vaporize
varcare: to cross
varicella: chicken pox
vasca: tub
vassoio: tray
vegetale: vegetable
vegliare: to be awake
veleno: poison
venerdì: Friday
veneto: inhabitant of Veneto
venticello: breeze
vento: wind
ventre: stomach
verde: green
verdetto: verdict
Vergine: Virgo
vergogna: shame, embarrassment
verme: worm
vero: true, genuine
versante: slope
verso: toward, near, about
vestito: dress, suit
veterinario: veterinary
vetro: glass
vetta: peak
vettura: car of a train
vezzo: habit
via: street
viaggio: trip
viale: avenue
vicinanza: nearness
vicino: near
vigile: watchful, vigilant, alert
Vigilia di Natale: Christmas Eve
vigna: vineyard
villaggio: village
vincere: to win
vino: wine
viola: purple
violincello: cello
violino: violin
viottolo: path
vipera: viper
visconte: viscount
viscoso: viscous

viso: face
visone: mink
vittoriano: Victorian
viuzza: narrow lane
vivaio: fish reserve
vivezza: liveliness, vivacity
vivificare: to enliven
vizio: vice
vizzo: withered, faded
vocabolo: word
vocazione: vocation
vogare: to row, to oar
voglia: wish, desire
volantino: leaflet
volare: to fly
volgo: common people
volo: flight
volpe: fox
voltaggio: voltage
voltavite: screwdriver
volteggiare: to circle, to vault
vomere: ploughshare, spade
vongola: clam
voragine: abyss
vorticare: to whirl, to swirl, to eddy
votaccio: bad mark
votare: to vote
vulcano: volcano
vuotare: to empty, to drain
vuoto: empty
zacchera: splash of mud
zaccherone: mud-bespattered person
zaffare: to stop up
zaffata: stench
zafferano: saffron
zaffirino: sapphire
zagara: orange blossom
zaino: backpack
zampa: paw, leg
zampare: to paw the ground
zampillante: gushing, spurting
zampirone: fumigator
zampogna: bagpipe
zana: basket
zangolare: to churn
zanna: fang, tusk
zanni: clown mask, fool, zany
zanzara: mosquito
zappa: hoe
zappare: to hoe
zattera: raft, slab
zavorro: ballast, dead weight
zazzera: mop of hair

zecca: mint
zecchino: sequin
zelante: zealous
zelo: zeal
zenzero: ginger
zeppa: wedge
zeppo: packed, crammed, bursting
zerbino: mat
zia: aunt
zibaldone: mixture, medley
zibellino: sable
zimbellare: to lure, to entice
zimbello: decoy
zincare: to coat with zinc
zinco: zinc
zio: uncle
zippolo: pin, peg
zitto: silence
zizzania: discord
zocollaio: clog maker
zocollare: to clatter about in clogs
zodiaco: zodiac
zolfo: sulfur
zolla: clod
zollette: sugar cube
zompare: to jump, to leap
zona: zone, band
zoo: zoo
zoologia: zoology
zoppaggine: lameness, shake, rickety
zoppicare: to limp
zoticaggine: roughness, boorishness
zoticone: boor, lout, rough person
zucca: pumpkin
zucchero: sugar
zuccheroso: sweet, sugary
zucchino: squash
zuccone: blockhead
zuffa: scuffle, fray
zufolare: to whistle
zuppa: soup
zuppiera: soup tureen
zuppo: soaked

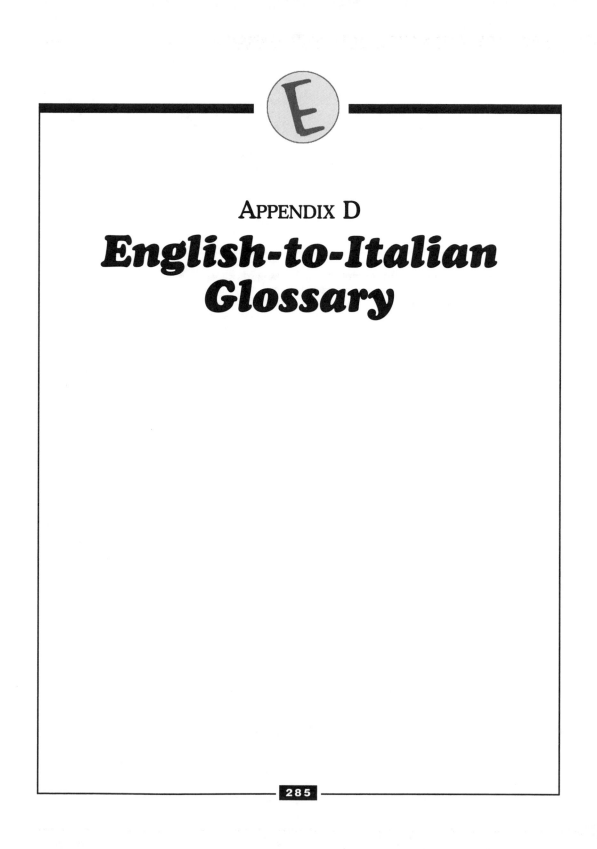

APPENDIX D

English-to-Italian Glossary

a: *un, una*
abbey: *badia*
abbot: *abate*
abdomen: *addome*
absent oneself, to: *assentarsi*
abyss: *voragine*
accompany, to: *accompagnare*
accordion: *fisarmonica*
ace: *asso*
acorn: *ghianda*
Aquarius: *Acquario*
act: *atto*
action: *querela*
actor: *attore*
additional charge: *supplemento*
address: *indirizzo*
advantage: *vantaggio*
advise against, to: *sconsigliare*
ago: *fa*
air: *aria*
airport: *aeroporto*
aisle: *corridoio*
alarm clock: *sveglia*
alas: *ahimè*
All Saint's Day (Nov. 1): *Ognissanti*
alliance: *alleanza*
allowed: *lecito*
almost: *quasi*
Alpine hut: *baita*
already: *già*
also: *anche*
although: *benché, quantunque, sebbene*
amber: *ambra*
ambulance: *ambulanza*
amethyst: *ametista*
amulet: *amuleto*
anchovy: *alice*
and: *e, ed* (before vowels)
angel hair pasta: *capellini*
annoy, to: *indispettire*
annul, to: *annullare*
Antarctic: *antartico*
antelope: *antilope*
anxious: *trepido*
any: *qualsiasi, qualunque*
apartment: *appartamento*
appetizers: *antipasti*
applaud, to: *applaudire*
apple: *mela*
appointment: *nomina*
apprenticeship: *tirocinio*
approve, to: *approvare*
apricot: *albicocca*

April: *aprile*
archaic: *arcaico*
archangel: *arcangelo*
area code: *prefisso*
argue, to: *litigare*
Aries: *Ariete*
arithmetic: *aritmetica*
arm: *braccio*
armpit: *ascella*
army: *esercito*
arrive, to: *arrivare*
arrow: *freccia*
as: *siccome*
asparagus: *asparago*
assign a share, to: *quotare*
Assumption Day (Aug. 15): *Ferragosto*
at least: *almeno*
attach, to: *agganciare*
attempt: *conato*
attempt, to: *tentare*
attend (to), to: *attenersi*
attic: *soffitta*
attract, to: *attirare*
audible: *udibile*
audience: *udienza, uditorio*
August: *agosto*
aunt: *zia*
autumn: *autunno*
avalanche: *valanga*
avenue: *viale*
aviary: *uccelliera*
avocado: *avocado*
avoid, to: *evitare*
awake, to be: *vegliare*
awkward: *goffo*
axe: *scure*
azalea: *azalea*
backpack: *zaino*
bacon: *pancetta*
bad: *malo*
bad mark: *votaccio*
bagpipe: *zampogna*
bakery: *panificio*
balance: *saldo*
ball: *palla*
ballast: *zavorro*
banal: *banale*
bank: *banca*
banker: *banchiere*
barber: *barbiere*
barn: *granaio*
barrel: *botte*
basil: *basilico*
bask, to: *crogiolarsi*

basket: *paniera, zana*
bass: *basso*
bassoon: *fagotto*
bathing suit: *costume da bagno*
bathrobe: *accappatoio*
bathroom: *bagno*
battery: *batteria*
bay: *baia*
bean: *fagiolo*
bear: *orso*
beard: *barba*
beast: *bestia*
become dark, to: *rabbuiarsi*
bed: *letto*
bedroom: *camera da letto*
bee: *ape*
beer: *birra*
begin, to: *iniziare*
beginners: *principianti*
Belgium: *Belgio*
bell: *campana*
belligerent: *bellicoso*
belong, to: *appartenere*
belt: *cinta*
bend, to: *uncinare, flettere*
bet, to: *scommettere*
better: *meglio*
between: *tra*
bevel: *quartabuono*
Bible: *Bibbia*
big toe: *alluce*
bill: *conto*
bind, to: *legare*
birch: *betulla*
bird: *uccello*
birthday: *compleanno*
black: *nero*
blacksmith: *fabbro*
block, to: *blocare*
blockhead: *zuccone*
blonde: *biondo*
blood bank: *emoteca*
blouse: *camicetta*
blue: *azzurro*
blunder: *gaffe*
board, to: *salire*
boat: *barca*
boil: *bollire*
bonfire: *falò*
book: *libro*
bookcase: *scaffale*
bookstore: *libreria*
boor: *zoticone*
boorishness: *zoticaggine*

boredom: *noia*
boring: *noioso, uggioso*
both: *entrambi*
bottle: *bottiglia*
bottle opener: *apribottiglia*
bounce: *sobbalzare*
bowler hat: *bombetta*
box: *scatola*
box seat: *palco*
boy: *ragazzo*
boycott, to: *boicottare*
braggart: *gradasso*
brake, to: *frenare*
brass: *ottone*
Brazil: *Brasile*
bread: *pane*
breadstick: *grissino*
breath: *soffio, respiro*
breeze: *venticello*
bribe: *bustarella*
brick: *mattone*
bricklayer: *muratore*
bridesmaid: *damigella*
bridge: *ponte*
brightness: *nitore*
broad bean: *fava*
brook: *rivo*
brother: *fratello*
brother-in-law: *cognato*
brown: *bruno*
buffalo: *bufalo*
bulletin: *bollettino*
bumper: *paraurti*
bunch: *grappolo*
bundle together, to: *affardellare*
burden, to: *onerare, gravare*
burst out, to: *prorompere, sbottare*
but: *tranne*
butler: *maggiordomo*
butter: *burro*
button: *bottone*
buttonhole: *occhiello*
by: *mediante*
cabbage: *cavolo*
cableway: *cabinovia, funivia*
calendar: *calendario*
calm: *calmo*
cameo: *cammeo*
can: *lattina*
can opener: *apriscatole*
Cancer: *Cancro*
canvas: *olona*
cap: *berretto*
Capricorn: *Capricorno*

carjack: *cricco*
carouse: *bagordare*
carpenter: *falegname*
carpet: *tappeto*
carrot: *carota*
carry, to: *recare*
carry on, to: *esplicare*
carve, to: *trinciare*
cashier: *cassiere*
cast iron: *ghisa*
castanet: *nacchera*
cat: *gatto*
catapult: *briccola*
caterpillar: *bruco*
cathedral: *duomo*
cave: *caverna, grotto*
ceiling: *soffitto*
cellar: *cantina*
cello: *violincello*
centigrade: *centogrado*
century: *secolo*
chalkboard: *lavagna*
challenge, to: *sfidare*
chandelier: *lampadario*
channel: *canale*
chaotic: *caotico*
chapel: *cappella*
charity: *beneficenza*
chaste: *illibato*
chat, to: *chiacchiere*
check: *assegno*
check, to: *controllare*
cheer up, to: *rallegrare*
cheese: *formaggio*
chemistry: *chimica*
cherub: *cherubino*
chess board: *scacchiera*
chest: *torace*
chest of drawers: *canterano*
chestnut: *castagna*
chicken: *pollo*
chicken pox: *varicella*
child: *bambino*
chimney sweeper: *spazzacamino*
chin: *mento*
China: *Cina*
chirp, to: *garrire*
choose, to: *scegliere*
chop, to: *tritare*
chowder: *cacciucco*
Christmas: *Natale*
Christmas Eve: *Vigilia di Natale*
chronic: *cronico*
church: *chiesa*

churn, to: *zangolare*
cinnamon: *canella*
circus: *circo*
citizen: *cittadino*
city hall: *municipio*
clam: *vongola*
clarinet: *clarinetto*
classroom: *aula, classe*
clatter about in clogs, to: *zocollare*
clay: *creta*
clean, to: *pulire*
clear: *chiaro, lampante*
clearing, glade: *radura*
climate: *clima*
cloak: *mantello*
clod: *zolla*
clog maker: *zocollaio*
closet: *armadio*
cloth: *panno*
cloud: *nuvola*
clown: *pagliaccio*
coat: *cappotto*
cockpit: *cabina di pilotaggio*
cockroach: *blatta*
cocoon: *bozzolo*
cod: *merluzzo*
colander: *colapasta*
collection: *raccolta*
come on: *orsù*
comic strip: *fumetto*
coming: *entrante*
commend, to: *encomiare*
commitment: *impegno*
common people: *volgo*
compel, to: *obbligare*
complete, to: *ultimare*
conclude, to: *concludere*
connection: *raccordo*
consider, to: *reputare*
continue, to: *perdurare*
contract, to: *contrarre*
cook, to: *cucinare*
cookie: *biscotto*
copper: *rame*
coriander: *coriandolo*
corkscrew: *cavatappi*
corner: *angolo*
cornet: *cornetto*
correct: *giusto*
costly: *costoso*
cotton: *cotone*
count: *conte*
counter: *banco*
countryside: *campagna*

cousin: *cugino*
covered roof terrace: *altana*
cow: *vacca*
crab: *granchio*
crackle, to: *crepitare*
crammed: *zeppo*
crank: *manovello*
cream: *crema*
credit card: *carta di credito*
crib: *lettino*
crop: *rapare*
cross, to: *varcare*
crossbow: *balestra*
crossroad(s): *quadrivio, crocicchio*
crossword puzzle: *cruciverba*
crouching: *quatto*
crowd: *calca, folla*
crucify, to: *crocifiggere*
crush, to: *maciullare*
cup: *tazza*
cure, to: *curare*
curse, to: *imprecare*
cursed: *maledetto*
curtain: *tenda*
customary: *solito*
customs: *dogana*
customs agent: *doganiere*
cut, to: *tagliare*
cymbal: *cembalo*
dad: *papà*
daddy: *babbo*
daily paper: *quotidiano*
dairy store: *latteria*
danger: *danno, pericolo*
dark: *buio*
dart: *darno*
dashboard: *cruscotto*
date: *dattero*
daughter: *figlia*
daughter-in-law: *nuora*
dawn: *alba*
dawning: *nascente*
day after tomorrow: *dopodomani*
deaf: *sordo*
dean: *decano*
debate: *dibattito*
debauched: *debosciato*
decade: *decenne*
December: *dicembre*
deceptive: *fallace*
decipher, to: *decifrare*
decorate, to: *parare*
decoy: *zimbello*
decrepit: *decrepito*

deep: *profondo*
deer: *cervo*
defeat, to: *debellare*
defect: *difetto*
deflation: *deflazione*
delicate: *cagionevole, gracile*
demagnetize, to: *demagnetizzare*
democratic: *democratico*
den: *covo*
Denmark: *Danimarca*
departure: *partenza*
deposit, to: *depositare*
deprecate, to: *deprecare*
deprive, to: *sfornire*
derisive: *irrisorio*
derive, to: *provenire*
desert: *deserto*
destiny: *destino*
destroy, to: *distruggere*
detour: *deviazione*
dew: *rugiada*
diabolical: *diabolica*
diary: *diario*
dictionary: *dizionario*
diesel oil: *gasolio*
diet: *dieta*
dining room: *sala da pranzo*
dinosaur: *dinosauro*
directive: *direttiva*
directory: *elenco*
dirge: *nenia*
dirty: *sporco*
discord: *discordia, zizzania*
discuss, to: *deliberare*
discussion: *dibattito*
dish drainer: *scolapiatti*
dishonor: *onta*
dishwasher: *lavapiatti*
dismiss, to: *dimettere*
distinguished: *illustre*
disturb, to: *turbare*
dive: *tuffo*
division: *reparto*
doctor: *medico*
dog: *cane*
doll: *bambola*
door: *porta*
double: *raddoppiare*
down here: *quaggiù*
down payment: *anticipo*
down there: *laggiù*
downhearted: *abbacchiato*
downstairs: *dabbasso*
dozen: *dozzina*

dragon: *drago*
dragonfly: *libellula*
drain, to: *scolare, vuotare*
drawer: *cassetto*
dream: *sogno*
drink: *bibita, bevanda*
drizzle, to: *piovigginare*
drug: *farmaco*
drum: *tamburo*
drunk: *ubriaco*
dry: *secco*
dry oneself, to: *asciugarsi*
duchess: *duchessa*
duck: *anatra*
duke: *duca*
dune: *duna*
during: *durante*
dusk: *tramonto*
dust: *spolverare*
dwarf: *nano*
dyslexia: *dislessia*
ear: *orecchio*
earth: *terra*
east: *est, levante*
Easter: *Pasqua*
eat, to: *mangiare*
eavesdrop, to: *origliare*
ebony: *ebano*
echo: *eco*
eclipse: *eclissi*
ecology: *ecologia*
edge: *orlare*
eel: *anguilla*
effort: *sforzo*
egg: *uova*
eggcup: *portauovo*
Egypt: *Egitto*
elaborate, to: *elaborare*
elbow: *gomito*
election: *elezione*
electric plug: *spina*
electrify, to: *elettrificare*
elephant: *elefante*
elevator: *ascensore*
eliminate, to: *eliminare*
else: *oppure*
emaciated: *emaciato*
embarrassment: *vergogna*
emergency: *emergenza*
emotional: *emotivo*
empty: *vuoto*
encore: *bis*
England: *Inghilterra*
enjoy, to: *gradire*

enliven, to: *vivificare*
enormous: *enorme*
enter, to: *entrare*
entice: *zimbellare*
entire: *intero*
entrance: *ingresso*
envelope: *busta*
epidemic: *epidemia*
Epiphany (Jan. 6): *Epifania*
epoch: *epoca*
equator: *equatore*
eraser: *gomma*
erode: *erodere*
escape, to: *eludere, evadere*
estuary: *estuario*
Etruscan: *etrusco*
eucalyptus: *eucalipto*
Europe: *Europa*
evasive: *evasivo*
evening: *sera*
event: *evento*
every: *ogni*
everybody: *ognuno*
everywhere: *dovunque, dappertutto*
evil: *malo*
evil eye: *iella*
evoke, to: *evocare*
exact: *esatto*
exactly: *appunto*
exactly the same: *uguale*
excel, to: *eccellere, primeggiare*
excellent: *ottimo*
except: *eccetto*
exceptional: *eccezionale*
exhibit: *mostra*
exit: *uscita*
exodus: *esodo*
exotic: *esotico*
expensive: *caro*
expert: *maestro*
explain, to: *spiegare*
explicit: *esplicito*
extraneous: *estraneo*
façade: *facciata*
face: *viso*
face to face: *quattrocchi*
facetious: *faceto*
factory: *fabbrica, opificio*
fail, to: *fallire*
falcon: *falcone*
fall, to: *cadere*
family: *famiglia*
famous: *famoso*
fang: *zanna*

far: *lontano*
fare: *tariffa*
fascism: *fascismo*
fast: *rapido*
fat: *grasso*
father: *padre*
father-in-law: *suocero*
faucet: *rubinetto*
faun: *fauna*
feather: *penna*
February: *febbraio*
feel, to: *palpare*
feline: *felino*
fellow: *tizio*
felt hat: *feltro*
fern: *felce*
fertility: *ubertà*
fervent: *fervente*
festival: *festa, sagra*
fever: *febbre*
fig: *fico*
fill (up), to: *empire*
filthy: *laido*
final: *ultimo*
find, to: *trovare*
finger: *ditto*
finish, to: *terminare*
fire: *fuoco*
fireplace: *caminetto*
first class: *prima classe*
fish: *pesce*
fish reserve: *vivaio*
fixed: *fisso*
flame-thrower: *lanciafiamme*
flask: *borraccia*
flight: *volo*
float, to: *galleggiare*
flock: *gregge*
flood: *alluvione*
floor: *pavimento*
flow, to: *fluire*
flute: *flauto*
fly, to: *volare*
foam: *schiuma*
fodder: *mangime*
fog: *nebbia*
foolish: *babbeo*
foot: *piede*
footstool: *sgabello*
ford: *guadare*
foreign: *estero*
forest: *bosco*
fork: *forchetta*
foul language: *turpiloquio*

four-leaf clover: *quadrifoglio*
fox: *volpe*
France: *Francia*
free: *libero*
freedom: *libertà*
freeze, to: *gelare*
freezing: *gelido*
Friday: *venerdì*
frog: *rana*
frost: *gelo*
frozen food: *surgelato*
fruit: *frutta*
frustrate, to: *frustrare*
fry, to: *friggere*
frying pan: *padella*
full: *pieno*
fumigator: *zampirone*
funnel: *imbuto*
furnish, to: *ammobiliare*
fuse: *miccia*
future: *futuro*
galaxy: *galassia*
gallery: *galleria*
gallop, to: *galoppare*
gang: *cricca*
gap: *lacuna*
garden: *giardino, orto*
garish: *pacchiano*
garlic: *aglio*
gasp, to: *boccheggiare*
gate: *cancello*
Gemini: *Gemelli*
genuflection: *genuflessione*
Germany: *Germania*
get dark, to: *imbrunire*
get drunk, to: *ubriacarsi*
ghost: *fantasma*
gift: *dono*
giggle, to: *ridacchiere*
ginger: *zenzero*
girl: *ragazza*
give a gift, to: *regalare*
give in, to: *demordere*
glacier: *ghiacciaio*
gland: *ghindola*
glass: *vetro*
glasses: *occhiali*
gloomy: *tetro*
gloves: *guanti*
glue: *colla*
gnaw, to: *morsicare*
go, to: *andare*
go mad, to: *ammattire*
goat: *capra*

god: *dio*
goddess: *dea*
godfather: *padrino*
godmother: *madrina*
goldsmith: *orafo*
goose: *oca*
gourmet: *buongustaio*
grain: *grana*
grand duke: *granduca*
grandfather: *nonno*
grandmother: *nonna*
grass snake: *biscia*
grater: *grattugia*
grave: *tomba*
gravel: *ghiaia*
gray: *grigio*
graze, to: *pascere*
grease, to: *ungere*
Greece: *Grecia*
green: *verde*
greet, to: *salutare*
gregarious: *gregario*
greyhound: *levriero*
grill: *griglia*
groan, to: *lagnarsi*
gross: *madornale*
ground floor: *pianterreno*
guess, to: *indovinare*
guitar: *chitarra*
gulf: *golfo*
habit: *tonaca*
habit: *vezzo*
half: *metà*
hammer: *martello*
handbook: *prontuario*
handkerchief: *fazzoletto*
hang, to: *appendere*
hanger: *stampella*
happen: *capitare*
happiness: *allegria*
happy: *allegro*
harm: *danneggiare*
harmful: *nocivo*
harmonica: *armonica*
harp: *arpa*
harpoon: *fiocina*
hat: *cappello*
hatchet: *accetta*
hateful: *odiabile*
hawk: *falco*
head: *testa*
healthy: *salubre*
heat: *caldo*
heat, to: *riscaldare*

heat: *scaldarsi*
heath: *landa*
heaven: *paradiso*
heavy: *greve*
Hebrew: *ebreo*
hectare: *ettaro*
heel: *calcagno, taco*
helicopter: *elicottero*
heliport: *eliporto*
helmet: *elmetto*
hem: *lembo*
hemisphere: *emisfero*
hen: *gallina*
herb: *erba*
here: *qua*
here: *qui*
hero: *eroe*
hiatus: *iato*
hide, to: *celare, nascondere,
    occultare*
high school: *liceo*
highway: *autostrada*
hill: *altura, colle*
hip: *fianco*
hit, to: *battere*
hoarse: *chioccio*
hoax: *gabbo*
hoe: *zappa*
hoe, to: *zappare*
holiday: *giorno festivo*
Holland: *Olanda*
homily: *omelia*
honest: *dabbene*
honesty: *onestà*
honey: *miele*
honor: *onore*
hook: *gancio, uncino*
hopeless: *inutile*
horde: *orda*
horizon: *orizzonte*
horoscope: *oroscopo*
horror: *orrore*
horse: *cavallo, equino*
hospital: *ospitale*
hostage: *ostaggio*
hostel: *ostello*
howl: *urlo*
howl, to: *ululare*
humanity: *umanità*
humble: *umile*
humor: *umore*
hunger: *fame*
hunt, to: *braccare*
hurricane: *uragano*

husband: *marito*
hydrofoil: *aliscafo*
hygiene: *igiene*
hymn: *cantico*
ice cream: *gelato*
icon: *icona*
idyll: *idillio*
if: *qualora*
ignore, to: *ignorare*
ill-omened: *nefasto*
illegal: *illegale*
illegible: *illeggibile*
illicit: *illecito*
imagine, to: *immaginare*
immense: *immenso*
immigrate, to: *immigrare*
import, to: *importare*
improper: *improprio*
in order that: *affinché*
inadequate: *incongruo*
incite, to: *incitare*
income: *reddito*
indeed: *davvero*
inexpensive: *economico*
inexperience: *imperizia*
infamy: *obbrobrio*
infinitive: *infinito*
inflate, to: *gonfiare*
inflation: *inflazione*
influence: *influsso*
inn: *osteria*
inside: *dentro*
insist, to: *insistere*
instead: *invece*
institute: *istituto*
intermission: *intermezzo, intervallo*
international: *internazionale*
intersection: *incrocio*
intravenous: *endovenoso*
intrigue: *tresca*
intrigue, to: *brogliare*
invitation: *invito*
Ireland: *Irlanda*
iron: *stirare*
irony: *ironia*
island: *isola*
issue: *questione*
Italy: *Italia*
itinerary: *itinerario*
ivory: *avorio*
jackal: *sciacallo*
jacket: *giacca*
jail: *carcere*
January: *gennaio*

Japan: *Giappone*
jar: *giara*
jasmine: *gelsomino*
jealousy: *gelosia*
jinx, to: *iettare*
job: *mestiera*
jockey: *fantino*
joke: *celiare*
journey: *tragitto*
jovial: *gioviale*
joy: *letizia*
jug: *bricco*
July: *luglio*
jump, to: *zompare*
jumpsuit: *tuta*
June: *giugno*
jungle: *giungla*
kayak: *caiaco*
keep, to: *mantenere*
key: *chiave*
kick, to: *calciare*
kidney: *rene*
kill, to: *uccidere*
kilogram: *chilogrammo*
king: *re*
kingdom: *regno*
kiss: *bacio*
kiss, to: *baciare*
kite: *nibbio*
knife: *coltello*
knock out, to: *tramortire*
knot: *nodo*
knuckle: *nocca*
label: *etichetta*
labyrinth: *labirinto*
lace: *merletto, pizzo*
lack: *mancanza*
lacquer: *lacca*
ladle: *mestola*
lake: *lago*
lamb: *agnello*
lameness: *zoppaggine*
lamp: *fanale, lampada*
lampshade: *paralume*
lance: *lancia*
land, to: *atterrare*
landlord: *affittacamere*
landslide: *frana*
lane: *corsia*
language: *lingua*
large: *grande*
latent: *latente*
later: *in ritardo*
laurel: *lauro*

lavish, to: *elargire, largire*
leaflet: *volantino*
leak: *falla*
learn, to: *imparare*
leather: *cuoio, pelle*
leave, to: *uscire*
leave one's country, to: *espatriare*
lecture: *conferenza*
leg: *gamba*
lemon: *limone*
lend, to: *imprestare*
lengthen, to: *dilungare*
Lent: *quaresima*
lentil: *lenticchia*
Leo: *Leone*
leopard: *gattopardo*
less: *meno*
lesson: *lezione*
letter: *lettera*
lettuce: *lattuga*
levitate, to: *levitare*
Libra: *Bilancia*
library: *biblioteca*
lick, to: *lambire*
lie: *menzogna*
lie down, to: *sdraiarsi*
light: *luce*
lightning: *fulmine*
limit, to: *limitare*
limp, to: *zoppicare*
line: *fila*
linen: *lino*
lip: *labbro*
listen, to: *ascoltare, udire*
liter: *litro*
living room: *soggiorno*
loaf: *pagnotta*
loan: *prestito*
lobster: *aragosta*
lock: *lucchetto*
locker room: *spogliatoio*
look: *piglio*
look for, to: *cercare*
look forward to, to: *pregustare*
lottery: *lotteria*
love: *amore*
loyal: *leale*
lullaby: *ninnananna*
lung: *polmone*
lute: *liuto*
macabre: *macabre*
machine: *macchina*
mackerel: *scombro*
magazine: *rivista*

magic: *magia*
magician: *mago*
magpie: *gazza*
mail, to: *imbucare, impostare*
mailbox: *cassetta postale*
main: *principale*
maize: *granturco*
majority: *maggioranza*
make a mess (of), to: *impasticciare*
make a reservation, to: *prenotare*
make lazy, to: *impigrire*
make official, to: *ufficializzare*
make ugly, to: *imbruttire*
mallet: *maglio*
man: *uomo*
manager: *gestore*
mandolin: *mandolino*
manner: *maniera*
maple: *acero*
marble: *marmo*
March: *marzo*
margin: *margine*
marionette: *fantoccio, burattino*
marjoram: *maggiorana*
market: *mercato*
marriage: *nozze*
marrowbone: *ossobuco*
marsh: *palude*
master: *padrone*
masterpiece: *capolavoro*
mat: *zerbino*
matches: *fiammiferi*
mattress: *materasso*
May: *maggio*
maze: *dedalo*
meager: *esiguo*
measure, to: *misurare*
medal: *medaglia*
melt, to: *liquefare*
melted: *sfuso*
Mexico: *Messico*
Middle Ages: *Medioevo*
midnight: *mezzanotte*
mild: *mite*
milk: *latte*
mind: *mente*
mink: *visone*
mint (spice): *menta*
mirror: *specchio*
misfortune: *sfortuna*
mist: *foschia*
mix, to: *mescolare, mischiare*
mixture: *zibaldone*
mole: *talpa*

Monday: *lundedì*
money: *denaro, quattrini*
money order: *vaglia*
monkey: *scimmia*
monologue: *monologo*
monotonous: *monotono*
monster: *mostro*
monument: *monumento*
moon: *luna*
mop of hair: *zazzera*
more: *più*
more than enough: *davanzo*
morning: *mattina*
mortgage: *ipoteca*
mortuary: *obitorio*
mosaic: *mosaico*
mosquito: *zanzara*
mother: *madre*
mother-in-law: *suocera*
motorcycle: *motocicletta*
mountain: *montagna*
mouse: *topo*
mouth: *bocca*
movie screen: *grande schermo*
Mr.: *signore*
Mrs.: *signora*
mud: *fango*
mummy: *mummia*
museum: *museo*
mushroom: *fungo*
musical: *musicale*
mussel: *cozza*
mustache: *baffi*
mustard: *senape*
myth: *mito*
name: *nome*
name-day: *onomastico*
nape: *nuca*
napkin: *tovagliolo*
narrate, to: *raccontare*
narrative: *narrativa*
narrow lane: *viuzza*
nation: *nazione*
native language: *madrelingua*
nature: *natura*
naughty: *birichino*
navel: *ombelico*
near: *verso, vicino*
nearly: *quasi*
nearness: *vicinanza*
neat: *nitido*
nectar: *nettare*
nectarine: *nocepesca*
need, to: *occorrere*

neglected: *negletto*
neighborhood: *quartiere*
nephew: *nipote*
nest: *nido*
neutral: *neutro*
new: *novello*
new moon: *novilunio*
New Year's Day: *Capodanno*
news: *notizia*
newsstand: *edicola*
nickname: *nomignolo*
niece: *nipote*
night: *notte*
nightingale: *usignolo*
nomadic: *nomade*
noon: *mezzogiorno*
north: *nord, settentrione*
north wind: *tramontana*
Norway: *Norvegia*
nose: *naso*
not: *non*
notary: *notaio*
note: *nota*
notebook: *quaderno*
nothing: *niente*
nourish, to: *nutrire*
November: *novembre*
now: *adesso*
nowadays: *oggigiorno*
nude: *nudo*
nuptial: *nuziale*
nurse: *infermiere*
nutmeg: *noce moscata*
oak: *quercia*
oasis: *oasi*
obelisk: *obelisco*
obey, to: *ubbidire*
object: *oggetto*
oblivion: *oblio*
oboe: *oboe*
obstruct, to: *ostruire*
obvious: *ovvio*
ocean: *oceano*
October: *ottobre*
octopus: *polpo*
odd: *insolito*
offend, to: *offendere*
offer, to: *offrire*
official: *ufficiale*
officiate, to: *officiare*
often: *spesso*
ogle: *occhieggiare*
ogre: *orco*
oilcloth: *incerata*

oiled: *unto*
ointment: *unguento*
olive: *olio*
olive grove: *oliveto*
omit, to: *omettere*
on top: *sopra*
once again: *daccapo*
one: *uno*
onerous: *gravoso*
onion: *cipolla*
only: *solamente, soltanto*
opal: *opale*
open: *aprire*
opinion: *parere*
opt, to: *optare*
orange: *arancia*
orange blossom: *zagara*
orbit: *orbita*
order, to: *ordinare*
oregano: *origano*
organ: *organo*
Orient: *Oriente*
outlaw: *fuorilegge*
outlet: *sfogo*
outside: *fuori*
outstanding: *esimio*
oval: *ovale*
overburden, to: *oberare*
owl: *gufo*
oyster: *ostrica*
pacify, to: *rabbonire*
package: *fardello, pacchetto*
page: *pagina*
paint, to: *dipingere*
painting: *quadro*
pair: *paio*
palate: *palato*
panting: *fiatone*
pantry: *dispensa*
pants: *pantaloni*
paper: *carta*
paprika: *paprica*
papyrus: *papiro*
parents: *genitori*
park: *parcheggiare, posteggiare*
partner: *socio*
pass, to: *passare*
pass over, to: *travalicare*
passport: *passaporto*
past: *scorso*
pastry shop: *pasticceria*
path: *sentiero, viottolo*
pavilion: *padiglione*
paw: *zampa*

pay, to: *pagare, sborsare*
payment: *pagamento*
peace: *pace*
peacock: *pavone*
peak: *vetta*
peanut: *arachide, nocciolina*
pear: *pera*
peat: *torba*
pedal: *pedale*:
peel, to: *pelare, sbucciare*
peg: *zippolo*
pencil: *matita*
penetrate, to: *compenetrare*
peninsula: *penisola*
people: *gente*
permit: *nullaosta*
petrified: *impietrito*
pharmacy: *farmacia*
phase: *fase*
pheasant: *fagiano*
phosphorus: *fosforo*
piano: *pianoforte*
pickle: *decapare*
pie: *timballo*
piece: *pezzo*
piercing: *lancinante*
pile: *mucchio*
pill: *pillola*
pillow: *guanciale*
pillowcase: *federa*
pincers: *tenaglia*
pinch, to: *pizzicare*
Pisces: *Pesci*
pistol: *pistola*
pitch: *pece*
place: *luogo*
place before, to: *preporre*
plague spreader: *untore*
play, to: *giocare*
plead, to: *perorare*
plot, to: *ordire*
ploughshare: *vomere*
plug: *tappo*
plumber: *idraulico*
plunge, to: *tuffare*
plushy: *felpato*
pocket: *tasca*
pocketknife: *temperino*
poison: *veleno*
poison, to: *avvelenare*
Poland: *Polonia*
police headquarters: *questura*
polish, to: *lucidare*
politeness: *creanza*

political exile: *confino*
pomp: *sfarzo*
Pope: *papa*
pork: *maiale*
portal: *portale*
porter: *usciere*
portray, to: *effigiare*
Portugal: *Portogallo*
positive: *positivo*
postage stamp: *francobollo*
postcard: *cartolina*
potato: *patata*
potato flour: *fecola*
praise, to: *decantare*
pray, to: *pregare*
predict, to: *pronosticare*
prefer, to: *preferire*
pregnant: *incinta, pregno*
prehistoric(al): *preistorico*
preview: *anteprima*
price: *prezzo*
pride: *orgoglio*
priest: *sacerdote*
primary school: *elementari*
prime minister: *primo ministro*
primer: *abbecedario*
prior event: *antefatto*
prison: *carcere, galera*
proclaim, to: *indire*
promise, to: *promettere*
promontory: *promontorio*
propeller: *elica*
prototype: *prototipo*
proverb: *proverbio*
public place: *locale*
pudding: *budino*
pull: *tirata*
pumpkin: *zucca*
punish, to: *castigare*
purify, to: *depurare*
purple: *viola*
pursue, to: *perseguire*
push, to: *spingere*
put before, to: *anteporre*
put on, to: *mettersi*
quadriceps: *quadricipite*
quadruplicate: *quadruplicare*
quail: *quaglia*
qualification: *qualifica*
quantity: *quantità*
quarantine: *quarantina*
quartz: *quarzo*
queen: *regina*
quintet: *quintetto*

quotient: *quoto*
rabbi: *rabbino*
rabbit: *coniglio*
race: *razza*
radish: *ravanello*
raft: *zattera*
rain: *pioggia*
rain, to: *piovere*
rainbow: *arcobaleno*
raincoat: *impermeabile*
raise, to: *ergere, levare*
rank: *rango*
raspberry: *lampone*
rat: *ratto*
rather: *piuttosto*
rave, to: *farneticare, vaneggiare*
raven: *corvo*
razor: *rasoio*
read, to: *leggere*
reality: *realtà*
reason: *motivo*
reassure, to: *rassicurare*
receipt: *quietanza, ricevuta*
recruit, to: *assoldare*
red: *rosso*
referee: *arbitro*
relative: *parente*
relax, to: *rilassare*
reliable: *attendibile*
relic: *reliquia*
remain, to: *rimanere*
Renaissance: *Rinascimento*
rent, to: *affittare, noleggiare*
repair, to: *raccomodare*
reprimand: *ramanzina*
resemble, to: *somigliare*
resentment: *rancore*
reside, to: *dimorare*
restaurant: *ristorante*
restore, to: *reintegrare, restaurare*
result: *esito*
rhapsody: *rapsodia*
rhubarb: *rabarbaro*
rhyme: *rima*
rhythm: *ritmo*
ribbon: *nastro*
rice: *riso*
rich: *ricco*
riddle: *indovinello*
right: *destra*
right hand: *dritta*
ring: *anello*
ring, to: *suonare*
ringleader: *capobanda*

ritual: *rito*
river: *fiume*
roast, to: *arrostire*
rob, to: *derubare*
robber: *predone*
robbery: *rapina*
roll: *panino*
roof: *tetto*
room: *stanza*
root: *radice*
rope: *corda*
round: *tondo*
row: *vogare*
royal palace: *reggia*
rubbish: *boiata*
rug: *tappeto*
rule: *norma, regola*
ruling: *decreto*
rumor: *fama*
rush hour: *ora di punta*
Russian: *russo*
sable: *zibellino*
sacrament: *sacramento*
sacristy: *sagrestia*
sad: *triste*
safe: *sicuro*
safety: *sicurezza*
saffron: *zafferano*
Sagittarius: *Sagittario*
sail, to: *salpare*
salacious: *salace*
salary: *salario*
sale: *svendita*
salmon: *salmone*
same: *medesimo*
sand: *rena, sabbia*
sapphire: *zaffirino*
satire: *satira*
Saturday: *sabato*
saucer: *piattino*
saxophone: *sassofono*
scale: *bilancia*
schedule: *orario*
scheme, to: *tramare*
scholarship: *borsa di studio*
science fiction: *fantascienza*
scissors: *forbici*
score: *punteggio*
Scorpio: *Scorpione*
Scotland: *Scozia*
scowl: *occhiaccio*
scrape, to: *scrostare*
scratch: *unghiata*
screwdriver: *cacciavite, voltavite*

scuffle: *zuffa*
scythe: *falce*
sea: *mare*
seafront: *lungomare*
seagull: *gabbiano*
sealing wax: *ceralacca*
secret: *segreto*
sedative: *sedativo*
self-portrait: *autoritratto*
send, to: *inviare, mandare*
sense of smell: *olfatto*
September: *settembre*
sequin: *zecchino*
sesame: *sesamo*
several: *parecchio*
sew, to: *cucire*
sex: *sesso*
shade: *ombra*
shadow: *pedinare*
shadowy: *umbratile*
shaky: *malfermo*
shark: *squalo*
shave oneself, to: *radersi*
sheep: *ovino, pecora*
sheet: *lenzuolo*
sheet metal: *lamiera*
shellfish: *crostaceo*
shipwrecked, to be: *naufragare*
shoe: *scarpa*
shoot: *tralcio*
shop: *bottega*
short story: *novella*
shortage: *penuria*
shoulder: *spalla*
shout, to: *urlare*
shove: *urtone*
show: *spettacolo*
shutter: *anta*
shy: *timido*
sideburns: *basette*
sign, to: *firmare*
silence: *zitto*
silent: *tacito*
silly: *grullo*
silver: *argento*
since: *dacché, poiché*
sincere: *sentito*
sink: *lavadino*
Sir: *signore*
sister: *sorella*
sister-in-law: *cognata*
ski, to: *sciare*
skillful: *valente*
skillfully: *abilmente*

skirt: *gonna*
skull: *cranio*
skyscraper: *grattacielo*
slang: *gergale*
sleep, to: *dormire*
slippers: *pantofole*
slope: *versante*
slowly: *adagio*
small picture: *quadretto*
smile, to: *sorridere*
snail: *lumaca*
snake: *serpente*
sneer, to: *ghignare*
snow: *neve*
snow, to: *nevicare*
snowdrop: *bucaneve*
snow-white: *niveo*
soaked: *zuppo*
soap: *sapone*
so-called: *cosiddetto*
soccer: *calcio*
socks: *calzini*
sofa: *divano*
soften: *blandire*
soldier: *fante*
sole: *sogliola*
someone: *qualcuno*
son: *figlio*
son-in-law: *genero*
sorceress: *maga*
soup: *minestra, zuppa*
soup spoon: *cucchiaio*
soup tureen: *zuppiera*
southwest wind: *libeccio*
spade: *paletta*
Spain: *Spagna*
spark: *favilla*
sparse: *rado*
speech: *favella*
spell out, to: *compitare*
spice: *spezia*
spider: *ragno*
spinach: *spinaci*
sponge: *spugna*
sprightly: *arzillo*
spring: *primavera*
spring lamb: *abbacchio*
spurting: *zampillante*
square: *quadrato*
squash: *zucchino*
squid: *calamaro*
squirrel: *scoiattolo*
stage: *palcoscenico*
stagger, to: *sfalsare*

staircase: *scala*
stamp: *bollo*
start, to: *incominciare*
station: *stazione*
steak: *bistecca*
stench: *fetore, zaffata*
stepbrother, half brother: *fratellastro*
stepfather: *patrigno*
stepmother: *matrigna*
stepsister, half sister: *sorellastra*
still: *ancora, tuttora*
stingy: *tirchio*
stomach: *ventre*
stop, to: *fermare*
stop up, to: *zaffare*
store: *negozio*
storm: *tempesta*
story: *racconto*
straight line: *dirittura*
straighten, to: *raddrizzare*
strain, to: *colare*
strainer: *colino*
strange: *strano*
strawberry: *fragola*
stray: *randagio*
stream: *rio, ruscello*
street: *strada, via*
stretcher: *lettiga*
strict: *severo*
strike off, to: *radiare*
strike: *sciopero*
string: *filza*
stroll about, to: *gironzolare*
strong: *forte, robusto*
struggle: *lotta*
stuffed: *ripieno*
stumble, to: *farfugliare*
stupendous: *stupendo*
subject: *materia, soggetto*
such: *tale*
sugar: *zucchero*
sugar cube: *zollette*
suggest, to: *suggerire*
suit: *vestito*
sulfur: *zolfo*
summer: *estate*
summer heat: *caldura, solleone*
sun: *sole*
Sunday: *domenica*
sunflower: *girasole*
supper: *cena*
supporter: *fautore*
surgeon: *chirurgo*
surrender: *resa*

swab, to: *radazzare*
swan: *cigno*
sweat, to: *sudore*
sweater: *maglione*
Sweden: *Svezia*
sweet: *zuccheroso*
swim, to: *nuotare*
swimming pool: *piscine*
swirl, to: *vorticare*
switchboard: *centralino*
Switzerland: *Svizzera*
table: *tavola*
tablecloth: *tovaglia*
taboo: *tabù*
tadpole: *girino*
take, to: *prendere*
take an oath, to: *giurare*
takeoff: *decollo*
take off, to: *decollare*
talcum powder: *borotalco*
tally, to: *quadrare*
tamburine: *tamburello*
tank: *serbatoio*
tapestry: *arazzo, tappezzeria*
taste: *gustare*
Taurus: *Toro*
taxes: *tasse*
team: *squadra*
tear: *lacrima*
teaspoon: *cucchiaino*
telepathy: *telepatia*
telephone: *telefono*
telescope: *telescopio*
temperament: *indole*
tenor: *tenore*
theater: *teatro*
theme: *tema*
therapy: *terapia*
therefore: *dunque*
thief: *ladro*
thigh: *coscia*
thimble: *ditale*
thin: *magro*
thing: *faccenda*
thirst: *sete*
threadbare: *liso*
throne: *soglio, trono*
Thursday: *giovedì*
thyme: *timo*
ticket: *biglietto, multa*
ticket window: *sportello*
tie: *cravatta*
tiger: *tigre*
tight: *stretto*

tine: *rebbio*
tinkle, to: *tintinnare*
tint: *tintura*
tip: *mancia*
tire: *pneumatico*
toad: *rospo*
tobacco: *tabacco*
today: *oggi*
toilet: *gabinetto*
token: *gettone*
toll: *pedaggio*
tomato: *pomodoro*
tomb: *tomba*
tomorrow: *domani*
tongue: *lingua*
tongue twister: *scioglilingua*
toothbrush: *spazzolino*
toothpaste: *dentrificio*
torch: *torcia*
tortoise: *tartaruga*
torture: *sevizia*
tourist: *turista*
toward: *verso*
tower: *torre*
toy: *balocco*
track: *binario*
traffic: *traffico*
traffic light: *semaforo*
tragedy: *tragedia*
train: *allenare, treno*
train car: *vettura*
trap: *trappola*
tray: *vassoio*
treasury: *zecca*
tributary: *immissario*
trifle: *nonnulla*
trigger: *grilletto*
trim: *rasare*
trip: *viaggio*
trite: *banale*
trophy: *trofeo*
troubador: *trovatore*
trouble: *grattacapo*
true: *vero*
trumpet: *tromba*
trust: *fiducia*
tub: *vasca*
tuba: *tuba*
Tuesday: *martedì*
tuna: *tonno*
Tunis: *Tunisia*
tunnel: *galleria*
turbulent: *turbolento*
turkey: *tacchino*

Turkey: *Turchia*
turn, to: *girare*
turnip: *rapa*
twilight: *crepuscolo*
typhoid: *tifoidea*
typhoon: *tifone*
ugly: *brutto, racchio*
unbutton, to: *sbottonare*
uncivilized, barbaric: *incivile*
uncle: *zio*
under: *sotto*
underworld: *malavita*
undo one's belt, to: *sbracarsi*
unexpected: *inatteso*
unhurt: *indene, illeso*
unicorn: *unicorno*
unify, to: *unificare*
uninhabitable: *inabitable*
union: *unione*
unit: *reparto*
unite, to: *unire*
United States: *Stati Uniti*
universe: *universo*
university: *università*
unknown: *ignoto*
unpack, to: *disimballare*
unusual: *insolito*
up (here): *quassù*
up (there): *lassù*
up till now: *finora*
uranium: *uranio*
urgent: *urgente*
used: *usato*
useful: *utile*
useless: *inutile*
usher, to: *usciere*
usual: *solito*
vacant: *vacante*
vacation: *vacanza*
vacuum cleaner: *aspirapolvere*
vague: *vago*
valet: *valletto*
valiant: *valoroso*
valid: *valevole*
valley: *valle*
vampire: *vampiro*
vandal: *vandalo*
vanilla: *vaniglia*
vanishing: *evanescente*
vaporize, to: *vaporizzare*
vault, to: *volteggiare*
vegetable: *ortaggio, vegetale*
vent: *sfogo*
verbose: *prolisso*

verdict: *verdetto*
veterinary: *veterinario*
vice: *vizio*
Victorian: *vittoriano*
vigilant: *vigile*
vigorous: *gagliardo*
village: *villaggio*
vinegar: *aceto*
vineyard: *vigna*
violent: *facinoroso*
violin: *violino*
viper: *vipera*
Virgo: *Vergine*
viscount: *visconte*
viscous: *viscoso*
vivacity: *vivezza*
vocation: *vocazione*
volcano: *vulcano*
voltage: *voltaggio*
vote, to: *votare*
waiter: *cameriere*
waiting room: *sala d'aspetto*
walk, to: *camminare*
wall: *muraglia, parete*
walnut: *noce*
wander, to: *vagare*
warehouse: *magazzino*
warhead: *ogiva*
warmth: *tepore*
wash oneself, to: *lavarsi*
washing machine: *lavatrice*
watch, to: *guardare*
watchful: *vigile*
water: *acqua*
water wheel: *noria*
waterfall: *cascata*
watermelon: *anguria*
wave: *onda*
weak: *debole, labile*
weaken, to: *debilitare*
wealth: *ricchezza*
wealthy: *facoltoso*
wedding: *nozze*
wedge: *zeppa*
Wednesday: *mercoledì*
weekday: *giorno feriale*
weekend: *fine settimana*
well: *pozzo*
well (then): *ebbene*
well-known: *noto*
well-mannered: *beneducato*
west: *occidente, ovest*
whale: *balena*
wharf: *imbarcadero*

whatever: *checchè*

when: *quando*

where: *ove*

whim: *fisima*

whirlpool: *gorgo*

whistle, to: *fischiare, zufolare*

white: *bianco*

wicked: *nefando, scellerato*

wide: *largo*

width: *larghezza*

wife: *moglie*

wiggle, to: *divincolarsi*

wild beast: *belva*

wild boar: *cinghiale*

willow: *salice*

win, to: *vincere*

winch: *manovello*

wind: *vento*

window: *finestra*

window sill: *davanzale*

windshield: *parabrezza*

windshield wipers: *tergicristallo*

wine: *vino*

wine bar: *enoteca*

wing: *ala*

wink, to: *ammiccare*

winter: *inverno*

wish: *voglia*

witch: *strega*

withered: *vizzo*

without: *senza*

woman: *donna*

wood: *legno*

word: *vocabolo*

worker: *operaio*

worm: *baco, verme*

worthless: *dappoco*

wrap, to: *incartare*

wrap up, to: *imballare*

wreath: *ghirlanda*

wrist: *polso*

writing desk: *scrittoio*

yawn: *sbadiglio*

year: *anno*

yearn for, to: *bramare*

yellow: *giallo*

yesterday: *ieri*

zeal: *zelo*

zealous: *zelante*

zinc: *zinco*

zodiac: *zodiaco*

zone: *zona*

zoo: *zoo*

zoology: *zoologia*

Index

THE EVERYTHING LEARNING FRENCH BOOK

By Bruce Sallee and David Hebert

Learning a foreign language can be both challenging and intimidating. Luckily, *The Everything® Learning French Book* makes it simple for everyone. It features easy-to-follow instructions on the French alphabet and pronunciation, how to greet people and ask questions, proper usage of nouns, verbs, pronouns, and articles, vocabulary lists, and French etiquette and style. Including many helpful exercises, self-tests, and an English to French dictionary, *The Everything® Learning French Book* will have anyone speaking—and understanding—French in no time.

Trade paperback, $12.95
1-58062-649-1, 320 pages

OTHER *EVERYTHING*® BOOKS BY ADAMS MEDIA CORPORATION

Everything® **After College Book**
$12.95, 1-55850-847-3

Everything® **American History Book**
$12.95, 1-58062-531-2

Everything® **Angels Book**
$12.95, 1-58062-398-0

Everything® **Anti-Aging Book**
$12.95, 1-58062-565-7

Everything® **Astrology Book**
$12.95, 1-58062-062-0

Everything® **Astronomy Book**
$14.95, 1-58062-723-4

Everything® **Baby Names Book**
$12.95, 1-55850-655-1

Everything® **Baby Shower Book**
$12.95, 1-58062-305-0

Everything® **Baby's First Food Book**
$12.95, 1-58062-512-6

Everything® **Baby's First Year Book**
$12.95, 1-58062-581-9

Everything® **Barbecue Cookbook**
$14.95, 1-58062-316-6

Everything® **Bartender's Book**
$9.95, 1-55850-536-9

Everything® **Bedtime Story Book**
$12.95, 1-58062-147-3

Everything® **Bible Stories Book**
$14.95, 1-58062-547-9

Everything® **Bicycle Book**
$12.00, 1-55850-706-X

Everything® **Breastfeeding Book**
$12.95, 1-58062-582-7

Everything® **Budgeting Book**
$14.95, 1-58062-786-2

Everything® **Build Your Own Home Page Book**
$12.95, 1-58062-339-5

Everything® **Business Planning Book**
$12.95, 1-58062-491-X

Everything® **Candlemaking Book**
$12.95, 1-58062-623-8

Everything® **Car Care Book**
$14.95, 1-58062-732-3

Everything® **Casino Gambling Book**
$12.95, 1-55850-762-0

Everything® **Cat Book**
$12.95, 1-55850-710-8

Everything® **Chocolate Cookbook**
$12.95, 1-58062-405-7

Everything® **Christmas Book**
$15.00, 1-55850-697-7

Everything® **Civil War Book**
$12.95, 1-58062-366-2

Everything® **Classical Mythology Book**
$12.95, 1-58062-653-X

Everything® **Coaching & Mentoring Book**
$14.95, 1-58062-730-7

Everything® **Collectibles Book**
$12.95, 1-58062-645-9

Everything® **College Survival Book**
$14.95, 1-55850-720-5

Everything® **Computer Book**
$12.95, 1-58062-401-4

Everything® **Cookbook**
$14.95, 1-58062-400-6

Everything® **Cover Letter Book**
$12.95, 1-58062-312-3

Everything® **Creative Writing Book**
$14.95, 1-58062-647-5

Everything® **Crossword and Puzzle Book**
$14.95, 1-55850-764-7

Everything® **Dating Book**
$12.95, 1-58062-185-6

Everything® **Dessert Cookbook**
$12.95, 1-55850-717-5

Everything® **Diabetes Cookbook**
$14.95, 1-58062-691-2

Everything® **Dieting Book**
$14.95, 1-58062-663-7

Everything® **Digital Photography Book**
$12.95, 1-58062-574-6

Everything® **Dog Book**
$12.95, 1-58062-144-9

Everything® **Dog Training and Tricks Book**
$14.95, 1-58062-666-1

Everything® **Dreams Book**
$12.95, 1-55850-806-6

Everything® **Etiquette Book**
$12.95, 1-55850-807-4

Everything® **Fairy Tales Book**
$12.95, 1-58062-546-0

Everything® **Family Tree Book**
$12.95, 1-55850-763-9

Everything® **Feng Shui Book**
$14.95, 1-58062-587-8

Everything® **Fly-Fishing Book**
$12.95, 1-58062-148-1

Everything® **Games Book**
$12.95, 1-55850-643-8

Everything® **Get-A-Job Book**
$12.95, 1-58062-223-2

Everything® **Get Out of Debt Book**
$12.95, 1-58062-588-6

Everything® **Get Published Book**
$12.95, 1-58062-315-8

Everything® **Get Ready for Baby Book**
$12.95, 1-55850-844-9

Everything® **Get Rich Book**
$12.95, 1-58062-670-X

Everything® **Ghost Book**
$14.95, 1-58062-533-9

Everything® **Golf Book**
$12.95, 1-55850-814-7

Everything® **Grammar and Style Book**
$12.95, 1-58062-573-8

Everything® **Great Thinkers Book**
$14.95, 1-58062-662-9

Everything® **Travel Guide to
    The Disneyland Resort®,
    California Adventure®,
    Universal Studios®, and
    Anaheim**
$14.95, 1-58062-742-0

Everything® **Guide to Las Vegas**
$12.95, 1-58062-438-3

Everything® **Guide to New England**
$14.95, 1-58062-589-4

Everything® **Guide to New York City**
$12.95, 1-58062-314-X

Everything® **Travel Guide to Walt Disney
    World®, Universal Studios®, and
    Greater Orlando, 3rd Edition**
$14.95, 1-58062-743-9

Everything® **Guide to Washington D.C.**
$12.95, 1-58062-313-1

Everything® **Guide to Writing
    Children's Books**
$14.95, 1-58062-785-4

Everything® **Guitar Book**
$14.95, 1-58062-555-X

Everything® **Herbal Remedies Book**
$12.95, 1-58062-331-X

Everything® **Home-Based Business Book**
$12.95, 1-58062-364-6

Everything® **Homebuying Book**
$12.95, 1-58062-074-4

Everything® **Homeselling Book**
$12.95, 1-58062-304-2

Everything® **Horse Book**
$12.95, 1-58062-564-9

Everything® **Hot Careers Book**
$12.95, 1-58062-486-3

Everything® **Hypnosis Book**
$14.95, 1-58062-737-4

Everything® **Internet Book**
$12.95, 1-58062-073-6

Everything® **Investing Book**
$12.95, 1-58062-149-X

Everything® **Jewish Wedding Book**
$12.95, 1-55850-801-5

Everything® **Judaism Book**
$14.95, 1-58062-728-5

Everything® **Job Interview Book**
$12.95, 1-58062-493-6

Everything® **Knitting Book**
$14.95, 1-58062-727-7

Everything® **Lawn Care Book**
$12.95, 1-58062-487-1

Everything® **Leadership Book**
$12.95, 1-58062-513-4

Everything® **Learning French Book**
$12.95, 1-58062-649-1

Everything® **Learning Italian Book**
$14.95, 1-58062-724-2

Everything® **Learning Spanish Book**
$12.95, 1-58062-575-4

Everything® **Low-Carb Cookbook**
$14.95, 1-58062-784-6

Everything® **Low-Fat High-Flavor
    Cookbook**
$12.95, 1-55850-802-3

Everything® **Magic Book**
$14.95, 1-58062-418-9

Everything® **Managing People Book**
$12.95, 1-58062-577-0

Everything® **Meditation Book**
$14.95, 1-58062-665-3

Everything® **Menopause Book**
$14.95, 1-58062-741-2

Everything® **Microsoft® Word 2000 Book**
$12.95, 1-58062-306-9

Everything® **Money Book**
$12.95, 1-58062-145-7

Everything® **Mother Goose Book**
$12.95, 1-58062-490-1

Everything® **Motorcycle Book**
$12.95, 1-58062-554-1

Everything® **Mutual Funds Book**
$12.95, 1-58062-419-7

Everything® **Network Marketing Book**
$14.95, 1-58062-736-6

Everything® **Numerology Book**
$14.95, 1-58062-700-5

Everything® **One-Pot Cookbook**
$12.95, 1-58062-186-4

Everything® **Online Business Book**
$12.95, 1-58062-320-4

Everything® **Online Genealogy Book**
$12.95, 1-58062-402-2

Everything® **Online Investing Book**
$12.95, 1-58062-338-7

Everything® **Online Job Search Book**
$12.95, 1-58062-365-4

Everything® **Organize Your Home Book**
$12.95, 1-58062-617-3

Everything® **Pasta Book**
$12.95, 1-55850-719-1

Everything® **Philosophy Book**
$12.95, 1-58062-644-0

Everything® **Pilates Book**
$14.95, 1-58062-738-2

Everything® **Playing Piano and
    Keyboards Book**
$12.95, 1-58062-651-3

Everything® **Potty Training Book**
$14.95, 1-58062-740-4

Everything® **Pregnancy Book**
$12.95, 1-58062-146-5

Everything® **Pregnancy Organizer**
$15.00, 1-58062-336-0

Everything® **Project Management Book**
$12.95, 1-58062-583-5

Everything® **Puppy Book**
$12.95, 1-58062-576-2

Everything® **Quick Meals Cookbook**
$14.95, 1-58062-488-X

Everything® **Resume Book**
$12.95, 1-58062-311-5

Everything® **Romance Book**
$12.95, 1-58062-566-5

Everything® **Running Book**
$12.95, 1-58062-618-1

Everything® **Sailing Book, 2nd Ed.**
$12.95, 1-58062-671-8

Everything® **Saints Book**
$12.95, 1-58062-534-7

Everything® **Scrapbooking Book**
$14.95, 1-58062-729-3

Everything® **Selling Book**
$12.95, 1-58062-319-0

Everything® **Shakespeare Book**
$14.95, 1-58062-591-6

Everything® **Slow Cooker Cookbook**
$14.95, 1-58062-667-X

Everything® **Soup Cookbook**
$14.95, 1-58062-556-8

Everything® **Spells and Charms Book**
$12.95, 1-58062-532-0

Everything® **Start Your Own Business Book**
$14.95, 1-58062-650-5

Everything® **Stress Management Book**
$14.95, 1-58062-578-9

Everything® **Study Book**
$12.95, 1-55850-615-2

Everything® **T'ai Chi and QiGong Book**
$12.95, 1-58062-646-7

Everything® **Tall Tales, Legends, and Other Outrageous Lies Book**
$12.95, 1-58062-514-2

Everything® **Tarot Book**
$12.95, 1-58062-191-0

Everything® **Thai Cookbook**
$14.95, 1-58062-733-1

Everything® **Time Management Book**
$12.95, 1-58062-492-8

Everything® **Toasts Book**
$12.95, 1-58062-189-9

Everything® **Toddler Book**
$14.95, 1-58062-592-4

Everything® **Total Fitness Book**
$12.95, 1-58062-318-2

Everything® **Trivia Book**
$12.95, 1-58062-143-0

Everything® **Tropical Fish Book**
$12.95, 1-58062-343-3

Everything® **Vegetarian Cookbook**
$12.95, 1-58062-640-8

Everything® **Vitamins, Minerals, and Nutritional Supplements Book**
$12.95, 1-58062-496-0

Everything® **Weather Book**
$14.95, 1-58062-668-8

Everything® **Wedding Book, 2nd Ed.**
$14.95, 1-58062-190-2

Everything® **Wedding Checklist**
$7.95, 1-58062-456-1

Everything® **Wedding Etiquette Book**
$7.95, 1-58062-454-5

Everything® **Wedding Organizer**
$15.00, 1-55850-828-7

Everything® **Wedding Shower Book**
$7.95, 1-58062-188-0

Everything® **Wedding Vows Book**
$7.95, 1-58062-455-3

Everything® **Weddings on a Budget Book**
$9.95, 1-58062-782-X

Everything® **Weight Training Book**
$12.95, 1-58062-593-2

Everything® **Wicca and Witchcraft Book**
$14.95, 1-58062-725-0

Everything® **Wine Book**
$12.95, 1-55850-808-2

Everything® **World War II Book**
$14.95, 1-58062-572-X

Everything® **World's Religions Book**
$14.95, 1-58062-648-3

Everything® **Yoga Book**
$14.95, 1-58062-594-0

*Prices subject to change without notice.

EVERYTHING KIDS' SERIES!

Everything® **Kids' Baseball Book, 2nd Ed.**
$6.95, 1-58062-688-2

Everything® **Kids' Cookbook**
$6.95, 1-58062-658-0

Everything® **Kids' Joke Book**
$6.95, 1-58062-686-6

Everything® **Kids' Mazes Book**
$6.95, 1-58062-558-4

Everything® **Kids' Money Book**
$6.95, 1-58062-685-8

Everything® **Kids' Monsters Book**
$6.95, 1-58062-657-2

Everything® **Kids' Nature Book**
$6.95, 1-58062-684-X

Everything® **Kids' Puzzle Book**
$6.95, 1-58062-687-4

Everything® **Kids' Science Experiments Book**
$6.95, 1-58062-557-6

Everything® **Kids' Soccer Book**
$6.95, 1-58062-642-4

Everything® **Travel Activity Book**
$6.95, 1-58062-641-6

Available wherever books are sold!
To order, call 800-872-5627, or visit us at everything.com

Everything® is a registered trademark of Adams Media Corporation.